The ASD Girls' Wellbeing Toolkit

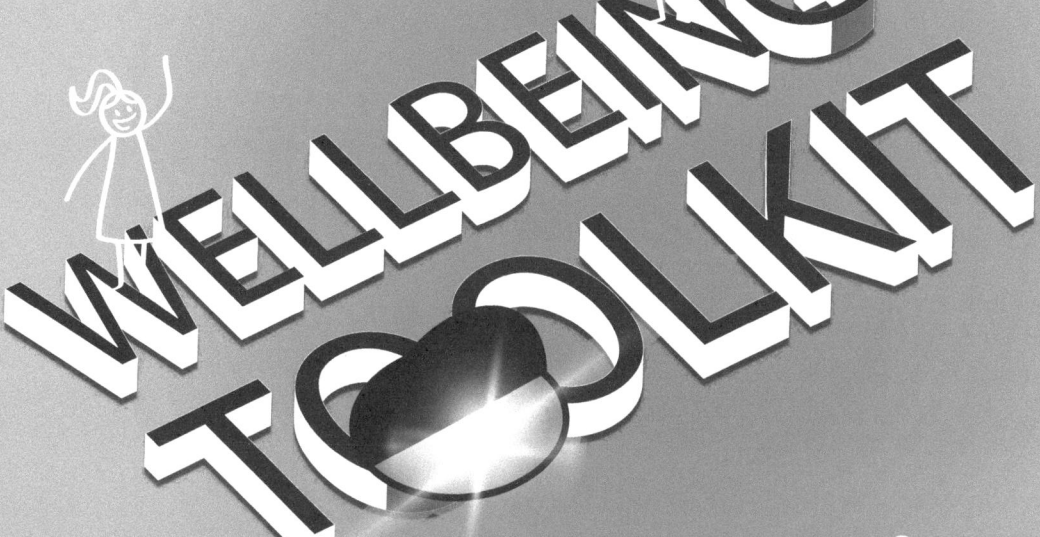

An Evidence-Based Programme Promoting Mental, Physical & Emotional Health

TINA RAE & AMY SUCH

HINTON HOUSE Mental Health Essentials

HINTON HOUSE

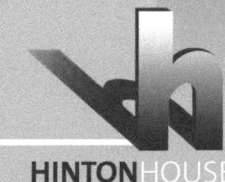

First published in 2019 by

Hinton House Publishers Ltd
T +44 (0)1280 822557 **E** info@hintonpublishers.com

www.hintonpublishers.com

© 2019 Tina Rae & Amy Such

Reprinted 2020, 2021, 2022

The right of Tina Rae and Amy Such to be identified as authors of this Work has been asserted by them in accordance with sections 77 and 78 of the Copyright, Designs and Patents Act 1988.

All rights reserved. The whole of this work including texts and illustrations is protected by copyright. No part of it may be copied, altered, adapted or otherwise exploited in any way without express prior permission, except in accordance with the provisions of the Copyright, Designs and Patents Act 1988 or in order to photocopy or make duplicating masters of those pages so indicated, without alteration and including copyright notices, for the express purpose of instruction and examination. No parts of this work may otherwise be loaded, stored, manipulated, reproduced, or transmitted in any form or by any means, electronic or mechanical, including photocopying or storing it in any information, storage or retrieval system, without prior written permission from the publisher, on behalf of the copyright owner.

Warning: The doing of an unauthorised act in relation to a copyright work may result in both a civil claim for damages and criminal prosecution.

British Library Cataloguing in Publication Data
A CIP catalogue record for this book is available from the British Library.

ISBN 978 1 906531 67 8

Printed and bound in the United Kingdom

Contents

List of Worksheets & Other Resources vi

About the Authors xi

Foreword by Professor Barry Carpenter xiii

Introduction 1

    Mental Health & Resilience 1

    Therapeutic Tools & Approaches in the Toolkit 2

    Contemporary Pressures: the Self-Harm Issue 3

    Tools to Cope with the Media & Sexualisation 4

    Aims of the Toolkit 5

    An ASD-Friendly Session Structure 6

    Outcomes 8

    Looking Ahead: Continuation of Support 11

    Working with Parents & Carers 11

    Notes for Facilitators 12

    Conclusion 16

Notes for the PowerPoint Presentation 17

1 Me & My Mental Health 21

    1.1 About Me 22

    1.2 Physical & Mental Health 31

    1.3 My Self Concept 37

    1.4 Resilience 48

1.5	Self-Esteem	56
1.6	Managing Stress & Anxiety 1	60
1.7	Managing Stress & Anxiety 2	67
1.8	Managing Stress & Anxiety 3	78
1.9	Self-Harm 1	84
1.10	Self-Harm 2	94

2 Relationships & Communication Skills … 103

2.1	Non-Verbal Communication	104
2.2	Verbal Communication	111
2.3	Relationships 1	120
2.4	Relationships 2	129
2.5	Relationships 3	134
2.6	Sexual Behaviours	142
2.7	Online Behaviours	149
2.8	Media & Other Influences 1	156
2.9	Media & Other Influences 2	166
2.10	Risk-Taking	170

3 My Toolbox for Wellbeing & Future Health … 177

3.1	Effective Thinking 1	178
3.2	Effective Thinking 2	184
3.3	Relaxation & Mindfulness 1	192
3.4	Relaxation & Mindfulness 2	197
3.5	Being Solution-Focused	207
3.6	Future Hopes, Dreams & Realities 1	218
3.7	Future Hopes, Dreams & Realities 2	226

3.8	Evaluation	234
3.9	My Targets 1	242
3.10	My Targets 2	249

4 Resources … 261

Facilitator Guides … 262

Templates & Information Sheets … 266

Useful Agencies, Websites & Support Systems … 289

References & Bibliography … 291

List of Worksheets & Other Resources

Part 1

1.1	Visual Timetable	27
1.2	Like or Dislike?	28
1.3	Circles	29
1.4	My Targets	30
1.5	Ideas for Physical & Mental Fitness	35
1.6	What Motivates Me?	36
1.7	Bingo!	41
1.8	Sources of Confidence	47
1.9	What Can I Say to Myself?	53
1.10	Control Spectrum	54
1.11	'Things' Bubbles	55
1.12	Celebrity Faces	59
1.13	Stress versus Anxiety	65
1.14	My Stress-Busting Plan	66
1.15	Stress & Anxiety Quiz	71
1.16	Definitions	74
1.17	Understand Panic	75
1.18	Body Scan	76
1.19	Challenging Anxious Thoughts	81
1.20	The Worry Tree	83
1.21	Self-Harm Facts & Myths	88
1.22	Amie's Story	93

List of Worksheets & Other Resources

1.23	Mindfulness Colouring	97
1.24	Mindfulness Sudoku	98
1.25	Mindfulness Doodling	99
1.26	A Letter from Sally	100
1.27	My Safety Plan	101

Part 2

2.1	More than Words	107
2.2	Photo Stories	108
2.3	Response Scripts	115
2.4	What is Assertiveness?	116
2.5	The Assertiveness Scale	117
2.6	Assertiveness Skills	118
2.7	Communication Slips	119
2.8	Name the Emotion	124
2.9	Intensity of Feeling	125
2.10	Speak & Guess Cards	126
2.11	Feeling Positive with Others	127
2.12	Relationships Rules	132
2.13	People Outlines	133
2.14	What Type of Abuse is This?	138
2.15	Ayisha & Naomi's Stories	139
2.16	Random Acts of Kindness	140
2.17	Random Acts of Kindness Diary	141
2.18	CSE Case Studies	145
2.19	Venn Diagram	153
2.20	Predator Tactics	154
2.21	Online Grooming Case Study	155
2.22	Social Media Images	159
2.23	Online Images: Fact or Fiction?	160

List of Worksheets & Other Resources

2.24	Young People & Pornography	162
2.25	Sexting Facts	165
2.26	Profile Page	169
2.27	No, Because …	173
2.28	High Risk	174
2.29	No Risk	175
2.30	Risky Scenarios	176

Part 3

3.1	PMA Scenarios	181
3.2	The Link …	182
3.3	Negative Internal Monologue	183
3.4	What If …?	188
3.5	NAT-Bashing	189
3.6	Socratic Questioning	191
3.7	Mindfulness	196
3.8	Beach	203
3.9	Meadow	204
3.10	Park	205
3.11	Mindful Timetable	206
3.12	Case Study: Lisa	211
3.13	Solution-Focused Cards	212
3.14	A Walk in the Wood	215
3.15	Autumn Wood…	217
3.16	Hand Template	222
3.17	Many Selves	223
3.18	Self-Awareness Profile	224
3.19	My Life Map	225
3.20	Preferred Future	229
3.21	Looking Forward	232

3.22	Bricks	238
3.23	Situations Circles	239
3.24	Decision Grid	240
3.25	Sources of Support	241
3.26	Stages of Change	246
3.27	Relapse Plan	247
3.28	Famous Goals	253
3.29	SMART Targets	254
3.30	Target-Setting	255
3.31	Front Cover	256
3.32	Things I Want in My Future	257
3.33	Sentence Stems	259
3.34	My Top Three	260

Facilitator's Guides

1	Reflections & Feedback	262
2	The Golden Scroll	263
3	Guided Relaxation	264

Letter Templates

1	Letter to Parents & Carers	266
2	Letter to Parents & Carers with Consent Form	267

Information Sheets

1	The ASD Girls' Wellbeing Toolkit: Information for Students	269
2	The ASD Girls' Wellbeing Toolkit: Information for Parents & Carers	270
3	Creating an ASD-Friendly Classroom	274
4	Parents & Carers: Autism in Girls	278
5	Tips for Teens Managing Stress & Anxiety	281
6	Parents, Carers & Staff: Self-Harm	283

About the Authors

Dr Tina Rae (BA (Hons), PGCE MA(Ed), Msc RSA Dip SpLD, Dip Psych ALCM, DAppChEdPsy MBPS), is an HCPC-registered child and educational psychologist, author and educational consultant. She has more than 30 years' experience working with children, adults and families in both clinical and educational contexts within local authorities and specialist educational services. She currently works as a consultant educational and child psychologist in a range of SEBD/SEMH and mainstream contexts and for Compass Fostering as a consultant psychologist supporting foster carers, social workers and looked-after children. From 2010 to 2016 she was also an academic and professional tutor for the Doctorate in Educational and Child Psychology at the University of East London.

Tina is a registered member of the Health and Care Professions Council and a full member of the British Psychological Society. She is also a member of ENSEC (European Network for Social and Emotional Competence) and, until recently, a trustee of the Nurture Group Network (NGN), now Nurtureuk. She is also a member of the editorial board for the journal *Emotional and Behavioural Difficulties* and for the *International Journal of Nurture in Education*.

Tina has published more than 100 titles with Hinton House, Sage Publications, Paul Chapman Publishing, Folens, JKP, Routledge, NGN and Optimus Education. She is currently working on research into staff wellbeing and resilience and peer group supervision systems.

Among her forthcoming and more recent publications are *The Wellbeing Toolkit for Mental Health Leads* (2019), *Supporting Teenagers with Anxiety & Stress* (2019), *Identifying & Supporting Children with Sensory Processing Difficulties* (2018), *The Essential Guide to Using CBT with Children & Young People* (2018), *Understanding & Preventing Self-Harm in Schools* (2107), *The Essential Guide to Using Mindfulness with Children & Young People* (2017), all from Hinton House Publishers.

Tina is a regular speaker at both national and international conferences including those run by Giraffe Training, Nurtureuk, BSA and Optimus. She provides training courses and consultancy on a wide range of wellbeing issues, and supervision for school-based staff in both special and mainstream contexts, Educational Psychology services and specialist teaching services across the UK and internationally.

tinarae@hotmail.co.uk

About the Authors

Dr Amy Such, BSc (Hons), DEdChPsy, is an HCPC-registered child and educational psychologist and author and is currently working as an independent educational and child psychologist, having obtained a doctorate from the University of East London in 2017. Amy has worked in a number of local authority Educational Psychology Services in and around London, meeting the social, emotional and mental health needs of children and young people. Whilst working at Buckinghamshire Educational Psychology Service, she took an active role in the Nurture Group Project, providing professional supervision, staff training and CPD for practitioners. She also assisted on the Emotional Literacy Support Assistant (ELSA) Project, providing supervision and training.

Prior to becoming an educational and child psychologist, Amy worked as a teaching assistant in the north of England and, more recently, received training as an applied behaviour analysis tutor at an autism-specific school. She has significant experience working with children and young people on the autism spectrum. In particular, her interests include the presentation of social communication difficulties within the female population. This became the topic of her doctorate thesis, and themes highlighted through the completion of her research have guided the information provided within this resource.

Amy is the co-author with Tina Rae of *The Wellbeing Toolkit for Mental Health Leads* (2019), published by Hinton House and *Emotion Coaching* and *The Well Being Tool Kit for Teens*, from Nurture Group Network.

a.such@hotmail.co.uk

Foreword
by Professor Barry Carpenter

Girls with autism are a misdiagnosed and misunderstood group. Recent research has exploded the myth that autism affects one girl to every four boys (Carpenter *et al*, 2019). The reality is it is likely to be at least one in three. So much of our research and diagnostic work has been orientated to the male profile of autism. This gender bias obscures the female lens we need to apply to truly assess girls with autism.

Girls with autism mask and camouflage. As a parent says, 'My teenager wears make-up, has her skirt rolled over, and is obsessed with social media, just like her friends ... except that she often does not understand the nuances of teenage girls' conversation' (Carpenter *et al*, 2019). Ultimately, girls with autism become exhausted at keeping up this pretence, and extreme anxiety appears.

As their mental health begins to erode, so their ability to keep up their mask evaporates; depression, hyper-anxiety, self-harm and eating disorders are often the indicators that first alert families and professionals to something deeper underlying these outward manifestations. Sadly, by then the mental ill health is embedded, and there is a major challenge to be overcome.

How can we divert these bleak outcomes? This *Wellbeing Toolkit*, specifically targeted at girls with autism is exactly what is needed to build emotional resilience. With so much new knowledge and insight into the needs of girls with autism, we are empowered by the *Toolkit* to make the girls emotionally strong, well before any of the negative issues emerge.

Styled to match the learning pathways of the girl with autism, the *Toolkit* encourages self-regulation and promotes self-image, self-esteem and self-confidence. There is a clear structure to the activities, and the topics in each session are carefully constructed. They work from the girl out, presenting issues around which she will have to make decisions that keep her mentally and physically safe, and in a state of emotional wellbeing.

Now is the time to resolve many of the injustices that have been heaped upon girls with autism, due to a lack of professional awareness and skill, and an inability to design interventions which were meaningful, and touched the girl at her point of need. *The ASD Girls' Wellbeing Toolkit* will do what it says on the label ... promote mental, physical and emotional health. Based on new

Foreword

research and evidence-based practice, this *Toolkit* will make a significant contribution to this work and enable a whole range of professionals in practice, and parents in their homes, to at long-last present material that has actually been designed with girls with autism in mind.

I hope that you will be one of those people.

Professor Barry Carpenter, CBE, OBE, PhD.
Chair, the National Forum on Girls with Autism
Professor of Mental Health in Education, Oxford Brookes University

Introduction

In recent years professionals working with young people with Autistic Spectrum Disorders (ASD) have become more aware of the need to ensure the timely and appropriate diagnosis of girls. Without such a diagnosis and the relevant support systems being put in place, such girls and young women are clearly at high risk of developing mental health difficulties such as anxiety, depression, self-harm and eating disorders.

Such disorders will ultimately put them at risk of disengaging with the learning process and school in general. Boys with ASD tend to be less social than their peers and display prominent and obvious areas of obsessive interests and compulsions. In contrast, girls with autism appear to be more able to follow or imitate social actions. In the early years they can mimic socially appropriate behaviour, without understanding what they are doing or why they are doing it. This can result in the masking of their difficulties and we feel that this is directly linked to the under-diagnosis of autism in girls.

> *The level of camouflaging that they may engage in on a daily basis alongside the repressing of their autistic behaviours, can be extremely tiring and stressful and is perhaps a direct cause of the high statistics of women on the continuum with mental health problems* (Yaull-Smith, 2007).

As Judy Eaton (2017, p. 9) states: 'Many girls and young women did not (and still do not) get a diagnosis of their difficulties and there is growing evidence that they will have an increased risk of experiencing issues with friendships and relationships, be prone to bullying and harassment, and may well experience significant mental health problems.'

Mental Health & Resilience

We know that mental health affects all aspects of a child's development, including their cognitive abilities, their social skills as well their emotional wellbeing. Many psychologists are now in agreement that building emotional resilience is key to preventing the escalation of such difficulties. They would support the development of the following key skills or attributes of resilience:

* The capacity to enter into and sustain mutually satisfying personal relationships
* A continuing progression of psychological development

Introduction

- An ability to play and to learn appropriately for their age and intellectual level
- A developing moral sense of right and wrong
- The capacity to cope with a degree of psychological distress
- A clear sense of identity and self-worth

(Weare, 2000)

We all want our children and young people to develop good mental health and overall wellbeing, as we are now fully aware that people with higher levels of good mental health and wellbeing have better general health, use health services less (Lyubomirsky *et al*, 2005; Pressman & Cohen, 2005), live longer (Chida & Steptoe, 2008), have better educational outcomes (NICE, 2009), are more likely to undertake healthier lifestyles (Lyubomirsky *et al*, 2005), including reduced smoking and harmful levels of drinking (Deacon *et al*, 2013), are more productive at work (NICE, 2009; Boorman, 2009), take less time off sick (Keyes, 2005; Mills *et al*, 2007), have higher income (Lyubomirsky *et al*, 2005), have stronger social relationships (Pressman & Cohen, 2005; Lyubomirsky *et al*, 2005) and are more social (Coid *et al*, 2006). Higher levels of mental wellbeing are also associated with reduced levels of mental ill health in adulthood (Lyubomirsky *et al*, 2005; Keyes *et al*, 2010).

Now that we have a greater awareness of the increased risk and raised levels of mental ill health in those with ASD generally (Crane *et al* 2018; Simonoff *et al*, 2008), it is surely vital that we develop interventions to specifically promote their mental health and wellbeing in both the school and home context. This is the main driver for us in developing *The ASD Girls' Wellbeing Toolkit*.

Therapeutic Tools & Approaches in the Toolkit

We are certain that there is a need to focus upon interventions to support the development of self-help and self-management strategies for our young people so that they can become autonomous, healthy young people who are able to self-manage their anxieties and stressors on a daily basis. We also know that specific therapeutic approaches (Cognitive Behaviour Therapy – CBT- and tools from Positive Psychology) can be adapted for use with girls on the autistic continuum, which is why they are included within our programme.

We know that all young people – particularly those going through the stage of adolescence, will frequently experience anxious and negative thoughts and doubts. These negative automatic thoughts (NATs) will often reinforce a state of inadequacy and/or low levels of self-esteem. CBT tools and strategies will help to support young people in reconsidering these negative assumptions and enable them to *learn how* to change their self-perceptions in order to improve their mental and emotional state.

This approach focuses on the role that thoughts play in regard to both emotions and behaviour, and advocates that change in thought processes can have a significant effect upon altering behaviours. Unlike many of the 'talking' treatments that traditional therapists have used, CBT focuses upon the here and now and ways to improve the individual state of mind in the present time. This is innovative in the sense that there is no focus on the causes of distress or past symptoms. There has been a great deal of recent research which concludes that CBT is an effective intervention for treating young people's psychological difficulties and problems.

CBT has been applied in educational settings in a range of ways – with individuals, small groups and whole classes, as well as informing whole-school policy and systems. There is evidence that school-based small group and individual sessions using cognitive behavioural approaches, including problem-solving and working with thoughts and behaviours, are effective mental health interventions (DfE, 2014). We also now know that there is more evidence to show the success of such interventions to treat anxiety amongst children and adolescents with ASD (Luxford *et al*, 2017; Kester *et al*, 2018).

In this programme we have therefore included tools from CBT approaches (Rae & Giles, 2018), alongside strategies from other evidence based therapeutic approaches such as Mindfulness (Rae *et al*, 2017), Resilience Theory, Solution Focused Brief Therapy (Rae et al, 2018) and Positive Psychology (MacConville & Rae, 2012, Rae et al., 2019) in order to provide the best possible intervention to support the mental wellbeing of our girls. These evidence- based interventions can provide us with tools to encourage and maintain effective thinking which will, in turn, promote wellbeing overall.

Contemporary Pressures: the Self-Harm Issue

Access to the online world has created more opportunities for young people to explore, experiment, socialise, create and educate themselves, but it has also exposed them to the risk of harm, including seeing extreme pornography and 'sexting' (Martellozzo *et al*, 2016). It is vital therefore, that we ensure they have the new skills and knowledge base in order to effectively navigate this new world and manage the levels of anxiety and stress that can so often result in a range of self-harming behaviours and other mental health difficulties such as anxiety disorders, social phobias, self-harm and eating disorders.

A common concern for parents, carers and staff is that by talking about self-harm, it might make more students think about doing it. We have included this topic in the *ASD Girls' Wellbeing Tool Kit* as we know that the evidence in fact suggests that the opposite is true and this is clearly an area of concern for many of our young people. While this can feel a sensitive topic, it is a very important and relevant one. Talking to young people about self-harm is going to give them knowledge, confidence and an understanding of how to support themselves and others. The role of the facilitator in the sessions is to demystify a topic that can be very powerful and upsetting

Introduction

for young people. By talking about it and sign-posting towards support, young people can be empowered.

The limited research focusing on ASD children and self-harm does point strongly to increased risk for this group in adolescence (Culpin *et al*, 2018; Hedley *et al*, 2018), and this is a key driver for us in including the topic in our programme of support. It is also vital to bear in mind that although few of those who engage in self-harming behaviours such as cutting will attempt suicide, most young people who attempt suicide have previously self-harmed and self-harm can be seen to considerably raise the risk of suicide (Olfson *et al*, 2018). It is therefore vital for both school-based staff and parents or carers to remain vigilant and be aware of the risk factors, such as physical, sexual or emotional abuse, low self-esteem, anxiety and difficulties in relationships. Gaining an informed understanding of this area is clearly an essential, which is why we have also included relevant and more detailed information in Part 4, 'Information Sheets'.

Tools to Cope with the Media & Sexualisation

As well as focusing on therapeutic and self-management skills in the *Toolkit*, we have also addressed the impact of the media and sexualisation of our young people, as we feel very strongly that these are both key areas of concern, specifically for the ASD girl. The report of the American Psychological Association's (APA) Task Force (2007) on the sexualisation of girls concludes that it is vital for psychologists, educators, carers and community organisations to work together in order to encourage the development of curricula that enhance self-esteem based upon young people's abilities and character, as opposed to their appearance, and also challenges the sexualisation of girls and young women in the media and online.

We know that the media provides us with a great deal of evidence of the sexualisation of women, including music videos, television, magazines, films, music lyrics, sports media, video games, internet and advertising (Krassas *et al*, 2001). These media images also further emphasise a narrow and unrealistic notion of physical beauty, which has evident implications for the development of girls' and young women's self-esteem and self-image (O'Donohue *et al*, 1997). This is a very real concern for those of us who work with or support girls and young women with ASD who may become fixated by specific images and media personalities, and over-anxious in terms of achieving the perfect body, appearance or life style. Again, this provides us with the rationale for including these topics in the programme.

We also know that male and female peers contribute to this process of sexualisation and associated body image issues. Peer pressure from both genders has been found to contribute to girls conforming to standards of thinness or 'sexiness' (Eder, 1995; Nichter, 2000). This kind of behaviour is also 'normalised' by the girls themselves via the process of self-objectification – the process whereby they learn to think of and treat themselves as the objects of other people's

Introduction

(mainly boys' and men's) desires (McKinley & Hyde, 1996). This is problematic for the ASD girl, because it does place her at additional risk as she tries to understand and navigate the responses and behaviours of others. The Toolkit pays special attention to this issue, since we know that girls on the autism continuum are more at risk of accepting and 'buying in' to this narrative and, as a result, may make incorrect and sometimes inaccurate judgements about the sexual behaviours of others, thus putting themselves at risk (Visser *et al.*, 2017).

Aims of the Toolkit

The overall aim of the 30-session group programme is to ensure that girls can, and do, develop good mental health, including appropriate levels of autonomy, emotional resilience and open communication. The three main objectives are as follows:

1. To promote emotional resilience in group members

2. To assist in the develop of the skills associated with positive communication

3. To support group members with a view to further developing self-regulation and awareness

The activities therefore aim to:

- promote personal and social skills development

- develop self-esteem and self-awareness

- empower young people to explore the many aspects of sexuality and healthy personal relationships

- encourage the acceptance of personal responsibility for keeping the mind and body safe and healthy

- help young people to evaluate and access confidently a range of local and national sources of information, support and advice

- address contemporary issues that are relevant to young people, including:

    * Consent in teenage relationships and recognising safe versus potentially exploitative relationships

    * The consequences of, and law relating to, sexual behaviour

    * The range of sexual attitudes, relationships and behaviours in society

    * Body image, obesity, self-respect, aspiration

    * The media portrayal of young people

Introduction

- The effects, risks and legal consequences of the use of psychoactive substances (i.e., legal 'highs', such as caffeine, alcohol, nicotine) and performance- and image-enhancing substances (e.g., steroids)

- Understanding and strengthening intergenerational relationships

- Understanding mental health as a concept and the stigma that may attach to someone labelled as having poor mental health

- Exploring the nature of stress and anxiety and understanding methods to minimise the impact of these

- Understanding the nature of and triggers to self-harming behaviours in young people

- Understanding how to maintain mental health, using tools from a range of evidence-based therapeutic approaches, including CBT and Mindfulness

An ASD-Friendly Session Structure

Care has been taken to ensure that the activities and structure are 'ASD-friendly' and therefore each activity considers and includes the following key elements:

1 **Reinforcement:** multiple opportunities to repeat and 'over-learn' key skills and concepts

2 **Explicit language:** clear communication at all times

3 **Concrete examples:** for each activity, to facilitate comprehension

4 **Role-play:** practice in key social skills and problem-solve challenges met in the real world of relationships with both genders

5 **Structure and routine:** each activity is structured in the same way to reduce anxiety

6 **Reading others' intentions:** role-plays are used, as appropriate, in order to try to develop skills in reading others' behaviours

7 **'I do not have to copy that':** used as a mantra throughout the sessions to reinforce the importance of taking control and not being manipulated by images in the media or others' behaviours and choices

8 **Self-awareness:** 'If I do not feel comfortable, what should I do?' Real life examples are given of other girls' experiences of being used or exploited due to not 'reading it right'. Supports the development of problem-solving skills by using structured frameworks

Introduction

The structure of the activity is made explicit at the start of each session and any changes are discussed and prepared for at the outset. The structure for each activity is:

1 Group Rules

2 Talk Time

3 Ice-Breaker

4 Core Activities

5 Reflections & Feedback

6 Target-Setting

7 Compliments to Close

8 Relaxation

Every activity includes a detailed plan for the facilitator, with notes on how to deliver each element, along with approximate timings. The sessions tend to last for 1 to 1.5 hours, but this can be adapted to suit the needs and requirements of each group of girls. Each plan lists the worksheets for the activity, which can be copied or printed prior to the start of the session. In addition, the plan refers the facilitator to guides in the Resources section ('Reflections & Feedback', 'The Golden Scroll' & 'Guided Relaxation'). The session notes indicate when, where and how to use each of the worksheets and facilitator guides. Each activity clearly lists any further resources that may be needed, for example, marker pens, paper, coloured pens. 'Notes' are also highlighted to alert you to any sensitive areas or specific points to look out for and consider more carefully.

The activities that make up the Toolkit are as follows:

Part 1 Me & My Mental Health

1 About Me
  Group Rules
  Layers of Myself

2 Physical & Mental Health
  Ideas for Physical & Mental Fitness
  My Energisers & Motivators

3 My Self Concept
  Building Confidence
  Learning from Failure

4 Resilience
  Control Spectrum
  Noticing Beliefs

5 Self-Esteem
  My Self-Esteem
  A Good Friend

6 Managing Stress & Anxiety 1
  What is Stress?
  Stress-Busting

Introduction

7 Managing Stress & Anxiety 2
Stress versus Anxiety
Understand Panic

8 Managing Stress & Anxiety 3
The Worry Tree 1
The Worry Tree 2

9 Self-Harm 1
Amie's Story
Keeping Safe

10 Self-Harm 2
A Letter from Sally
My Safety Plan

Part 2 Relationships & Communication Skills

1 Non-Verbal Communication
Non-Verbal Communication
Photo Stories

2 Verbal Communication
What is Assertiveness?
My Scripts

3 Relationships 1
Speak & Guess Cards
Other People

4 Relationships 2
Beliefs about Relationships
Good Partners versus Toxic Partners

5 Relationships 3
Challenging Controlling Behaviour
The Effects of Kindness

6 Sexual Behaviours
Exploitation
Sources of Support

7 Online Behaviours
Online Grooming
Online Grooming Case Study

8 Media & Other Influences 1
Online Images
Sexting

9 Media & Other Influences 2
Who Are You Talking To?
Safe Profiles

10 Risk-Taking
Saying 'No'
Risk

Part 3 My Toolbox for Wellbeing & Future Health

1 Effective Thinking 1
Positive Mental Attitude (PMA)
Thoughts, Feelings, Behaviours

2 Effective Thinking 2
NAT-Bashing
Socratic Questioning

3 Relaxation & Mindfulness 1
Explaining Mindfulness
Mindful Mouthful

4 Relaxation & Mindfulness 2
Relaxation Techniques
My Mindful Timetable

5 Being Solution-Focused
Problem-Free Talk
Forgiveness

6 Future Hopes, Dreams & Realities 1
Many Selves
My Life Map

7   Future Hopes, Dreams & Realities 2
    A Preferred Future
    Looking Forward

8   Evaluation
    Situations Circles
    Trust Map

9   My Targets 1
    The Stages of Change
    Relapse Planning

10 My Targets 2
    Target-Setting
    My Positive Future

It is important that you make yourself aware of the contents and aims of each activity to ensure that their selection (if you choose not to deliver all of the activities in sequence) is appropriate to your group. It may be appropriate to select a more focused set of activities that highlights key areas, for instance, relationships or self-image. You will also need to take time constraints into account in order to allocate sufficient time to deliver all of these activities in sequence.

Outcomes

It is hoped that the success of the programme can be measured in the following areas:

* prompting school staff to reflect upon their practices and how these may impact upon students' behaviour, self-esteem and social and emotional development – particularly in terms of developing personal coping strategies and problem-solving skills

* prompting a review of policies on self-esteem, emotional literacy and emotional support for students in order to further develop more inclusive whole-school approaches that take into account the specific needs of ASD girls

* identifying any staff and student training needs in the areas of emotional awareness, mentoring, stress and anger management, assertiveness skills and basic counselling approaches for those with ASD in particular

* enabling students to develop a more in-depth awareness of, and understanding of, their own feelings, attitudes and behaviours

* encouraging students to reflect more specifically upon their own feelings and behaviours, being able to recognise and articulate both negative and positive patterns

* increasing students' self-esteem/self-concept

* supporting the students' ability to understand and articulate the nature and causes of stress, in both personal and more general terms, and to acknowledge the fact that stress is person-specific

* assisting the students' understanding of the ways in which positive thinking and challenging and reframing negative automatic thoughts (NATs) can minimise stress and anxiety

Introduction

- increasing confidence, listening skills, assertive behaviours, cooperation and empathy
- increasing students' ability to recognise their own and others' optimal stress levels and the reactions and behaviours that both increase and reduce stress
- promoting an understanding of the importance of emotional support, a healthy lifestyle, the development of organisational skills, relaxation techniques and assertiveness skills in coping effectively with anxiety and to make use of this range of strategies in the process
- enabling students to develop skills of reflection and consequently to develop and set realistic personal goals and targets
- removing the risk of students suffering from extreme levels of anxiety and withdrawing from the school context
- supporting the students in their understanding of the risks involved in some online behaviours and relationships
- supporting the students in their understanding of the concept of consent in sexual relationships
- developing students' ability to transfer the skills and strategies taught into a range of social contexts
- increasing staff knowledge and awareness of the specific needs of ASD girls and to feel more confident in referring students on to appropriate specialist agencies at the appropriate time.

Confidentiality: an important note

It is essential that young people who participate in the programme feel safe, comfortable and secure in the knowledge that their contributions will be treated with respect and in confidence. When setting up the group and agreeing a set of group rules, each person needs to be made aware of the necessity to keep conversations private to the group. Divulging other people's views or problems outside the group would be a total betrayal of trust and damage the self-esteem and confidence of those involved. You will need to explicitly state that such behaviour will not be tolerated. Any students who chose to break this rule would, as a consequence, be required to give up their place on the course. Although this may appear quite harsh, it is essential to maintain such a position if all participants are to benefit from the group problem-solving work and to develop the mental health self-management skills that they need within a truly supportive framework.

Looking Ahead: Continuation of Support

Once students have completed the programme, it may be necessary to continue to monitor progress and to provide access to an appropriate support system. This may include ongoing mentoring or involvement of outside agencies. Clearly, whatever decisions are made, the individual needs and requirements of the students will need to be carefully assessed. Many of the students who will have been targeted via the course will have certainly appreciated the increase in their access to real 'Listening Time'. A mentoring scheme would at least continue to ensure weekly one-to-one sessions, during which students could discuss specific stress-related problems that they have encountered and will ensure that they have a confidential forum in which to problem-solve and further develop their skills in managing stress and remaining solution-focused and positive in outlook.

The mentoring approach could, in turn, also form the basis of a whole-school policy and approach to 'listening time': this may well include the setting up of peer support groups, for instance, self-help groups that focus on sharing and developing mental health/wellbeing self-management skills. This would necessarily have resource and training implications, for example: training for staff and students in basic counselling skills, a review of the PSHE curriculum, the setting up of mentoring programmes and the creation of specific 'listening' environments.

Referring on & raising awareness

However school-based staff choose to further support students in their care, it is essential that they are aware of those who may require additional support from a specialist therapeutic agency. It is also important that all adults involved in working with young people become increasingly aware of mental health issues in general and the ways in which these are currently experienced by adolescents in our complex and ever-changing society.

Working with Parents & Carers

Families, and in particular parents, play a major role with regard to supporting adolescent girls with ASD in mainstream education and, as a result, this intervention places a high value on working supportively with families. It is proposed that educating families on how ASD might present in a young person and how to manage more challenging behaviours could have a positive impact on home life.

Despite the identification of parents as key supporters, it would appear that there is a limited amount of help available for the parents of children with ASD. Additionally, given the presentation of ASD as a predominantly male disorder (Sayal *et al*, 2006), much of the support available appears to be targeted at boys, isolating girls with ASD further still (Cridland *et al*,

Introduction

2014). When interviewing the mothers of adolescent girls with ASD, a common theme identified by Cridland *et al* (2014) was the lack of support following diagnosis. Many mothers felt that there were limited services available to assist their understanding, or help them adapt to their daughters' diagnoses. It is felt that this understanding of the needs of their daughters is essential in order for parents to support them fully.

Therefore, whilst focusing specifically on the female population, *The ASD Girls' Wellbeing Toolkit* aims to provide support for the parents of girls with ASD. This is encouraged through the provision of the information sheets in Part 4, as well as the opportunity for schools to host an introductory evening, using the PowerPoint presentation.

Notes for Facilitators

Each activity plan includes clear notes regarding the delivery of that activity. However, we would strongly recommend that prior to delivering this (or any similar) intervention, staff should make reference to the facilitator's checklist below. It is important to be aware of your own views and attitudes and the ways in which these should and should not impact upon delivery and outcomes.

NB In some sessions there are activities which make reference to specific websites and / or online links. We have tried to ensure that these are all currently available but there may be occasions where the link has been deleted. This should not happen frequently so we would suggest that the facilitator might need to check prior to delivering the session and ensure that they have sourced an alternative should this be necessary. We would always also advise to check such links to also ensure that you feel they are entirely appropriate for your specific group.

The facilitator's checklist

Preparation for delivery of this programme must include both practical considerations relating to room use, resources and so on, as well as reflection on your own experience of behavioural change and wellbeing, your skills as a facilitator, and the need to reduce risk and create a learning environment that feels safe for your students.

The checklist below (adapted from Rae & Weymont, 2006) has been developed to help you prepare thoroughly. It may be useful as an exercise to help you establish priorities for discussion or action. It is not definitive and it may be appropriate to add other points that relate more specifically to your situation.

While it is not essential that you have all the knowledge, skills and experience implied below, it is essential that you are aware of your strengths and weaknesses and that you take the necessary steps to ensure you are well prepared.

Remember, mental health can be an emotional topic and may arouse strong feelings and reactions. It is important that you feel able to 'hold' a group and are prepared to deal with difficulties that arise. It is important that the learning process itself is 'emotionally literate' and that a supportive, empathic and caring ethos is promoted from the outset.

Ideally, it would be helpful for two facilitators to run the programme. This could be a 'lead facilitator' (for example, a learning mentor, teacher or visiting professional), supported by a learning support assistant. If there are two facilitators, you can withdraw individuals if necessary; it also means one of you can take on an observer role if appropriate.

The lead facilitator should:

- Have experience or a secure understanding of group processes and basic therapeutic techniques
- Have a sound knowledge of ASD and strategies and interventions to support students in school
- Have experience of delivering group work and Circle Time
- Have a positive approach and proven skills in relation to social inclusion
- Be committed to developing their own emotional literacy
- Have a reflective approach to their teaching and learning
- Understand how emotional literacy promotes mental health and school achievement

Before starting this programme, facilitators should discuss any personal experience, helpful or unhelpful, of behavioural change and mental health issues with each other. Consideration should also be given to ways in which you will support each other during the programme.

1 Whole-school readiness

- In your opinion, has the school dealt well with wellbeing issues amongst staff and students?
- Does the school have an active policy on behaviour and bullying?
- Who is the member of staff responsible for SEN, travellers, homeless, looked-after, adopted children and refugees?
- Are school exclusions dealt with systematically, fairly and as a last resort?

Introduction

- Will you be supported by senior management?
- How will you deal with colleagues or parents/carers who have a strong negative reaction to this work?
- How will you explain the work to parents/carers?
- Is there a whole school policy on wellbeing and mental health?
- To whom are you accountable in this role?

2 Reducing risk

- Think about writing a letter to parents and carers to either secure their consent, or inform them of your intentions (see Part 4, 'Information Sheets', for suggested templates).
- Identify potentially vulnerable students prior to starting the group.
- Do you feel confident to manage the contributions of those at risk of exclusion?
- Do you feel confident to manage the contributions of those underachieving?
- Do you feel confident to manage the contributions of those engaged in youth offending?
- What self-management strategies will you use to prepare yourself for each activity?
- Can you provide one-to-one time for students who need it? How will you identify those pupils?
- Will you evaluate each activity on the same day as it is held?
- How will 'lessons learned' when running this group be fed into future planning for this work?
- When planning the programme, identify 'What if …?' worst case scenarios. This will help you to anticipate and prevent problems.
- Who will provide supervision for you? Do you have access to an experienced colleague who could take on this role? How would this support ensure your safety and how will you access and find this support?

3 Inclusion

- Are the classroom and the curriculum accessible to all learners? Will your sessions include everyone, or will you target young people in specific groups?
- How will you manage the introduction of differentiated tasks for some learners?
- How will you pay attention to different learning styles?

Introduction

- How will you ensure that resources and anecdotes do not portray the world as exclusively young, white, middle-class, able-bodied and heterosexual?

- Will your displays represent the cultural diversity of our society? Will they challenge stereotypes?

- Will you challenge the discriminatory attitudes and practices of some students constructively?

- How are the needs of bilingual and ethnic minority learners met?

- What are your own beliefs about behavioural change and the use of evidence-based interventions to achieve this?

- What are the dominant cultural values and/or religious beliefs in the school? In what ways will this help or hinder the effective delivery of the programme?

4 Groupwork & team-teaching

- Do you understand the difference between groupwork and working in groups?

- Have you and your co-facilitator discussed:

    * How much you will disclose
    * How and when you will evaluate each activity
    * What happens if one of you is absent
    * What you will do if a student is absent
    * The benefits of having one of you taking an observer role for some activities
    * A draft opening statement for your first session
    * Suggested group rules
    * How you will manage any resulting paperwork
    * Strategies for managing difficult individuals and behaviour in groups
    * A shared view on how you will manage difficulties
    * How you would like to give each other feedback?

Conclusion

'Experiencing tension and stress is a normal part of everyday life and, to a certain extent, a necessary one, if individuals are to effectively grow and effect change. What is essential is that such stress is managed effectively and kept to a manageable level so that individuals can maintain a healthy balance of tension, growth, rest and self-nurturing.' (Rae, 2001)

The fostering and maintenance of students' wellbeing and ability to cope effectively with the usual and less usual stressors of adolescent life remains the key objective for us in developing this intervention. It is essential that we ensure more vulnerable populations, such as girls and young women with ASD, have the necessary support to effectively manage and maintain their own wellbeing and levels of anxiety in an increasingly complex and stressful social and learning context. This cannot be disputed, given the fact that there is now such an awareness of the increased risk and elevated levels of mental ill health in those with ASD generally (Crane *et al*, 2018; Simonoff *et al*, 2008). It is hoped that *The ASD Girls' Wellbeing Toolkit* will begin to provide the necessary resources and support for professionals and carers to begin to meet such an objective.

Notes for the PowerPoint Presentation

The following notes are designed to facilitate using the PowerPoint presentation. Slides which will benefit from further clarification, information from the presenter, or a group discussion are taken in turn.

2 Go through the key aims as listed in the slide.

3 This lack of a diagnosis for some of our girls has been a problem for some time. You may wish to ask the group is they have been aware of such concerns and to perhaps discuss these together to identify areas of agreement.

In recent years, professionals working with young people with Autistic Spectrum Disorders (ASD) have become more aware of the need to ensure the timely and appropriate diagnosis of girls. Without such a diagnosis and the relevant support systems being put in place, such girls and young women are clearly at high risk of developing mental health difficulties such as anxiety, depression, self-harm and eating disorders.

Such disorders will ultimately put them at risk of disengaging with the learning process and school in general. Boys with ASD tend to be less social than their peers and display prominent and obvious areas of obsessive interests and compulsions. In contrast, Girls with autism appear to be more able to follow or imitate social actions. In the early years they can mimic socially appropriate behaviour, without understanding what they are doing or why they are doing it. This can result in the masking of their difficulties and we feel that this is directly linked to the under-diagnosis of Autism in Girls.

4 Reinforce the fact that the level of camouflaging that girls may engage in on a daily basis alongside the repressing of their autistic behaviours, can be extremely tiring and stressful and is perhaps a direct cause of the high statistics of women on the continuum with mental health problems (Yaull-Smith, 2007). It may also be helpful to highlight some examples from the group. What have they observed in their girls? How does this impact upon behaviours in the home?

5 Social isolation and anxiety can be a problem for the ASD girl.

A high level of anxiety is common among girls with autism for whom the world can be a confusing and unpredictable place. To minimize this, they may need to exert a high level of control on their environment and the people in it. This can result in quite ritualised behaviour, inflexible routines and meltdowns when unplanned events occur.

Autistic girls are often 'people pleasers' and will spend all day at school trying very hard to do the right thing and conform. As a result, home life often suffers as they vent their frustration and anxiety for hours at the end of every school day when they are in a context in which they feel that they do not have to conform and hole in all the anxiety that they have been experiencing.

Notes for the PowerPoint Presentation

6 Essentially, what we want for these girls is good mental health. This slide illustrates the key aspects of this.

8 Logically of course, the key characteristics of poor mental health are the opposite of those of good mental health.

9 It is important to also introduce the idea of mental health upon a continuum and perhaps facilitate a discussion around recovery and the fact that it is possible to have good mental and emotional wellbeing despite having a diagnosis of a mental health disorder.

Also highlight why it is so vital to ensure mental health in our children and young people to develop good mental health as we are now fully aware that people with higher levels of good mental health and wellbeing have better general health, use health services less, live longer, have better educational outcomes, are more likely to undertake healthier lifestyles, including reduced smoking and harmful levels of drinking, are more productive at work, take less time off sick, have higher income, have stronger social relationships and are more social. Higher levels of mental wellbeing are also associated with reduced levels of mental ill health in adulthood (Centre for Mental Health, 2009; Coid et al, 2006; Lyubomirsky et al, 2005; Boorman, 2009; Deacon et al, 2013; Dolan et al, 2006; Keyes et al, 2005 & 2010; Mills et al, 2007; NICE, 2009; Pressman & Cohen, 2005; Chida & Steptoe, 2008).

The emphasis is on the fact that we all have mental health challenges and various things affect our equilibrium. At any time in our lives we may be moving along the continuum.

Activity Participants are asked to consider events and occurrences that would move them along the continuum.

You could make some suggestions e.g., bereavement pushing a person along towards the vulnerable end and winning the lottery placing you at the resilient end - or not?

Additional factors should be introduced and considered such as being made redundant, being bullied, achieving success in exams, feeling safe and secure and having someone to talk to who you can trust.

10 You can next ask the group to discuss the different types of mental health problems that children and young people in school may experience throughout their education and to also discuss how is this different or similar for those with ASD?

11 You can ask the group what they feel about this. What are their concerns and what do they think their girls and most young people are worried about? What are we trying to prevent by intervening in this way?

12 This is important as these are the so-called neurotypical girls. It stands to reason that the ASD girl will also be at risk.

Now that we have a greater awareness of the increased risk and raised levels of mental ill health in those with ASD generally (Crane et al, 2018; Simonoff et al, 2008), it is surely vital that we develop interventions to specifically promote their mental health and wellbeing both at school and home. This is the main driver for *The ASD Girls' Wellbeing Tool Kit*.

13 The statistics are clearly alarming for all our young people.

14   Key concerns are the ways in which young people are engaging in self-harm as a means of managing psychological pain and the fact that ASD girls are included in such a statistic, and are more at risk of the impact of social media in this area.

A common concern for parents/carers and staff is that by talking about self-harm it might make more students think about doing it. This topic is included in The ASD Girls' Wellbeing Tool Kit as the evidence in fact suggests that the opposite is true and this is clearly an area of concern for many of our young people. While this can feel a sensitive topic, it is a very important and relevant one. Talking to young people about self-harm is going to give them knowledge, confidence and an understanding of how to support themselves and others. The role of the facilitator in the sessions is to de-mystify a topic which can be very powerful and upsetting for young people. By talking about it and sign-posting towards support young people can be empowered.

15   Social media is now an addiction for some, and the ASD girl is at risk due to the nature of online contact and the problems in misreading messages and information and/or becoming obsessed with specific individuals or ideas.

16   The online world is clearly a daily diet for many children and young people, including our girls.

17   Self-harm websites remain a concern too.

The limited research focusing on ASD children and self-harm does point strongly to increased risk for this group in adolescence (Culpin et al 2018, Hedley et al 2018) which is also a key driver for including the topic in this programme of support. It is also vital to bear in mind that although few of those who engage in self-harming behaviours such as cutting will attempt suicide, most young people who attempt suicide have previously self-harmed and self-harm can be seen to considerably raise the risk of suicide (Olfson et al, 2018). It is therefore vital for both school-based staff and parents/carers to remain vigilant and be aware of the risk factors such as physical, sexual or emotional abuse, low self-esteem and anxiety and difficulties in relationships. Gaining an informed understanding of this area is also clearly an essential and relevant and more detailed information on this area is included in the Resources section.

18   For all teenagers, there will be a sense that adults do not and cannot understand them or their perspective.

Access to the online world has created more opportunities for young people to explore, experiment, socialise, create and educate themselves but it has also exposed them to the risk of harm, including seeing extreme pornography and sexting (NSPCC Report: Martellozzo et al, 2016). It is vital therefore, that we ensure they have the new skills and knowledge base in order to effectively navigate this new world and mange the levels of anxiety and stress which can so often result in a range of self-harming behaviours and other mental health difficulties such as anxiety disorders, social phobias and eating disorders.

19   It may be helpful at this point to ask the group what their own experience is of this area. Are there any similarities or shared concerns and what are the tolls or strategies they are currently using to help and support their girls?

Notes for the PowerPoint Presentation

21 These types of activities all form part of the contents and approaches of this programme.

22 It is important for schools to have effective tools and mechanisms to identify those at risk and also to monitor progress and the outcomes of any interventions. It may be helpful to ask the group how they currently do this. What are the tools they use and how are they effective for ASD girls?

23 These are the underpinning philosophical principles underlying the approach of this programme.

24 Key tools and strategies from Cognitive Behavioural Therapy (CBT) and Positive Psychology are used in this programme.

There is a need to focus upon interventions to support the development of self-help and self-management strategies for our young people so that they can become autonomous, healthy young people who are able to self-manage their anxieties and stressors on a daily basis. We also know that specific therapeutic approaches (CBT and tools from Positive Psychology) can be adapted for use with girls on the autistic continuum which is why they are included within this programme.

25 We know that all young people – particularly those going through adolescence - will frequently experience anxious and negative thoughts and doubts. These negative automatic thoughts (NATs) will often reinforce a state of inadequacy and/or low levels of self-esteem. Cognitive behaviour therapy (CBT) tools and strategies will help to support young people in reconsidering these negative assumptions and enable them to learn how to change their self-perceptions in order to improve their mental and emotional state.

26 The CBT approach breaks the problems into smaller parts. This enables the student to see how they're connected and how they affect them. This follows a process of A, B, C as follows:

A: activating event, is often referred to as the 'trigger' – the thing that causes you to engage in the negative thinking.

B: negative beliefs, which can include thoughts, rules and demands, and the meanings the individual attaches to both external and internal events.

C: consequences, or emotions, and the behaviours and physical sensations accompanying these different emotions. It is important to highlight and discuss with the students how the way that they think about a problem can affect how they feel physically and emotionally. It can also alter what they do about it. This is why the key aim for CBT is to break the negative, vicious cycle that some students may find themselves in. For example, if you think that you will get your work wrong you feel angry, and then you don't give it a try in case it is wrong.

The aim is to help the girls to reframe and challenge their NATs, replacing them with more effective thinking patterns which disrupt this vicious circle and support behaviour change which decreases the tendency to blow things out of proportion – sadly a very typical adolescent behaviour.

When working with students in identifying such faulty thinking, the main aim is to encourage them to break the negative cycle. These NATs can arise from a number of errors in our thinking, including the following six types of faulty thinking:

Doing ourselves down – only focusing on the negatives and seeing bad things about ourselves.

Blowing things up or catastrophising – making things worse than they really are.

Predicting failure – setting your mind ready to predict failure at all costs.

Over-emotional thoughts – this is when your emotions become extremely powerful and cloud your judgement.

Setting yourself up – setting yourself targets that are too high so that you know then you will fail.

Blaming yourself – thinking that everything that goes wrong is your own fault.

When working with young people, it is important to allow them time to consider the effects that these NATs can have prior to them beginning to implement some changes.

27 What we do not do is present stress as something bad. We are explicit that it is a normal part of life and can be positive. It is how we respond to it that matters the most.

'Experiencing tension and stress is a normal part of everyday life and, to a certain extent, a necessary one, if individuals are to effectively grow and effect change. What is essential is that such stress is managed effectively and kept to a management level so that individuals can maintain a healthy balance of tension, growth, rest and self-nurturing'. (Rae, 2001)

28 These are key concerns in terms of supporting ASD girls, and all the above topics are incorporated into the programme. The aim is to ensure that they have the skills to effectively meet such challenges and manage any associated stressors and anxieties.

29 The whole programme is designed to be ASD friendly – adopting a nurturing approach within a safe and contained context with facilitators who are aware of and differentiate for the specific needs of this group.

31 In *The Toolkit*, all of the activities and structure are 'ASD friendly' and each session considers and includes the key elements listed in this slide.

32 The group is a powerful mechanism to address the girls' concerns but we do need to ensure safety and confidentiality.

It is essential that students who participate in the programme feel safe, comfortable and secure in the knowledge that their contributions will be treated with respect and in confidence. When setting up the group and formulating and agreeing a set of group rules, all involved need to be made aware of the necessity to keep conversations private to the group. Divulging other's views/problems outside the group would simply be a total betrayal of trust and damage the self-esteem and confidence of those involved. The facilitator will need to explicitly state that such behaviour will not be tolerated. Any students who chose to break this rule would, as a consequence, be required to give up their place on the course. Although this may appear somewhat harsh, it is essential to maintain such a position if all the students are to benefit from the group problem-solving work and to develop the mental health self-management skills that they need within a truly supportive framework.

33 The following 3 slides detail the key elements of the 30 sessions.

Notes for the PowerPoint Presentation

36 The format for each session is the same, ensuring a sense of safety and predictability for the girls.

37 This remains the key aim of the programme.

38 Explain that you will now work through a couple of the activities that are included in the intervention.

39 This activity requires Worksheet 2.10 'Speak & Guess Cards'

Ask participants to form pairs. One must then select a 'Speak & Guess' card (cut into strips and folded in half). Ask them to read out the phrase on the card, whilst keeping in mind the alternative emotion. Person 2 must try to work out what Person 1 is thinking.

After, discuss how easy/difficult that was. What did Person 2 use as clues to work out what was happening for Person 1?

40 The group should consider each statement listed on the 'Relationship Rules Sheet' (Worksheet 2.12 – shown on the slide) and discuss whether they agree or disagree, and why. These statements act as prompts to encourage deeper discussion about why people hold different beliefs about relationships. The discussion should be nuanced, with some feeling that they agree or disagree with statements sometimes, or under certain conditions.

41 Provide participants with a piece of A4 paper folded in half. Ask them to draw around both of their hands on the piece of paper. The left hand represents the past and the right hand represents the future.

Give the participants a few minutes to reflect on where they have been and where they are going. Then, asked them to decorate each hand to represent their past and future wishes. They might want to draw pictures or write key words onto their hands. The value of this activity is in looking back into the past, safely, and then into the future.

42 The key to this programme is achieving wellbeing in our ASD girls.

43 The key objective of this programme is the development and maintenance of students' wellbeing and their ability to cope effectively with both the usual, and less usual, stressors of adolescent life. It is essential that we ensure more vulnerable populations such as girls and young women with ASD have the necessary support to effectively manage and maintain their own wellbeing and levels of anxiety in increasingly complex and stressful social and learning environments. This increase cannot be disputed as there is now such an awareness of the increased risk and raised levels of mental ill health in those with ASD generally (Crane et al 2018, Simonoff et al, 2008). It is hoped that *The ASD Girls' Wellbeing Tool Kit* will begin to provide the necessary resources and support for professionals and carers to meet such an objective.

44 End by thanking the group and allow sufficient time to address any concerns or answer questions.

Part 1
Me & My Mental Health

1 About Me
Group Rules
Layers of Myself

2 Physical & Mental Health
Ideas for Physical & Mental Fitness
My Energisers & Motivators

3 My Self Concept
Building Confidence
Learning from Failure

4 Resilience
Control Spectrum
Noticing Beliefs

5 Self-Esteem
My Self-Esteem
A Good Friend

6 Managing Stress & Anxiety 1
What is Stress?
Stress-Busting

7 Managing Stress & Anxiety 2
Stress versus Anxiety
Understand Panic

8 Managing Stress & Anxiety 3
The Worry Tree 1
The Worry Tree 2

9 Self-Harm 1
Amie's Story
Keeping Safe

10 Self-Harm 2
A Letter from Sally
My Safety Plan

Activity 1.1
About Me

Aims

* To build rapport within the group
* For the group to feel safe and confident to participate in the session
* To familiarise the group with *The ASD Girls' Wellbeing Toolkit*

Talk Time   5 mins

Materials: Worksheet 1.1 'Visual Timetable' (p. 27).

Welcome everyone to the *ASD Girls' Wellbeing Toolkit* sessions, then explain that attendance is voluntary and the range of activities are to help boost how the group feel about themselves and provide them with resources for coping with challenges in the future. Use Worksheet 1.1 to explain how each session will be structured (see also 'Introduction: An ASD-Friendly Session Structure).

Ice-Breaker   5 mins

Ask the group to sit in a circle and introduce themselves in turn, providing three 'personal' facts about themselves to the group. Role-model an introduction before the group begins, for example: 'I am Mrs Rae. I am 58 years old and I like writing and going to the gym.'

> If a student is reluctant to talk, they should be given the opportunity to pass. Make this very clear now and underline that this rule applies throughout every session they will experience together.

Core Activity 1: Group Rules   5 mins

Materials: A3 paper, or whiteboard, or flip chart, with appropriate pens.

Emphasise the importance of setting appropriate group rules in order to ensure that everyone can contribute and feel safe and secure within the group. If the students have difficulty in thinking of rules, you could start them off with some suggestions: read out the ideas below and let them select the ones they feel most appropriate to their group. Create a Group Rules Chart by writing the chosen rules on a large sheet of paper, flip chart or white board. Rules could include:

- It is important that we listen to each other and show each other respect.
- We should not judge each other or put each other down.
- We need to be tolerant and not think ourselves in any sense superior to someone else or their culture.
- We need to empathise and think about other people's feelings in the group.
- We need to keep things confidential to the group and not talk about them outside of the room.
- Any person can pass on any question or activity if they need to.

Emphasise that everyone needs to agree to the rules and adhere to them throughout the remaining sessions. Stress that if a group member does break any of the rules this means that they will be challenged about their responses or behaviours.

Mention that the group rules will be underlined at the start of every session.

Core Activity 2: Layers of Myself 20 mins

Materials: Worksheets 1.2 'Like or Dislike?' (p.28) & 1.3 'Circles' (p. 29).

Shoe boxes (one each), small sandwich bags (two each), paper plates, box of postcards and other visual images, coloured pens, scissors, safe internet access. Craft & collage materials, including: glue, coloured paper, plain paper, glitter, straws, pipe cleaners, polystyrene, balls, 'googly' eyes, fabric, beads, ribbon, string, wool, large sticky labels to write and draw on.

Explain that this activity is about slowly and gently identifying our core beliefs about ourselves, while building up our own picture of ourselves, layer by layer. Core beliefs can be thought of as a buried deep within us and it can take some time and effort to identify what they might be. Identifying them can be useful, because it can help us to understand some of our thoughts, feelings and behaviours, as well as starting to think about how we might control them.

Tell the students that the first step in the activity is to decorate their shoe box as they wish. Their box is going to bring together their view of themselves, so they have complete control over decorating and personalising their own box. It may have their name on it, or be labelled 'Me', or simply be decorated with things that they like, or feel represent them. You might say, 'As we work through the activity, this box will hold representations of the various 'layers' of you – different things about you that make you, you.' Mention also that the students may wish to continue to add layers of information in later sessions.

Guide the students as they add different 'layers' to their box:

>   **Layer 1: physical appearance**   This first layer can be: a picture that you draw of yourself, or a photograph; a picture of your face stuck onto, or drawn onto, a paper plate; a list of

words that you feel describe what you look like; a model or puppet representing yourself, or a Bitmoji. Place the picture or model in the box.

Layer 2: likes and dislikes   Choose items to cut out from Worksheet 1.2 – things that you like and dislike. Make two piles and put a pile in each sandwich bag. Label the bags 'Like' and 'Dislike' and put them in the box.

Layer 3: places I like   Use the internet to find pictures of places that you like to print off and place in your box.

Layer 4: people I like and admire   Use Worksheet 3.1 to note down people you like or admire, or are important to you in some way. (Everyone should be encouraged to do this in their own way, for example: the different circles may represent different types of relationship, or levels of closeness.) Put the sheet in the box.

Layer 5 beliefs   Identify one helpful or positive belief about yourself. When you have identified your belief, write it on a sticky label, illustrate it, and put it in the box.

Remind students what a belief is: something you think is true, in this case about yourself. Group members are looking for positive beliefs, so make time for a sensitive and individualised discussion and try to steer it in a positive direction when appropriate. This can be done by using 'I am', 'I can' and 'I have' as prompts.

You might also like to consider things the student has done that have gone well or things that have been said to them about their strengths. Encourage them to wonder what it was about them (e.g., 'I am tough', 'I am kind') that meant that the thing went well. This, in turn, may indicate beliefs (e.g., you should never show weakness; you should always treat people as you would like to be treated).

Sometimes beliefs seem to be negative, but on examination this is not so clear. What is important is to start a group conversation about beliefs and come up with a belief that may have helped each student succeed or survive at some point in their life.

Some examples of positive beliefs about the self:

- I can make new friends easily
- I can cook
- I am tough
- Everything will be alright
- I can work my way through this
- I should try my best
- I am smart
- I should keep on trying, even when it is hard

Reflections & Feedback 5 mins

Materials: Facilitator Guide 1 'Reflections & Feedback' (p. 262).

Ask the students to focus on the questions on the facilitator guide.

Target-Setting 5 mins

Materials: Worksheet 1.4 'My Targets' (p. 30) (one each); pens.

Use Worksheet 1.4 to help each student set their targets for the coming week. They can do this in pairs and support each other to identify what they would like to work on.

Compliments to Close 5 mins

Materials: Prepare a 'Golden Scroll' for each person (a 1m length of paper) and a gold permanent marker each.

To close the session, the aim is to provide each of the students with positive feedback. It will be important to ensure that each student is given a compliment and this may include highlighting the following behaviours or responses:

- Listening well and attentively
- Taking turns/waiting for a turn
- Showing empathy or concern for others
- Being thoughtful
- Supporting someone who found responding or contributing difficult
- Working hard on the activities
- Building on others' ideas and not putting anyone down
- Overcoming any initial embarrassment or fear and trying to contribute
- Being honest and reflective about themselves
- Making a contribution
- Having a go and being positive

Compliments can be given by you or by other members of the group: it is helpful to reinforce these positives by encouraging students to identify one thing that each member of the group has done well in the session.

Compliments can be recorded on the students' own Golden Scrolls. The name of each student should be written at the top of their scroll; you then can go around the circle asking students to say something positive about each other. They can choose an attribute or a specific skill, or something that the student has done well during the session.

The scrolls will be added to each week and given to the students at the end of the series of sessions.

Relaxation   10 mins

Materials: Facilitator Guide 3 'Guided Relaxation' (p. 264).

Use the script on the facilitator's guide to support the students in deep relaxation.

Worksheet 1.1
Visual Timetable

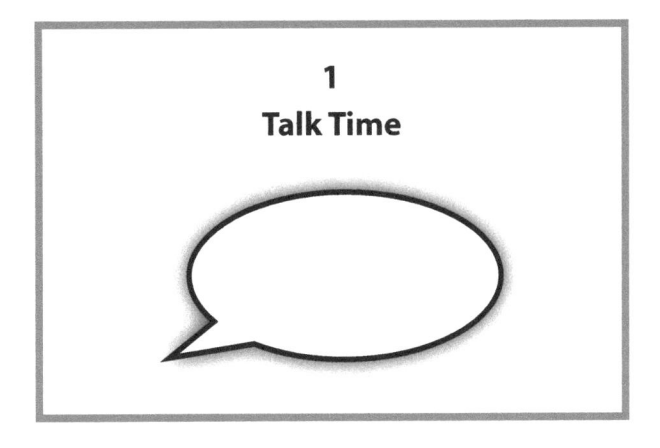

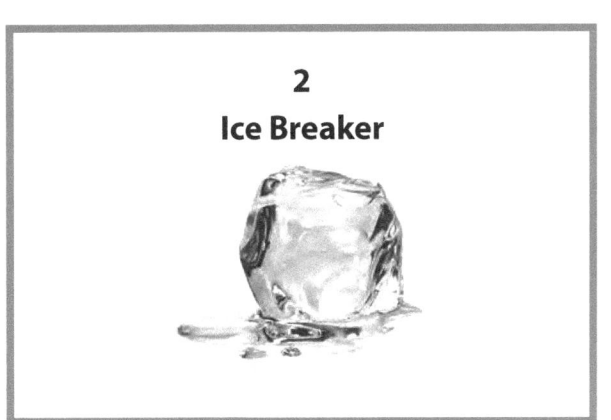

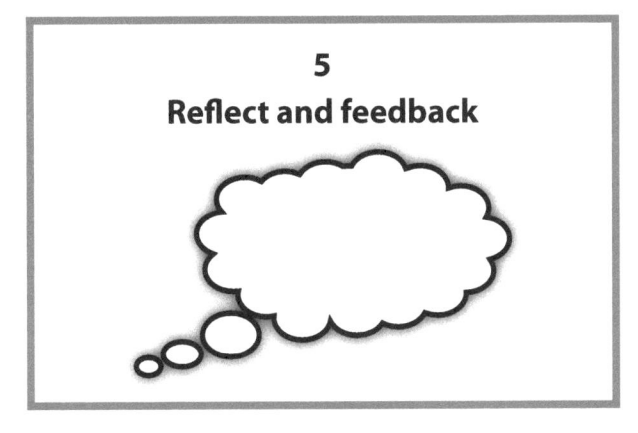

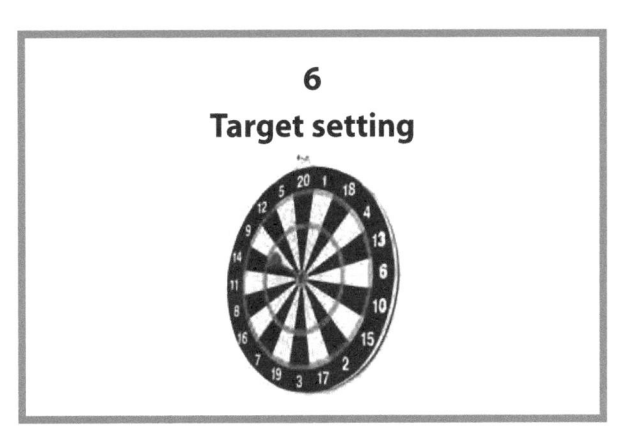

All activities

1 Talk Time	2 Ice Breaker
3 Core Activity 1	4 Core Activity 2
5 Reflect and feedback	6 Target setting
7 Golden Scroll	8 Relax

Worksheet 1.1

This page may be photocopied for instructional use only. *The ASD Girls' Wellbeing Toolkit* © Tina Rae & Amy Such 2019

Worksheet 1.2

Like or Dislike?

Activity 1.1

Make your own	Make your own	Make your own

Worksheet 1.3
Circles

Activity 1.1

Worksheet 1.4
My Targets

All activities

```
 0
 1
 2
 3
 4
 5
 6
 7
 8
 9
10
```

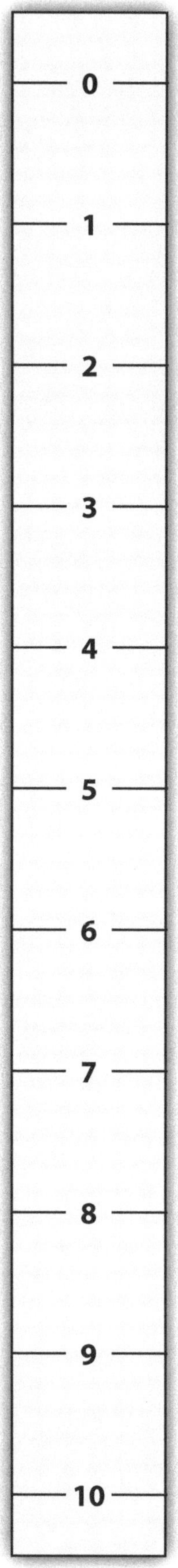

Mark where you are now on the scale.

I am at point _____

What have you done to get as far as that?

I have done these things:

✳ _____

✳ _____

✳ _____

✳ _____

Where would you like to be?

I would like to reach point _____

How can you get there?

My targets to reach that point are:

✳ _____

✳ _____

✳ _____

✳ _____

Activity 1.2
Physical & Mental Health

Aims

- To build rapport between students
- For the students to feel safe & confident to participate in the session
- To remind the students of the purpose of *The ASD Girls' Wellbeing Toolkit*
- To introduce the idea of keeping ourselves healthy

Group Rules   2 mins

Materials: Worksheet 1.1 'Visual Timetable' (p. 27); Group Rules Chart created in Activity 1.1.

Using Worksheet 1.1 and the Group Rules Chart, remind the group of the structure of each session and of the rules that were agreed in Activity 1.1. It might be useful to have these displayed on the wall of the room in which you are meeting so they can be referred back to when necessary. Ask the students if there are any additional rules they feel it would be appropriate to add, or if they would like any of the rules to be explained again.

Talk Time   5 mins

Materials: Post-it notes.

Ask the students: 'What can people do to keep themselves healthy?' Give the group the opportunity to discuss their answers, to write them on post-its, or to reflect on their responses without sharing with the group.

Ice-Breaker   5 mins

Materials: Ball of wool or string

Ask the students to stand in a circle. Holding the end of a ball of wool or string in your hand, throw the ball to a student. Whoever catches the ball must pick a number from 1 to 15.

Each number corresponds to a question that they are invited to answer. They may choose not to answer if they would rather not.

1. What is your favourite colour?
2. What is your favourite film?
3. Which radio station do you listen to the most?
4. What book/magazine are you reading at the moment?
5. If you were on a desert island, what one item would you want to have with you?
6. If you could go anywhere on holiday, where would you most like to go?
7. What is your favourite subject at school?
8. Would you rather watch soaps or sport on the TV?
9. If you were an animal, which animal would you like to be?
10. What do you like doing at the weekend?
11. Who is your favourite cartoon character?
12. What is the weirdest thing you have ever eaten?
13. If you could only eat one thing for the rest of your life, what would you pick?
14. What is the best thing that has happened so far this week?
15. How many brothers and sisters do you have?

They must then keep hold of a section of the wool or string whilst throwing the ball on to another student. Ensure that each student has the opportunity to hold a piece of the wool or string.

Ultimately, a web of wool or string will have formed: reflect on this, explaining that it was important for each member to be a part of the group otherwise the web would look different. Hopefully, the students have also become more familiar with each other through answering the questions.

Core Activity 1: Physical & Mental Fitness   10 mins

Materials: Worksheet 1.5 'Ideas for Physical & Mental Fitness' (p. 35) (one each); scissors.

This activity is designed to encourage the students to identify ways in which they can maintain both physical and mental health into the future. Provide each student with a copy of Worksheet 1.5.

Instruct students to cut out the statements and then sort them into order, in terms of the most healthy options and least healthy options for maintaining positive physical and mental health. Allow time for them to compare their sequence with others.

Use the following prompts to aid discussion:

* Do you agree on what constitutes a healthy lifestyle that promotes and maintains wellbeing?
* Can you justify your ideas?

Core Activity 2: Energisers & Motivators   15 mins

Materials: Worksheet 1.6 'What Motivates Me?' (p. 36) (one each); pens.

Research suggests that many teenagers have high aspirations and ideas for their future, but they have low expectations. If they have high ambitions, but no expectation of attaining them, there is disconnect between what they want and what they are doing. What will help in this situation is for the young person to develop the habits required to reach their aspirations.

1 **Determine Goals.** First we need to identify what it is we want to achieve.

2 **Identify energisers & motivators.** To remain positive about the future and continue working toward our goals, we need to keep motivated and it is crucial to identify our key energisers and motivators. These can be people, situations, particular hobbies, passions and interests. The students are therefore asked to consider their top motivators and record them on Worksheet 6.1. In other words, 'what is important to you?'

3 **How healthy are my motivators?** They should then think about how healthy these motivators are, and if they contribute to achieving the best possible outcome for their lives.

It will be important to distinguish between healthy and unhealthy energisers and motivators, as you will really want the group to recognise the fact that wellbeing can only be maintained via promoting the use of positive tools. For example, some students may say that they are energised and motivated by taking drugs or smoking and that this helps to maintain their overall wellbeing.

This page may be photocopied for instructional use only. *The ASD Girls' Wellbeing Toolkit* © Tina Rae & Amy Such 2019

> It is important not to judge contributions of unhealthy energisers, whilst also encouraging the group to consider the negative outcomes these may incur in the longer term.

Explain to the students that in the longer term it is vital that their key energisers have healthy benefits, both physically and emotionally.

Reflections & Feedback — 5 mins

Materials: Facilitator's Guide 1 'Reflections & Feedback' (p. 262).

Ask the students to focus on the questions on the guide.

Target-Setting — 5 mins

Materials: Worksheet 1.4 'My Targets' (p. 30) (one each); pens.

Use Worksheet 1.4 to support each student in setting their weekly targets. They can do this in pairs and support each other to identify what they would like to work on during the coming week. Allow a little time for reflection on the achievement (or otherwise) of the previous week's targets.

Compliments to Close — 5 mins

Materials: Each individual's 'Golden Scroll' & a gold permanent marker each; Facilitator's Guide 2 'The Golden Scroll' (p. 263).

The guide will support you in directing the group as they add positive comments to their Golden Scrolls.

Relaxation — 10 mins

Materials: Facilitator's Guide 3 'Guided Relaxation' (p. 264).

Use the script on the facilitator guide to support the students in deep relaxation.

Worksheet 1.5

Ideas for Physical & Mental Health

Activity 1.2

Taking regular exercise	Not eating junk food
Going to lots of parties	Unprotected sex
Sleeping for 7–9 hours a night	Feeling happy
Low self-esteem	Feeling confident
Using stress-busters	Enjoying hobbies
Eating fruit and vegetables	Reframing those Negative Automatic Thoughts
Not smoking or taking drugs	Liking other people and doing things for them
Eating a low-fat diet	Being optimistic
Not eating sweets or too much sugar	Eating at regular times
Having good friends	Doing acts of kindness
Eating fibre each day	Being able to relax
Sharing with other people	A high-fat diet
Being the 'right' weight for your height	Not getting anxious about things

Worksheet 1.6

What Motivates Me?

Activity 1.2

WHAT MOTIVATES ME?

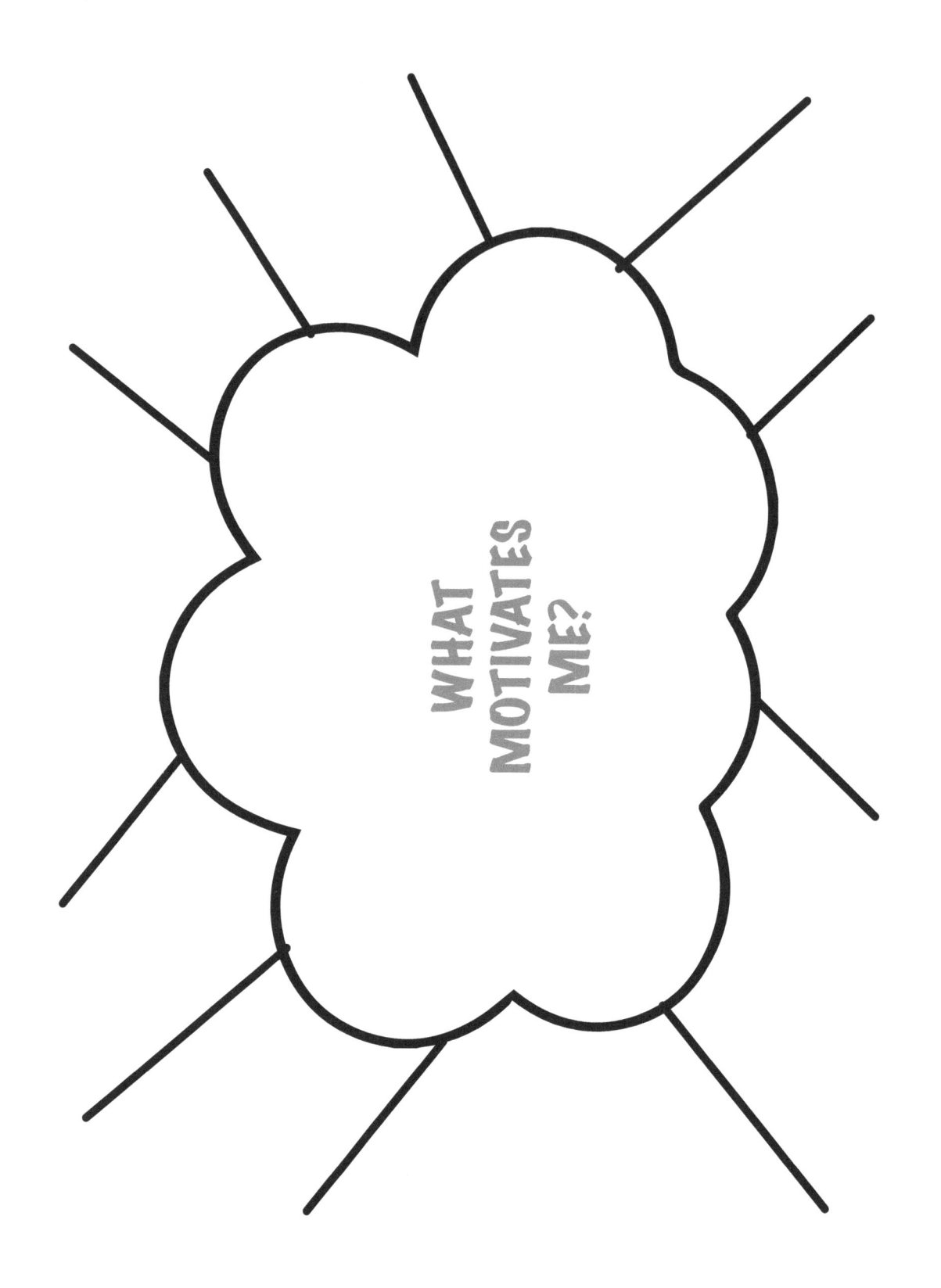

Activity 1.3
My Self Concept

Aims

* To build rapport between students
* For the students to feel safe & confident to participate in the session
* To develop our understanding of 'self-concept'
* To discuss strategies for increasing confidence in ourselves

Group Rules   2 mins

Materials: Worksheet 1.1 'Visual Timetable' (p. 27); Group Rules Chart created in Activity 1.1.

Using Worksheet 1.1 and the Group Rules Chart, remind the group of the structure of each session and of the rules that were agreed in Activity 1.1.

Talk Time   5 mins

Materials: Post-it notes.

Ask the students: 'When do you feel confident?' Give the group an opportunity to discuss their answers, write them on post-its, or to reflect on their responses without sharing with the group.

Ice-Breaker   5 mins

Materials: Worksheet 1.7 'Bingo!' (p. 41) (one different sheet for each person; suitable for a group of up to six).

Worksheet 1.7 consists of six Bingo sheets, on which Bingo numbers are replaced by 16 different kinds of people; each of the 16 is repeated on the six sheets, but in a different sheet position.

Give each student a different bingo sheet and then encourage the students discuss the ways in which the members of their group are different or similar, in light of the qualities, characteristics or interests of the people that appear on the Bingo sheet. If they decide that someone in the group shares a quality, characteristic or interest with a personality on the Bingo sheet, ask them to write the name of the group member the correct box.

The first student to fill a full row, column or diagonal shouts out 'Bingo!' and is the winner.

Core Activity 1: Building Confidence   10 mins

Materials: Worksheet 1.8 'Sources of Confidence' (p. 47) (one each); paper & pens.

Give Worksheet 1.8 to each member of the group. On the worksheet they will see listed the four main sources of confidence, as follows:

1   **Experience:** Previous success will make you feel confident

2   **Role models:** Positive people who are confident will inspire you

3   **Encouragement:** People who believe in you will make you feel confident

4   **Managing feelings:** Your ability to manage stress and cope when it goes wrong will help you to feel confident

This activity helps them to see that their ability to manage stress and cope when things go wrong will give them confidence and that people, places, situations and memories can all give and take away our confidence. The group are asked to consider and then record their own examples of each category – verbally or in writing, as appropriate.

Within this activity, you may wish to discuss confidence givers and confidence takers. This will reinforce the need for us to try to surround ourselves with those who are confidence givers and not confidence takers. The students may be asked to identify these people in their lives.

There may be times when the girls realise that someone very close to them is a confidence taker and that the relationship is not particularly good. It is their decision to share this realisation or not, but the facilitator may provide some additional one-to-one advice after the session, in order to support the student's problem-solving skills as they find their path ahead.

Core Activity 2: Learning from Failure   15 mins

Materials: Lined paper, pens, envelopes.

Young people who have had trauma in their past often struggle to find and acknowledge any positive outcomes from difficult situations. This exercise is about celebrating even apparently small positives and studying their legacy. It may also highlight how the young person coped with adversity and trauma. Given the sensitivity of the subject, it is important to allow time for processing.

1. Ask the group to identify a 'good failure'; in other words, one that they have learnt from. Sometimes we forget that failures can be positive. Remind the group that Henry Ford (founder of Ford Motor Company) said that the only bad mistake was the one we do not learn from.

2. Tell the students that you are going to help them write a letter. The letter is to their younger self. It is going to tell their younger self what was positive, funny, chatty, helpful, kind, cute, smart, wise, or adventurous about them when younger.

They may struggle to find things to write and/or find it difficult to stay in the role, so you will need to have prepared some suggestions about their good qualities in advance. Either they can pick the age of the younger self they will write to, or you may suggest one. You may need to start them off and try to find positives for character formation in their stories. Here is an example:

> Dear 5-[7/10]-year-old me, you are third in the family and everyone loves you because you are always laughing [make people happy/ are naturally outgoing]. One time you secretly tried to drink a whole bottle of juice when no one was looking and spilt it all over the carpet. That's how adventurous [determined/mischievous] you are. But always fun!

This activity is designed to get them thinking about the fact that they have had certain positive qualities for a long time, qualities that they can depend upon and use as a resource.

To support this process:

- It may be helpful to ask them to describe how they looked at that age, as this can help jog memories.
- It may be necessary to move away from family environment to find the positive.

Ask them if they would like to read their letters out loud at the end of the activity.

3. It is important to emphasise that we can all learn from the past. Focus in the discussion here on positives and ask each member of the group to identify three things that they have learnt and three things that they would do differently in the future if they had the chance to go back and be their 'best self'.

Reflections & Feedback   5 mins

Materials: Facilitator's Guide 1 'Reflections & Feedback' (p. 262).

Ask the students to focus on the questions on the guide.

Target-Setting 5 mins

Materials: Worksheet 1.4 'My Targets' (p. 30) (one each); pens.

Use Worksheet 1.4 to support each student in setting their weekly targets. They can do this in pairs and support each other to identify what they would like to work on during the coming week. Allow a little time for reflection on the achievement (or otherwise) of the previous week's targets.

Compliments to Close 5 mins

Materials: Each individual's 'Golden Scroll' & a gold permanent marker each; Facilitator's Guide 2 'The Golden Scroll' (p. 263).

The guide will support you in directing the group as they add positive comments to their Golden Scrolls.

Relaxation 10 mins

Materials: Facilitator Guide 3 'Guided Relaxation' (p. 264).

Use the script on the guide to support the students in deep relaxation.

Worksheet 1.7
Bingo!

Activity 1.3

Someone who likes to relax listening to music	Someone who is good at hockey	Someone who likes spending time with their siblings	Someone who enjoys making things
Someone who loves animals	Someone who has the same favourite colour as you	Someone who has their ears pierced	Someone who has lived in a different country
Someone who can swim	Someone who thinks Michael McIntyre is funny	Someone who has blue eyes	Someone who has dyed their hair
Someone who can ride a horse	Someone who knows what they want to do when they are older	Someone who can speak more than one language	Someone who likes shopping

Worksheet 1.7
Bingo!

Activity 1.3

Someone who has blue eyes	Someone who likes to relax listening to music	Someone who loves animals	Someone who can swim
Someone who has the same favourite colour as you	Someone who can ride a horse	Someone who is good at hockey	Someone who thinks Michael McIntyre is funny
Someone who knows what they want to do when they are older	Someone who has their ears pierced	Someone who likes shopping	Someone who likes spending time with their siblings
Someone who enjoys making things	Someone who has lived in a different country	Someone who has dyed their hair	Someone who can speak more than one language

Worksheet 1.7
Bingo!

Activity 1.3

Someone who likes to relax listening to music	Someone who is good at hockey	Someone who likes spending time with their siblings	Someone who enjoys making things
Someone who loves animals	Someone who has the same favourite colour as you	Someone who has their ears pierced	Someone who has lived in a different country
Someone who can swim	Someone who thinks Michael McIntyre is funny	Someone who has blue eyes	Someone who has dyed their hair
Someone who can ride a horse	Someone who knows what they want to do when they are older	Someone who can speak more than one language	Someone who likes shopping

Worksheet 1.7
Bingo!

Activity 1.3

Someone who has the same favourite colour as you	Someone who has blue eyes	Someone who is good at hockey	Someone who can speak more than one language
Someone who knows what they want to do when they are older	Someone who can swim	Someone who can ride a horse	Someone who thinks Michael McIntyre is funny
Someone who has lived in a different country	Someone who likes to relax listening to music	Someone who likes spending time with their siblings	Someone who has dyed their hair
Someone who has their ears pierced	Someone who loves animals	Someone who likes shopping	Someone who enjoys making things

Worksheet 1.7
Bingo!

Activity 1.3

Someone who can speak more than one language	Someone who can ride a horse	Someone who can swim	Someone who thinks Michael McIntyre is funny
Someone who likes spending time with their siblings	Someone who has their ears pierced	Someone who has blue eyes	Someone who is good at hockey
Someone who has the same favourite colour as you	Someone who likes shopping	Someone who likes to relax listening to music	Someone who knows what they want to do when they are older
Someone who enjoys making things	Someone who has lived in a different country	Someone who loves animals	Someone who has dyed their hair

Worksheet 1.7
Bingo!

Activity 1.3

Someone who likes spending time with their siblings	Someone who has their ears pierced	Someone who can speak more than one language	Someone who has dyed their hair
Someone who enjoys making things	Someone who likes to relax listening to music	Someone who knows what they want to do when they are older	Someone who has the same favourite colour as you
Someone who loves animals	Someone who has lived in a different country	Someone who thinks Michael McIntyre is funny	Someone who can swim
Someone who has blue eyes	Someone who likes shopping	Someone who can ride a horse	Someone who is good at hockey

Worksheet 1.8
Sources of Confidence

Activity 1.3

Experience Previous success will make you feel confident	**Role Models** Positive people who are confident will inspire you
Encouragement People who believe in you will make you feel confident	**Managing Feelings** Your ability to manage stress and cope when it goes wrong will help you feel confident

Activity 1.4
Resilience

Aims

- For the students to feel safe & confident to participate in the session
- To understand the difference between a fixed and a growth mindset
- To recognise there is a connection between thoughts, feelings and behaviour
- To think about the amount of control we have over our thoughts, feelings and behaviour

Group Rules — 2 mins

Materials: Worksheet 1.1 'Visual Timetable' (p. 27); Group Rules Chart created in Activity 1.1.

Using Worksheet 1.1 and the Group Rules Chart, remind the group of the structure of each session and of the rules that were agreed in Activity 1.1. Ask if anyone would like to add a rule, or have a rule explained again.

Talk Time — 5 mins

Materials: Post-it notes.

Ask the students: 'What things do people have control over?' Students have the opportunity to discuss their answers, write them on post-its, or to reflect on their responses without sharing with the group.

Ice-Breaker — 5 mins

Materials: Worksheet 1.9 'What Can Say to Myself?' (p. 53) (one only).

This activity is underpinned by psychologist Carol Dweck's 'growth mindset approach' (2006). Dweck suggests that we all hold stories about ourselves, which she calls 'self-theory'/self-perception. Some examples might include:

- Someone who believes that they are 'intelligent' or 'unintelligent'
- Someone who believes: 'I am a good friend/parent/daughter'

People are unaware of these mindsets, but they have a deep and complex impact on all areas of our lives, including our personal relationships, learning, how we pick up new skills and how successful we feel. Dweck argues that all individuals can be put on a spectrum from 'growth mindset' to 'fixed mindset', depending on where they believe that their ability comes from:

* **Fixed mindset:** believing that abilities are innate.
* **Growth mindset:** believing that success is based on learning, hard work and determination.

Identifying our own mindset is complex and requires support. Most people are not aware of their mindset, however, it still influences behaviour. This impacts how we manage challenges, such as stress, anxiety and failure. Particularly notable are our different reactions to failure. For example, someone with a fixed mindset may find failure more difficult as they will see it as a negative comment on their personal talents. By contrast someone with a growth mindset may not find failure so difficult, because they are aware that they can learn from it and feel that they can improve their skills.

As a whole group, consider some possible examples of what someone might say when they feel anxious or stressed and then what they could possibly say instead. Use Worksheet 9.1 to record the group's reflections.

Core Activity 1: Control Spectrum   15 mins

Materials: Worksheet 1.10 'Control Spectrum' (p. 54) (one each, copied onto A3 paper); Worksheet 1.11 'Things Bubbles' (p. 55) (2 each, copied onto two different colours of card); Blu Tack or sellotape.

* Experiencing an **internal Locus of Control** makes us attribute outcomes to internal factors, for example: 'I did well in the maths test because I worked hard.'
* Experiencing an **external Locus of Control** makes us attribute outcomes to external factors, for example: 'I did well in the maths test because it was an easy test.'

The idea of Locus of Control is best thought of as a continuum, rather than something pre-determined and difficult to change.

A strongly internal or a strongly external Locus of Control can both be seen as undesirable. In the former there is a tendency to blame oneself for factors outside of one's control. The latter can bring the assumption that we have no control over our lives and therefore should not try. A balance is desirable, and a healthy awareness that we sometimes have control over things, and we sometimes don't.

Activity 1.4

It is important to remember that there are things in life over which we have little or no control. However, it is important to communicate to the students that exerting control over our own feelings, thoughts and behaviours can support our mental health. The activity is about exploring this.

Start by explaining that the session is about how much control we think we have over:

- Things that happen to us
- What we do
- How we feel
- What we say
- What others do, think or feel.

1. Give each person their own copy of Worksheet 1.10 and use it to introduce the idea of a 'spectrum' of control: generally, we neither have complete control, nor no control at all – there is variation.

    Get some ideas from the group about the kinds of things we have control over, and the kinds of things we do not control, as well as how we might know we have some control, or not. It is especially worth considering how much control we have over the thoughts, feelings and behaviours of others.

2. Now give two copies of Worksheet 1.11 to each person (each of the pair should be copied onto a different colour of paper or card).

3. Tell the group that the two different colours represent:

    - How much control they **think they have** over this bubble (Colour 1)
    - How much control they **would like to have** over this bubble (Colour 2)

4. Ask the group to cut out the bubbles on their pair of worksheets, then ask them to place each of their bubbles on their Control Spectrum, according to how much control they think they have (Colour 1) and how much they would like to have (Colour 2).

5. To avoid confusion, you may start with a Colour 1 worksheet and allow time for decision. Then give out the Colour 2 worksheet to consider. Blu Tack or similar could be used to stick the bubbles onto the Control Spectrum.

6. Encourage the group to share and discuss their ideas throughout, if they are happy to. The aim of sharing and discussion is to open up the possibility of exceptions and change with regard to how much control we feel we have over our own feelings, actions and thoughts, and those of others. It is vital to recognise and discuss that we have very little control over others, so the key thing to work on is ourselves. Our wellbeing is best supported if we only try

to control our own thoughts, feelings and actions, rather than those of others, and if we have a Locus of Control that is not too extreme.

7   To end the activity, recap the Locus of Control concept and ask the group to identify the pairs of bubbles that have been placed furthest apart on the Control Spectrum (those where there is the biggest discrepancy between the control represented by the bubbles in Colour 1 and Colour 2). Discuss as a group if appropriate. They may wish to think about positive changes or steps they could take to move towards their desired amount of control and how this might feel.

> The facilitator role is vital here, to support the group to make realistic and positive changes.

Core Activity 2: Noticing Beliefs   10mins

Materials: Selection of accessible and varied newspaper and magazine articles about a range of different people (including news stories, real life stories, interviews with famous people, cartoons, made-up stories), highlighters, scissors, glue.

This shorter activity is about looking for clues about beliefs in magazine and newspaper articles. The clues will come from what people do and what people say. Start by asking the group to define the meaning of 'beliefs', 'thoughts' and 'feelings'.

This activity may be done individually, in a pair, or as a group. In a group, different people may analyse different articles and feed back to their group, leading to discussion. A framework for discussion and feedback might be:

- Who are the characters in this story?
- Which character is most interesting to you and why?
- Retell the story briefly in pictures or words.
- What does your character do? Describe one action.
- How does your character feel? Describe one feeling.
- What kind of beliefs might your character have? How do you know?
- What kind of childhood might this person have had and why?
- What kind of future do you think they might have and why?

Try to encourage the students to use the words 'belief' and 'thought' in their discussion and make sure that people have the chance to talk about any worries that have come up during the session.

Reflections & Feedback 5 mins

Materials: Facilitator Guide 1 'Reflections & Feedback' (p. 262).

Ask the students to focus on the questions on the facilitator guide.

Target-Setting 5 mins

Materials: Worksheet 1.4 'My Targets' (p. 30) (one each); pens.

Use Worksheet 1.4 to support each student in setting their weekly targets. They can do this in pairs and support each other to identify what they would like to work on during the coming week. Allow a little time for reflection on the achievement (or otherwise) of the previous week's targets.

Compliments to Close 5 mins

Materials: Each individual's 'Golden Scroll' & a gold permanent marker each; Facilitator's Guide 2 'The Golden Scroll' (p. 263).

The guide will support you in directing the group as they add positive comments to their Golden Scrolls.

Relaxation 10 mins

Materials: Facilitator Guide 3 'Guided Relaxation' (p. 264).

Use the script on the facilitator guide to support the students in deep relaxation.

Worksheet 1.9

What Can I Say to Myself?

Activity 1.4

Instead of saying … *Try saying …*

- I give up
- I'm rubbish at this
- I'm too stressed
- It is impossible
- I can't do science
- She's so pretty. I'll never be pretty like her

Worksheet 1.10
Control Spectrum

Activity 1.4

External control – I am not in control

Internal control – I am in control

Worksheet 1.11
'Things' Bubbles

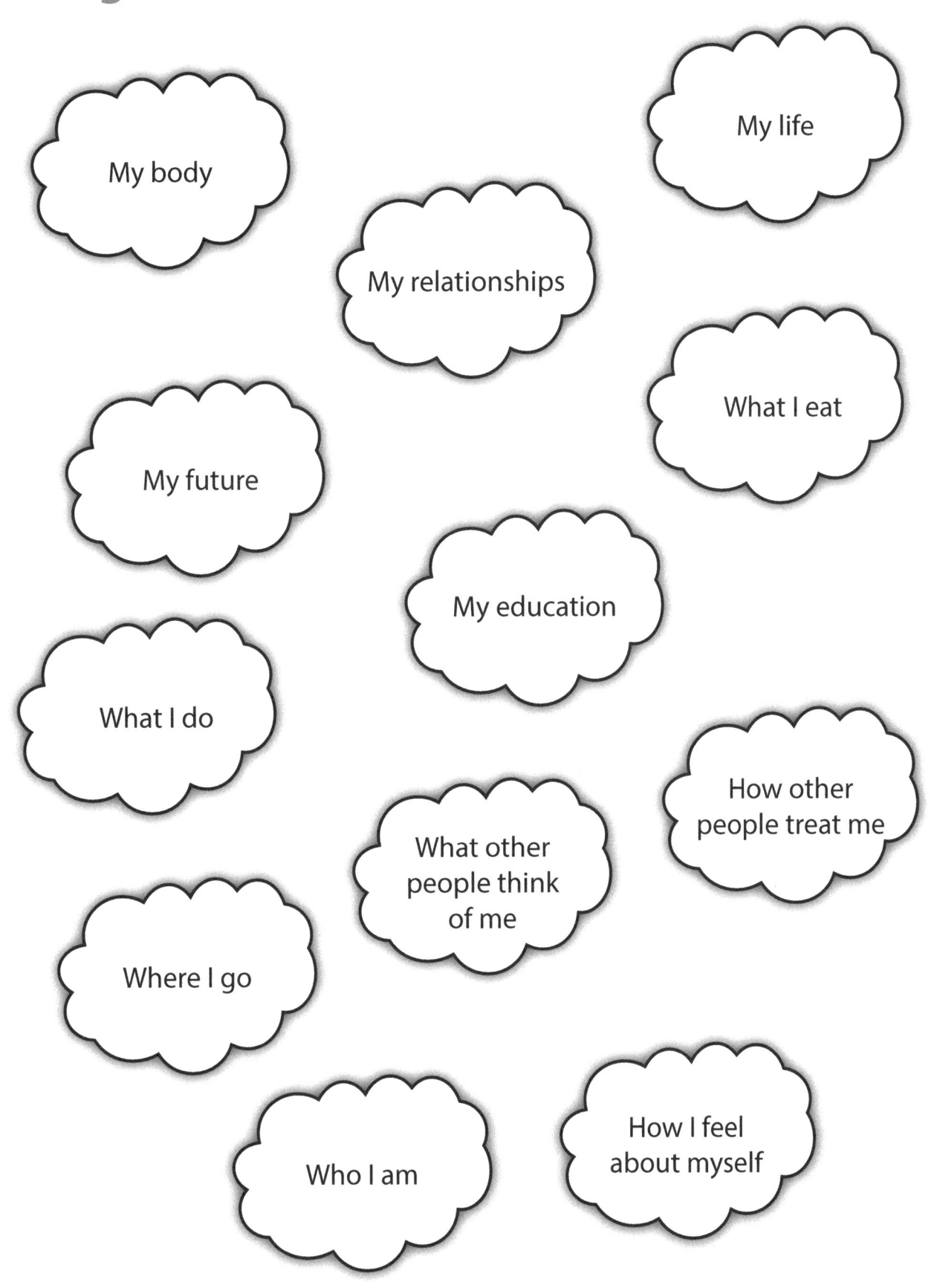

Activity 1.4

- My body
- My life
- My relationships
- What I eat
- My future
- My education
- What I do
- How other people treat me
- What other people think of me
- Where I go
- Who I am
- How I feel about myself

This page may be photocopied for instructional use only. *The ASD Girls' Wellbeing Toolkit* © Tina Rae & Amy Such 2019

Activity 1.5
Self-Esteem

Aims

- For the students to feel safe & confident to participate in the session
- To be able to describe 'self-esteem'
- To consider characteristics of someone with good and bad self-esteem
- To explore methods for boosting self-esteem

Group Rules   2 mins

Materials: Worksheet 1.1 'Visual Timetable' (p. 27); Group Rules Chart created in Activity 1.1.

Using Worksheet 1.1 and the Group Rules Chart, remind the group of the structure of each session and of the rules that were agreed in Activity 1.1. Ask if anyone would like to add a rule, or have a rule explained again.

Talk Time   5 mins

Materials: Post-it notes.

Ask the students: 'What makes you feel good about yourself?'

Students have the opportunity to discuss their answers, write them on post-its, or to reflect on their responses without sharing with the group.

Ice-Breaker   5 mins

Materials: Flip chart & paper, flip-chart pen.

Introduce the topic of self-esteem and ask the group:

- What does self-esteem mean to you?
- How does your self-esteem at different times of your life relate to your decision-making?
- Does it impact on your personal, physical, mental, or sexual health?

- How can people's self-esteem be damaged?
- Note the group's responses on a flip chart.

Core Activity 1: My Self-Esteem — 15 mins

Materials: Worksheet 1.12 'Celebrity Faces' (p. 59) (add images of famous people of your choosing); plain A4 paper, an assortment of coloured pens and/or pencils.

The purpose of this activity is to raise awareness of the importance of good self-esteem in relation to positive personal physical, mental and sexual health.

Ask the group to identify people in the media, such as characters from films/soaps/other TV programmes, who have good or bad self-esteem, or whose self-esteem levels have changed. Facilitate group discussion on what influences the self-esteem of their chosen characters. It might be useful to provide some examples for the students, you could add some pictures to Worksheet 1.12.

Hand out some plain paper and pens and ask the group to design a logo or image that represents having a high level of self-esteem. This could include representations of ways self-esteem could be raised or just a period when they felt they had good self-esteem.

Allow the young people time to complete their images. Then ask those who are willing to share their images and thoughts with the group.

Core Activity 2: A Good Friend — 10 mins

Materials: flip chart & paper, flip-chart pen; A4 paper & pens.

This activity focuses on supporting young people to think about what they value in a friendship. Students will be engaged to think about their friendships and the qualities that they consider to be important to them.

1. Using the flip chart, write the title: 'A Good Friend'.

2. In pairs or small groups the young people are asked to work together to list as many qualities of a good friend that they possibly can. Once they have generated and recorded their ideas in pairs or small groups, present the following prompting questions:

   - What are the actions/behaviours of a good friend?
   - What kind of things might a good friend say?
   - Do they like the same things as you?
   - Do they care about you?

- Do they stand up for you?
- Can you trust them? How do you know?
- Is being a good listener an important part of being a good friend?
- Is a good friend honest with you?

3 Discuss these as a whole group. As each group shares their comments, record the answers on the flip chart. It is important for the final activity that there is a comprehensive list of all of the suggestions made during the group discussion.

4 Ask the group to compare their own current or previous friendships to the list of things they have identified that define a 'good friend'. How many of the statements on the flip chart does this relationship tick? Are they happy about this, or has it made them think differently about some of their friendships?

Reflections & Feedback   5 mins

Materials: Facilitator Guide 1 'Reflections & Feedback' (p. 262).

Ask the students to focus on the questions on the facilitator guide.

Target-Setting   5 mins

Materials: Worksheet 1.4 'My Targets' (p. 30) (one each); pens.

Use Worksheet 1.4 to support each student in setting their weekly targets. They can do this in pairs and support each other to identify what they would like to work on during the coming week. Allow a little time for reflection on the achievement (or otherwise) of the previous week's targets.

Compliments to Close   5 mins

Materials: Each individual's 'Golden Scroll' & a gold permanent marker each; Facilitator's Guide 2 'The Golden Scroll' (p. 263).

The guide will support you in directing the group as they add positive comments to their Golden Scrolls.

Relaxation   10 mins

Materials: Facilitator Guide 3 'Guided Relaxation' (p. 264).

Use the script on the facilitator guide to support the students in deep relaxation.

Worksheet 1.12
Famous Faces

Activity 1.5

NAME

NAME

NAME

NAME

Worksheet 1.12

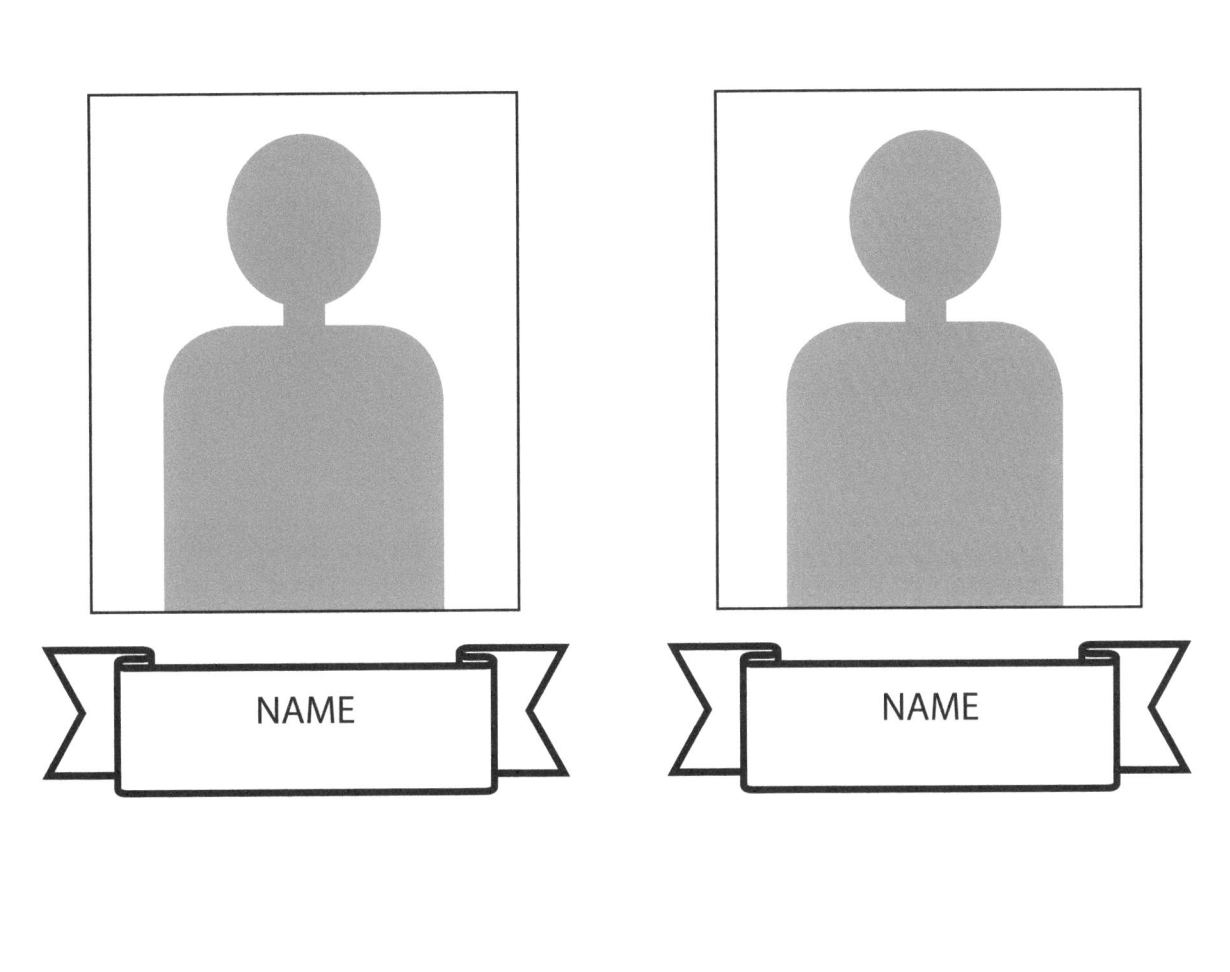

Activity 1.6
Managing Stress & Anxiety 1

Aims

* For the students to feel safe & confident to participate in the session
* To be able to describe 'stress'
* To identify areas of stress within the students' own lives
* To discuss techniques that can be used to reduce stress

Group Rules   2 mins

Materials: Worksheet 1.1 'Visual Timetable' (p. 27); Group Rules Chart created in Activity 1.1.

Using Worksheet 1.1 and the Group Rules Chart, remind the group of the structure of each session and of the rules that were agreed in Activity 1.1. Ask if anyone would like to add a rule, or have a rule explained again.

Talk Time   5 mins

Materials: Post-it notes.

Ask the students: 'When do people feel stressed?'

Students have the opportunity to discuss their answers, write them on post-its or to reflect on their responses without sharing with the group.

Ice-Breaker   15 mins

Materials: Flip chart & paper, flip-chart pen; A4 paper & pens. Optional: source of meditative music.

In this activity, aspects of one of three women's stories will be used to explore the idea of resilience in the face of abuse and adversity.

Before starting this session, you should watch all video clips given below and select one, considering the suitability for your group. The group may wish to choose an alternative clip as appropriate to the needs and interests of their group.

1. Re-introduce the idea of resilience to the group: it is the ability to thrive in adversity, to bounce back when things are difficult.

2. Put the following question up on a board or flip chart for people to think about when they watch the clips: 'What was it about these people that helped them to survive and thrive?'

3. Now watch one of the following clips:

   a. Aleesha Dixon: Performer and television personality who witnessed domestic violence as a child.
   https://www.youtube.com/watch?v=3nfi5G_0Q1M (4 mins)

   b. Oprah Winfrey: Global megastar who grew up in poverty, was sexually abused and became pregnant at 14.
   https://www.youtube.com/watch?v=zr0gMn2dLts (2.4 mins)

   c. Maya Angelou: World famous author who was raped at 7.
   https://www.youtube.com/watch?v=stAOpg71vK4 (3.02 mins)

   (*Videos last accessed 29/09/2019*)

4. Discuss the clip generally, perhaps including:
   - How did the group feel whilst watching the clip?
   - What did the group think of the woman?
   - What did they think of the woman's story?
   - Are there any themes within the story?
   - Do they consider the woman resilient? Why/why not?
   - What do they think they might have in common with the woman and why?

5. Now, as a group, compile a list of every possible source of resilience for any of these women on the flip chart. Discuss the list. Are there certain themes that people notice? Do they feel they share some of these resilience factors or could develop them?

6. Finally, allow some space, possibly with music on, for people to reflect in silence on possible sources of their own resilience. After reflection give everyone a blank piece of A4 paper and ask them to show one or more of these sources in their own way, for instance in drawings, notes, doodles, names.

Activity 1.6

A debrief will be needed at the end of the activity to reflect back on the clips that have been shown and the ideas that have come up about resilience. Ask if anyone is willing to share their private work with the group.

Core Activity 1: What is Stress?   10 mins

Materials: Worksheet 1.13 'Stress versus Anxiety' (p. 65); post-it notes, pens.

The aim of this activity is to begin to explore and define a commonly used word: stress. This activity should help group members understand the difference between stress and anxiety. It is helpful to hold in mind the difference between stress and anxiety, because once we can understand the two, we can use the most effective strategies to cope with them.

Worksheet 1.13 includes definitions of stress and anxiety. You can read these to the group and then share the worksheet with them to facilitate a discussion.

As a group, discuss different examples of when we feel stress and when we feel anxiety. These examples could be imagined, or from the students' own lives. Ask the group to consider each situation in turn and address questions that explore the example in detail:

- How long do you think the feeling of stress and/or anxiety would last?
- How common do you think it is for someone to feel stressed and/or anxious in this situation?
- Might different people react in different ways to this situation?

The final stage of the activity is for individuals to write examples from their own lives of when they feel stressed and/or anxious, each on a different post-it note. Once they have at least five different examples, they need to rank these from 'worst' to 'least bad'. This part of the activity allows the young people to start identifying how feelings of anxiety and stress can be recognised and to consider the way in which this understanding can strengthen their ability to manage stress and anxiety.

Core Activity 2: Stress-Busting   15 mins

Materials: Worksheet 1.14 'My Stress-Busting Plan' (p. 66); flip chart & paper, flip-chart pen, source of calming music.

Discuss the idea of 'good/healthy' stress. Pressure can help us try things and do things that then make us feel good. How can we tell when stress becomes unhealthy? Introduce the idea of a 'threshold' of stress. It is important to mention that this threshold is different for each individual and that it is important to think about what our own thresholds are.

1. Each young person now takes up to two minutes of 'thinking time': this is a reflective time in silence, or with calming music playing. Key words can be written up on the flip chart to remind the young people what they are being asked to think about/reflect on:

   - What makes you stressed?
   - What are your triggers?
   - How do you feel when you are experiencing unhealthy stress?

     * Physically: headaches; nausea; sleeping badly

     * Behaviour with others: irritable/grumpy with your friends; withdrawal from your friends/family

     * Behaviour: biting nails; self-harming; lack of concentration

     * Changes in your eating habits: eating more or less than usual

   > Note that these are personal reflections and the young people will not need to share these with the group. However, they may wish to access additional support away from the group in order to further explore their stressors.

2. Come back together as a group to consider what might help to reduce stress. Either you or a member of the group can record these ideas on a flip chart. Ask the group to keep going and come up with as many ideas as possible. Suggestions might include:

   - Doing exercise
   - Seeing friends/people who are positive and supportive
   - Keeping a diary
   - Asking for help from someone you trust
   - Doing things that make you feel good, e.g. going out, or having a bath, or eating chocolate
   - Having a good routine
   - Being organised
   - Listening to music that makes you feel good
   - Distracting yourself with something you like, e.g. a TV show/film

3. The activity will then focus on bringing together the ideas discussed in order to give the young people the opportunity to create their own Stress-Busting Plan, using Worksheet 1.14.

Take time to consider how you would complete it for yourself, which will give you a helpful insight when you come to working it through with the young people. You may wish to complete a copy alongside them. It might help to start with the end point (the outcome – how I want to feel) and work backwards.

Activity 1.6

Give them some examples to get them started:

* *How I want to feel:* calm, in control, happy
* *What I want to think:* I have enough time to do things I want, I can do my school work

Reflections & Feedback   5 mins

Materials: Facilitator Guide 1 'Reflections & Feedback' (p. 262).

Ask the students to focus on the questions on the facilitator guide.

Target-Setting   5 mins

Materials: Worksheet 1.4 'My Targets' (p. 30) (one each); pens.

Use Worksheet 1.4 to support each student in setting their weekly targets. They can do this in pairs and support each other to identify what they would like to work on during the coming week. Allow a little time for reflection on the achievement (or otherwise) of the previous week's targets.

Compliments to Close   5 mins

Materials: Each individual's 'Golden Scroll' & a gold permanent marker each; Facilitator's Guide 2 'The Golden Scroll' (p. 263).

The guide will support you in directing the group as they add positive comments to their Golden Scrolls.

Relaxation   10 mins

Materials: Facilitator Guide 3 'Guided Relaxation' (p. 264).

Use the script on the facilitator guide to support the students in deep relaxation.

Worksheet 1.13
Stress versus Anxiety

Activity 1.6

'Stress is a feeling of emotional or mental strain.

Stress can cause mental health problems, and make existing problems worse.

For example, if you often struggle to manage feelings of stress, you might develop a mental health problem like anxiety or depression. Mental health problems can cause stress'

(www.mind.org.uk/stress)

'Anxiety is a word we use to describe feelings of unease, worry and fear. It incorporates both the emotions and the physical sensations we might experience when we are worried or nervous about something … We all know what it is like to feel anxious from time to time. It is common to feel tense, nervous and perhaps fearful at the thought of a stressful event or decision you're facing – especially if it could have a big impact on your life. For example:

- Sitting an exam
- Going to hospital
- An interview
- Starting a new job
- Moving away from home
- Having a baby
- Being diagnosed with an illness
- Deciding to get married or divorced'

(www.mind.org.uk/information-support/types-of-mental-health-problems/anxiety-and-panic-attacks)

Worksheet 1.14
My Stress-Busting Plan

Activity 1.6

Name _____

How I want to feel:
* _____
* _____
* _____

What I want to think:
* _____
* _____
* _____

My Stressors

Actions/activities that make me feel calm:

My thoughts when I am stressed:

Places that make me feel calm:

People that make me feel calm:

How I feel when I'm stressed:

My Plan:
1 _____
2 _____
3 _____

Activity 1.7
Managing Stress & Anxiety 2

Aims

* For the students to feel safe & confident to participate in the session
* To be able to define 'stress' and 'anxiety'
* To be able to identify the differences between stress and anxiety
* To understand the physical and psychological symptoms of a panic attack
* To consider person-centred responses to panic attacks

Group Rules   2 mins

Materials: Worksheet 1.1 'Visual Timetable' (p. 27); Group Rules Chart created in Activity 1.1).

Using Worksheet 1.1 and the Group Rules Chart, remind the group of the structure of each session and of the rules that were agreed in Activity 1.1. Ask if anyone would like to add a rule, or have a rule explained again.

Talk Time   5 mins

Materials: Post-it notes.

Ask the students: 'What happens when people feel anxious?'

Students have the opportunity to discuss their answers, write them on post-its or to reflect on their responses without sharing with the group.

Ice-Breaker   5 mins

Materials: Worksheet 1.15 'Stress & Anxiety Quiz' (p. 71) (one each of p.1, one copy of p. 2 for facilitator); pens.

Each student is given Worksheet 1.15; the second page of the worksheet consists of answers to assist the facilitator. They are encouraged to read through each statement and determine whether they believe it is true or false. Students can work individually or in pairs/small groups.

This page may be photocopied for instructional use only. *The ASD Girls' Wellbeing Toolkit* © Tina Rae & Amy Such 2019

Once the group have completed the quiz, reveal the correct answers to the students. Take a few minutes to discuss any statements that the students appear surprised or confused by.

Core Activity 1: Stress versus Anxiety   10 mins

Materials: Worksheet 1.16 'Definitions' (p. 74) (one each).

This activity builds on the ice-breaker. The students are given Resource Sheet 3.7 to read through in pairs. All of the definitions are valid and the students are asked to read and discuss each one, before decide which they think are most relevant.

The main focus of the session is then on the pairs sharing why they picked their particular definitions.

* Where there any definitions that they didn't agree with or did not think were helpful?
* What is the difference between anxiety and stress?

This activity can be extended by asking the young people to create their own definitions.

Core Activity 2: Understand Panic   20 mins

Materials: Worksheet 1.17 'Understand Panic' (p. 75) & 1.18 'Body Scan' (p. 76) (one each); pens.

This activity makes use of Worksheet 1.17 to assist students in assessing how they think and feel during a panic attack. This then allows them to reflect on how they already cope with them and if there is anything that will help them to cope with them more effectively.

Introduce the topic of panic attacks. A panic attack is a rush of intense anxiety with physical symptoms, for example, shortness of breath. You may want to start by asking the group what they know about panic attacks already and then build on this to be sure that all of the key information below has been shared.

Key information to share

* A panic attack is a brief period of overwhelming fear or anxiety. The intensity of a panic attack goes well beyond normal anxiety, and can include a number of physical symptoms. During panic attacks, people often fear that they are having a heart attack, they cannot breathe, or they are dying. Some possible symptoms include:
    * Pounding or racing heart
    * Fear of dying

- * Feeling sick
- * Pain in chest
- * Sense of fear
- * Trembling/shaking
- * Fear that you are 'going mad'
- * Feeling detached/separate from what is going on
- * Sweating
- * Shallow breathing/struggling to breathe
- * Many other symptoms – these are just some of the possibilities.

* Panic attacks feel very frightening, but do not cause physical harm – however, people often feel as if they cannot breathe, or that they are having a heart attack, even though they are not.

* Panic attacks usually last for a relatively short period of time, but are very intense. Typically they peak within 10 minutes and are over in about 30 minutes. Sometimes the lingering symptoms continue for an hour or even longer.

* Sometimes panic attacks can be linked to something specific, for example, small spaces, crowded spaces, driving, being in crowds. But sometimes panic attacks can seem to occur randomly.

* Relaxation techniques help to support people with panic attacks. You can train your body to relax, just as you can train your body with exercise. Spending time using relaxation techniques like deep breathing or the Body Scan (given on Worksheet 1.18) can help to tackle and manage panic attacks.

* Cognitive Behavioural Therapy is useful for treating panic attacks. It works by helping the person to notice and change negative patterns of thinking.

This is an individual activity for each young person that they will not be asked to share. Towards the end of the activity, you should speak individually with each student to provide an opportunity to talk through the exercise and debrief, as necessary. It may be helpful to provide the students with an opportunity to discuss this activity during an individual session, to take place outside of the group sessions.

Reflections & Feedback   5 mins

Materials: Facilitator Guide 1 'Reflections & Feedback' (p. 262).

Ask the students to focus on the questions on the facilitator guide.

Target-Setting   5 mins

Materials: Worksheet 1.4 'My Targets' (p. 30) (one each); pens.

Use Worksheet 1.4 to support each student in setting their weekly targets. They can do this in pairs and support each other to identify what they would like to work on during the coming week. Allow a little time for reflection on the achievement (or otherwise) of the previous week's targets.

Compliments to Close   5 mins

Materials: Each individual's 'Golden Scroll' & a gold permanent marker each; Facilitator's Guide 2 'The Golden Scroll' (p. 263).

The guide will support you in directing the group as they add positive comments to their Golden Scrolls.

Relaxation   10 mins

Materials: Facilitator Guide 3 'Guided Relaxation' (p. 264).

Use the script on the facilitator guide to support the students in deep relaxation.

Worksheet 1.15
Stress & Anxiety Quiz

Activity 1.7

Which statements are true and which are false?

1   Stress and anxiety are the same thing   T / F

2   Anxiety can be specific (e.g., fear of heights), or general   T / F

3   Stress is not necessarily a bad thing   T / F

4   Anxiety and stress can affect your physical health   T / F

5   Boys never suffer from anxiety   T / F

6   If you suffer from anxiety there is nothing you can do about it   T / F

7   Anxiety disorders are the most common type of mental health
    problem for teenagers   T / F

8   Phobias are a type of anxiety disorder   T / F

9   The only way to get over a phobia is to face it head on   T / F

10 Adults never get stressed   T / F

page 1 of 3

Worksheet 1.15

Facilitator's Answer Sheet: Stress & Anxiety Quiz

Activity 1.7

1	Stress and anxiety are the same thing	**FALSE** Stress is a feeling of mental strain that can affect your day-to-day functioning; anxiety is a feeling of intense and overwhelming fear that stops you functioning. Stress is not always a bad thing, it depends how you cope with it/manage it.
2	Anxiety can be specific (e.g., fear of heights), or general	**TRUE** You may want to discuss some specific examples of anxiety, e.g.: fear of heights, being in crowds, small spaces. It is important to explore the idea that these are individual: for example, one person may love dogs and another person might be very afraid of them (a phobia). Sometimes a phobia can be more severe and people will change their behaviour to avoid what they are afraid of, e.g.: someone who was afraid of dogs may not visit a much-loved relative because that relative has a dog. Anxiety can be mild or much more severe. Everyone has feelings of anxiety at some point in their lives. Some people find it more difficult to control their worries and their feelings of anxiety can be more constant and affect their daily lives. A more general anxiety would be if someone feels anxious most of the time and finds it difficult to remember when they last felt relaxed. They might feel anxious about a range of issues, not one specific thing.
3	Stress is not necessarily a bad thing	**TRUE** There are a number of times when it is appropriate to feel stressed or when feeling stressed might be helpful, e.g.: an actor/musician might feel stressed before a big show/performance, or an athlete might feel stressed before a race/event.
4	Anxiety and stress can affect your physical health	**TRUE** Stress and anxiety can have mental and physical symptoms. These will be different for every person, but examples might include: trouble sleeping, trouble concentrating, feeling worried/restless, dizziness, heart palpitations, high blood pressure.

Worksheet 1.15

Facilitator's Answer Sheet: Stress & Anxiety Quiz

Activity 1.7

5	Boys never suffer from anxiety	**FALSE** Boys and girls both experience anxiety. Fewer boys are diagnosed with anxiety problems, but some are, and it may also be that boys are less likely to come forward with an anxiety problem. Why might that be?
6	If you suffer from anxiety there is nothing you can do about it	**FALSE** This is a very important point to emphasise. There are many things that can be done to cope with anxiety, particularly if you seek help through a professional intervention, or preventative work. These sessions will suggest many ways to recognise and combat anxiety.
7	Anxiety disorders are the most common type of mental health problem for teenagers	**FALSE** This is only true for girls.
8	Phobias are a type of anxiety disorder	**TRUE** A phobia is an intense fear of something that poses little or no actual danger. A fear becomes a phobia when you have to change your lifestyle to manage it.
9	The only way to get over a phobia is to face it head on	**FALSE** This is false. Steady 'de-sensitising' can work really well, e.g., if you are scared of spiders you could (with support) start by being in the same room as a picture of one and build it up from there. However, this is not the only way to tackle phobias, there are a wide variety of approaches and different things work for different people.
10	Adults never get stressed	**FALSE** Adults do get stressed and experience the same physical and emotional symptoms as young people. They also sometimes need support in order to manage their feelings and symptoms.

Worksheet 1.16
Definitions

Activity 1.7

Stress:

The response of a living thing to a *stressor* in the environment (e.g., lack of food)

Anxiety:

An emotion characterised by dread, uneasiness and worry

Stress:

Having too many things to do in the time available

Anxiety:

When fear becomes unmanageable and affects how you function

Stress:

The feeling of being under too much physical, mental or emotional pressure. Pressure turns into stress when you feel unable to cope. A bit of stress is normal and can help push you to do something new or difficult, but too much stress can take its toll.

* a response to daily pressure

* a physical and mental reaction to having too much going on in your life and not being able to manage it.

Anxiety:

* a feeling of worry, nervousness or unease about something with an uncertain outcome

* a nervous disorder marked by excessive uneasiness and apprehension, typically with compulsive behaviour or panic attacks

Worksheet 1.17
Understand Panic

Activity 1.7

What were you <u>thinking</u> about before your most recent panic attack?

_____

How were you <u>feeling</u> before your most recent panic attack?

_____

What were you <u>doing</u> before your most recent panic attack?

_____

Are you worried about having another panic attack? (Circle how worried you are.)

1	2	3	4	5
Not worried				Very worried

How distressing do you find your panic attacks?

1	2	3	4	5
Not distressing				Very distressing

Circle any of the symptoms you experience when you have panic attacks and add any others.

- Feeling sick
- Feeling hot or cold
- Sweating
- Shallow breathing/finding it hard to breathe
- Heart racing or beating loudly
- Feel as if you are 'going mad'
- Feeling dizzy/faint
- Pain in chest
- Feeling numb

- Feeling very scared
- Shaking
- Feeling detached
- _____
- _____
- _____

Worksheet 1.18
Body Scan

Activity 1.7

The Body Scan should take about 15 to 20 minutes.

You may want to lie on a mat on the floor, making sure you are warm and comfortable, covering yourself with a blanket and resting your head on a cushion or pillow. You can also do this sitting upright. Take care to ensure you will not be disturbed for the period of the Body Scan.

1. First, check in with your body just as it is right now, noticing the sensations that are present, feeling the contact the body is making with the floor.

2. Then start to 'scan' the body, sweeping your awareness through different parts of the body, without judging what you are aware of, but simply bringing attention to your experience, moment to moment.

3. Start with the crown of the head and notice any sensations here: tingling, numbness, tightness, or relaxation. Then include the head, feeling the weight of the head as it rests on the cushion; then include awareness of the forehead, noticing whether or not you can feel the pulse in the forehead, whether there is tightness or ease. Then include the eyes, the nose, cheeks, mouth and chin and finally the ears, including any sounds that you notice coming to the ears. Be aware of, moment by moment, the changing pattern of sensations, feelings of warmth, coolness, ease. If you notice your mind wandering, then this is perfectly natural and what minds do. Noticing your mind has wandered is a moment of awareness – just gently guide your mind back to the part of the body you are focusing on.

4. Then let go of the head and face, moving your awareness into the neck and shoulders, noticing the strong muscles in this part of the body, having awareness of any tension in the neck and throat, perhaps becoming aware of the sensation of air in the throat.

5. Move your awareness now to the shoulders, the places where there is contact between the shoulders and the floor, stretching your awareness into the arms, elbows, wrists, hands and fingers, aware of what is here in each moment.

6. Shift the focus now to the chest area, noticing the subtle rise and fall of the chest with the in and out breath, turning your awareness to the ribcage, front and back of the ribs, sides of the ribs, the upper back resting on the floor. Notice any aches and pains here and see if you can bring a sense of gentleness and kindness to these areas.

page 1 of 2

Worksheet 1.18
Body Scan

Activity 1.7

7. Turn your awareness now to the abdomen and stomach, the place where we feel our 'gut feelings', noticing your attitude to this part of your body, seeing if you can allow it to be as it is, taking a relaxed and accepting approach to this part of the body. Then stretch your awareness to the lower back, the lumber spine, feeling the gentle pressure as the back meets the floor before moving your awareness to the pelvis area, the hip bones, and sitting bones, genitals and groin, noticing any sensations or lack of sensations that are here, perhaps being aware of the breath in this part of the body. Bringing a kindly attention here.

8. Now let go of the torso as the centre of your awareness and move your attention into the thighs of both legs, feeling the weight of the legs, gently noticing what other sensations there are here, tuning into the skin, bone and muscle of the legs here. If your mind has wandered into thinking, planning, worrying, daydreaming, then just gently guiding it back to this part of the body.

9. Next turn your attention gently towards the knees, bringing a friendly attention; notice if there is any discomfort here and, if there is none, then notice what is present already here.

10. Stretch your attention into the calves of both legs, noticing how your muscles feel here, feeling this part of the legs from the inside out, the flesh and bone of the lower legs. And again, checking in where your attention is from time to time and noticing the quality of your attention, seeing if it is possible to bring a gentleness and kindliness into your awareness, not forcing yourself, bringing a lightness of touch to your attention in this part of the body.

11. Finally move your attention into both feet, the heels of the feet, the instep, the balls of the feet, the tops of the feet, skin and bone and finally the toes, seeing if it is possible to distinguish one toe from another. Notice whether there is tension here, sensations, numbness, tingling and allow any tension to soften as you bring a gentle attention to it.

12. Now take one or two deeper breaths and widen your focus, filling the whole body with awareness, noticing whatever is present, sweeping the body with your awareness from top to bottom, experiencing the body from the inside out. Notice whether there is any lack of acceptance towards any parts of the body as you fill the body with a gentle awareness and see if you can have compassion for any judgments, or for any tensions or pain that might be present as and when you notice it. Feel the energy of life flowing through you. And rest in awareness of this amazing body that you have, compassion for its pains and appreciation for its capacities and the wonder of it.

Taken from Mindfulness for Students: http://mindfulnessforstudents.co.uk/resources/the-body-scan/

page 2 of 2

Activity 1.8
Managing Stress & Anxiety 3

Aims

- For the students to feel safe & confident to participate in the session
- To introduce the concept of cognitive behavioural therapy
- To begin to challenge negative thoughts
- To share a variety of anxieties and concerns

Group Rules — 2 mins

Materials: Worksheet 1.1 'Visual Timetable' (p. 27); Group Rules Chart created in Activity 1.1.

Using Worksheet 1.1 and the Group Rules Chart, remind the group of the structure of each session and of the rules that were agreed in Activity 1.1. Ask if anyone would like to add a rule, or have a rule explained again.

Talk Time — 5 mins

Materials: Post-it notes.

Ask the students: 'What negative thoughts do you have?'

Students have the opportunity to discuss their answers, write them on post-its or to reflect on their responses without sharing with the group.

Ice-Breaker — 10 mins

Materials: Worksheet 1.19 'Challenging Anxious Thoughts' (p. 81); pens.

This activity uses a cognitive behavioural therapy approach to look at irrational thoughts and how these can make us feel more anxious. Without a structure and support it is very difficult to identify our irrational thoughts: Worksheet 19.1 is designed to work through the stages of identifying these thoughts.

The session can be opened by introducing the idea of irrational thoughts – when our anxious thoughts get out of control. When we experience this, we find it very difficult to feel calm and solve our problems.

Core Activity 1: The Worry Tree 1   10 mins

Materials: Worksheet 1.20 'The Worry Tree' (p. 83); coloured paper, pens, crayons, colouring pencils, a variety of collage materials (including magazines, newspaper articles, safe access to the internet & a printer), scissors.

In 'The Worry Tree' activity students draw a tree that represents their worries.

To begin with, the students must make leaves to represent their worries. They may wish to make leaves from scratch or, alternatively, you may give them the leaf template on Worksheet 1.20. Encourage the students to make as many leaves as they want and to write the worries they have on each leaf. The young people should be encouraged to be creative and represent their worries using symbols, words, colours and images.

Core Activity 2: The Worry Tree 2   15 mins

Materials: A3 paper, on which to construct the tree. Optional: rolls of wallpaper, glue, sellotape, coloured pencils/pens, crate paper, a variety of collage materials.

The second part of this activity requires the students to begin to build their trees.

As the young people are creating their trees, the questions to consider (either with you and the young person individually, or for pairs to discuss if appropriate) are:

- The height of the tree
- The roots of the tree
- The stability of the tree
- The number of the leaves

The purpose of exploring these issues is to begin to unpick some of the young person's worries. This creative activity allows the young person the opportunity to safely name things that are worrying them, as well as evaluating the magnitude of the worry.

Reflections & Feedback   5 mins

Materials: Facilitator Guide 1 'Reflections & Feedback' (p.262).

Ask the students to focus on the questions on the facilitator guide.

Target-Setting   5 mins

Materials: Worksheet 1,4 'My Targets' (p. 30) (one each); pens.

Use Worksheet 1.4 to support each student in setting their weekly targets. They can do this in pairs and support each other to identify what they would like to work on during the coming week. Allow a little time for reflection on the achievement (or otherwise) of the previous week's targets.

Compliments to Close   5 mins

Materials: Each individual's 'Golden Scroll' & a gold permanent marker each; Facilitator's Guide 2 'The Golden Scroll' (p. 263).

The guide will support you in directing the group as they add positive comments to their Golden Scrolls.

Relaxation   10 mins

Materials: Facilitator Guide 3 'Guided Relaxation' (p. 264).

Use the script on the facilitator guide to support the students in deep relaxation.

Worksheet 1.19
Challenging Anxious Thoughts

Activity 1.8

Give an example of a situation that makes you feel very anxious
e.g., being in a crowded place, giving a speech in public, and so on …

_____

_____

_____

When we are anxious, it is like looking in a circus mirror that distorts the size of things. When we feel anxious, something can look much bigger/worse than it actually is. We need to take time to recognise when we might be experiencing irrational thoughts.

Imagine how you feel in the example you have just given.

What is the worst outcome?

_____

What is the best outcome?

_____

What is the likely outcome?

_____

page 1 of 2

Worksheet 1.19
Challenging Anxious Thoughts

Activity 1.8

Imagine that the worst outcome comes true. Would it still be a problem …

in one week?
_____

in one month?
_____

in one year?
_____

When we feel anxious, it is normal to focus on the worst thing that might happen, even if it is not likely at all. For example, someone who needs to give a speech in front of lots of people might think: 'I am going to be totally embarrassed and everyone will laugh at me. I will be so ashamed and I will never forget it.'

But a friend might say have a more rational thought: 'What is more likely to happen? Probably the speech will fine.'

Another example of a rational thought might be: 'My speech will probably be fine, but even if I do really badly and mess it up, everyone will forget about it quite quickly.'

Go back to your example. Look at what you have written for your 'worst outcome' and 'likely outcome' and then identify what is your …

Irrational thought _____
_____

Rational thought _____
_____

page 2 of 2

Worksheet 1.20
The Worry Tree

Activity 1.8

Worksheet 1.20

P This page may be photocopied for instructional use only. *The ASD Girls' Wellbeing Toolkit* © Tina Rae & Amy Such 2019

Activity 1.9
Self-Harm 1

Aims

* For the students to feel safe & confident to participate in the session
* To become aware of some of the myths that surround self-harm
* To consider the most effective ways of supporting a peer who is self-harming
* To share information about keeping safe with peers

Group Rules — 2 mins

Materials: Worksheet 1.1 'Visual Timetable' (p. 27); Group Rules Chart created in Activity 1.1.

Using Worksheet 1.1 and the Group Rules Chart, remind the group of the structure of each session and of the rules that were agreed in Activity 1.1. Ask if anyone would like to add a rule, or have a rule explained again.

Talk Time — 5 mins

Materials: Post-it notes.

Ask the students: 'Why might someone self-harm?'

Students have the opportunity to discuss their answers, write them on post-its or to reflect on their responses without sharing with the group.

Ice-Breaker — 5 mins

Materials: Worksheet 21.1 'Self-Harm Facts & Myths' (p. 88): one copy of the first page (cut up) for the group to sort, one copy of the pages that follow for you. Flip chart & paper, flip-chart pen (or use of whiteboard & dry-wipe pen), Blu Tack.

The important focus in this activity is to develop a clear and evidence-based understanding of self-harm.

To do this, the first question is: What are the facts about self-harm?

Self-harm is a topic surrounded by myths and misunderstandings that make it even more difficult for young people to seek the help that they need. Challenging these myths and developing confidence is vitally important.

Self-harm isn't usually a suicide attempt, or a cry for attention. Instead, it is often a way for young people to release overwhelming emotions. It is a way of coping. So, whatever the reason, it should be taken seriously.

Before the activity starts, write two headings on the flip chart or whiteboard: 'Facts' and 'Myths'. The young people will read and discuss the eight statements about self-harm on Worksheet 1.21 and, once they have decided whether each is a fact or a myth, they will stick it underneath the heading they have selected.

All of these statements are myths and the second part Worksheet 1.21 is for you, as facilitator, to feed the facts back to the students.

Core Activity 1: Amie's Story   10 mins

Materials: Worksheet 1.22 'Amie's Story' (p. 93) (one each). Optional: Flip chart & paper, flip-chart pen, printed copy of the questions below.

In this activity the students are presented with a scenario involving Amie and the concerns of others that she is self-harming.

The students are asked to read the story on Worksheet 1.22 and think about what action they might take. This can work well as a whole-group activity, as this enables you to guide some of the discussion and work through the key questions. However, the questions can also be written up or printed out and handed to the young people who can work in small groups or pairs.

Key questions

- What might be causing Amie to feel distressed?
- Could you talk to Amie?
- Who else could you talk to?
- What support does Amie need?

If the young people have worked in pairs or small groups, then invite them to share their thoughts, comments and ideas with the whole group.

The purpose of the activity is for the young people to go understand Amie's thought process in her situation and to develop the idea that self-harm is a behaviour caused by emotional distress, a way of coping with difficult situations and emotions.

Central to this activity is the fact that the most likely person to receive a disclosure of self-harm is a peer. This leaves many young people in an incredibly difficult and stressful situation. Young people who have been confided in, in this way, can feel isolated, extremely anxious and powerless. They may feel that telling an adult would be betraying their friend and that this friend will no longer trust them. Engage with this idea in discussion and **explore the idea that the priority is helping Amie to be safe, well and happy** – to achieve this, what might she need?

They may also feel that they can help Amie by themselves. To do so alone may be far too overwhelming. The key message is that the safe and responsible thing for a good friend to do in this situation is to tell an adult they trust about their concerns, so that Amie can get the help that she needs.

Core Activity 2: Keeping Safe   15 mins

Materials: A4 paper, coloured pencils/pens, scissors, glue, magazines, safe access to the internet.

> Attention: The activity is deliberately designed so that the young people are thinking about key information for other young people, rather than themselves. This creates some distance, which can allow the students to explore a wide variety of ideas and strategies.

This session links closely to the core activity in Activity 1.10, in which the young people will create their own safety plan. The purpose of the present activity is to allow the young people to think about ways to stay safe. They are asked to design an A4 poster with key pieces of information about self-harm for other young people. They might want to include:

* Key facts that they think are important for other young people to know
* Myths that need to be challenged
* Where to go to get help
* Information on how to develop a safety plan, including alternative coping methods

Use the websites below and the information from the session:

* https://www.selfharm.co.uk/
* https://youngminds.org.uk/find-help/feelings-and-symptoms/self-harm/
* https://youngminds.org.uk/find-help/feelings-and-symptoms/self-harm/
* https://www.mind.org.uk/information-support/types-of-mental-health-problems/self-harm/#.WTP1f2yrPRM

Note: the resource from Mind is designed for people of all ages, not specifically for young people.

Key words that young people might want to include or refer to:

- Myths
- Facts
- Support
- Social media
- Causes
- Staying safe

Reflections & Feedback   5 mins

Materials: Facilitator Guide 1 'Reflections & Feedback' (p. 262).

Ask the students to focus on the questions on the facilitator guide.

Target-Setting   5 mins

Materials: Worksheet 1.4 'My Targets' (p. 30) (one each); pens.

Use Worksheet 1.4 to support each student in setting their weekly targets. They can do this in pairs and support each other to identify what they would like to work on during the coming week. Allow a little time for reflection on the achievement (or otherwise) of the previous week's targets.

Compliments to Close   5 mins

Materials: Each individual's 'Golden Scroll' & a gold permanent marker each; Facilitator's Guide 2 'The Golden Scroll' (p. 263).

The guide will support you in directing the group as they add positive comments to their Golden Scrolls.

Relaxation   10 mins

Materials: Facilitator Guide 3 'Guided Relaxation' (p. 264).

Use the script on the facilitator guide to support the students in deep relaxation.

This page may be photocopied for instructional use only. *The ASD Girls' Wellbeing Toolkit* © Tina Rae & Amy Such 2019

Worksheet 1.21

Self-Harm Facts & Myths

Activity 1.9

It's just a phase – they will grow out of it
Self-harm is to get attention
Self-harm is only done by girls
If the injury is small, it is no problem
Self-harm is a 'suicide attempt'
Self-harm is a 'fashion', or a 'trend'
Self-harming means that you are mentally ill
The only form of self-harm is cutting

page 1 of 5

Worksheet 1.21

Activity 1.9

Facilitator's Sheet: Self-Harm Facts & Myths

Statement		What are the FACTS?
It's just a phase – they will grow out of it	Myth	Self-harm is not about being young or immature. When someone self-harms they are coping with more than they feel that they can manage. People of any age can self-harm as a way of trying to cope with emotional pain, trauma, stress, or other issues. Some people who have self-harmed as young people will turn to this coping mechanism again in adulthood when they experience stress or difficult life events. People do not 'grow out' of self-harming behaviours. The way to make progress is through developing alternative coping mechanisms. To develop alternative coping mechanisms people need time and support. It is vital to understand self-harm as a coping mechanism. Some young people will self-harm infrequently and others do so regularly. Some people will self-harm consistently for a number of years, or when they experience particular difficulties or stresses in their life. Self-harm is not a phase, it is a coping mechanism and therefore, to properly address self-harm, it is vital to address the underlying issues that are causing distress. Therefore, if you tell someone who is self-harming to 'just stop it', this will not be helpful, but is likely to alienate them further. It will not work, because it does not help the person to address what is causing them to self-harm. Also, it is likely to make a young person feel guilty, ashamed and/or pressured. To make positive progress young people need support to develop alternative coping strategies.

Worksheet 1.21

Facilitator's Sheet: Self-Harm Facts & Myths

Activity 1.9

Statement		What are the FACTS?
They are doing it to get attention	Myth	Seeing self-harm as 'attention-seeking' is incredibly common. The opposite is true and it is important to start seeing self-harm as 'attention needing'. Self-harm is a very personal and private thing and considerable research has shown that people who self-harm will make lot of effort to hide it. The vast majority of self-harm is never reported. When self-harm does bring attention, that attention is usually negative attention. For some young people self-harm is to cope with a difficult situation – they will deal with it in private and cover it up. Self-harm is not a manipulative behaviour. Sometimes it is seen that way, because it is upsetting for those around the young person who is self-harming. However, many young people are not aware of the impact that their self-harm is having on those around them. Sometimes young people do not know how to ask for the help that they need. So instead they might show a friend an injury they have caused themselves, or send them a photo. This can feel very overwhelming and young people need to know that it is okay to tell a trusted adult when this happens and that this is not a betrayal of their friend's trust. Others are very aware of this and find it even more isolating and upsetting to know that they are upsetting those they care about. This results in feelings of guilt and shame and makes it even harder for young people to talk about what is happening for them. It is important to focus on the fact that seeking help usually will come after weeks, months or even years of hiding self-harm and feeling shame and guilt. When someone does disclose self-harm it requires real bravery. Self-harm can be usefully seen as a communication – a young person who is self-harming is expressing (to themselves): 'This is a bad situation, I am not in a good place and I am finding it hard to cope.'
Self-harm is only done by girls	Myth	It is not at all true that only girls or women self-harm. It is also not true that it is 'mostly' women who self-harm. A number of studies show that both men and women will self-harm. Self-harm is a behaviour people use to cope with emotional difficulties or stressful situations. Self-harm is not based on whether you are a man or woman.

Worksheet 1.21

Facilitator's Sheet: Self-Harm Facts & Myths

Activity 1.9

Statement		What are the FACTS?
If the injury is small, it is no problem	Myth	It can be easy to think that if the damage done to a person's body is bad, then this means someone is more seriously emotionally distressed. This is not true at all. The seriousness of the self-harm does not link to the level of distress. The physical side of self-harm does not necessarily reflect the emotional issues/stresses. Someone can feel extremely distressed and their self-harm can appear relatively minor. It is important to care for any wounds or other injuries. The focus needs to be on the factors that caused the young person to self-harm. If a young person is self-harming, this is never okay, even if they do not leave damage on their body. If someone is self-harming it means that they are in distress and all people in distress need help and support.
Self-harm is a 'suicide attempt'	Myth	Self-harm is a coping behaviour to try to manage emotional distress – a way of coping, rather than a 'suicide attempt'. It is a way of staying alive and coping; it is, in fact, the opposite of a 'suicide attempt'. The reasons that people self-harm do not include the desire to take their own life. The reasons are complex. ChildLine and other support lines for young people think that unaddressed emotions such as unhappiness, anger and frustration may often be reasons for self-harm. Stresses at home, or feeling powerless, are the reasons that young people use to explain their self-harm. Think about occasions where you have felt distressed, or that you have no control. You may have cried, or gone to someone for help – these are ways of coping with upsetting feelings and events. For some young people self-harm is their way of coping with these emotions.
It is a 'fashion', or a 'trend'	Myth	This is an important misunderstanding/myth. Self-harm is not a lifestyle choice – it is a way of coping with emotional difficulties. Young people do not self-harm because of the music they listen to, the clothes they wear, or the friends that they hang out with. Self-harm is because someone is trying to cope with difficult and stressful issues. Self-harm is done by people of all ages, genders, backgrounds, races. Anyone can be affected by self-harm.

Worksheet 1.21
Facilitator's Sheet: Self-Harm Facts & Myths

Activity 1.9

Statement		What are the FACTS?
Self-harming means that you are mentally ill	Myth	Self-harm is a behaviour; a behaviour to cope with emotional distress or stress. Self-harm is not a diagnosis. Self-harm does not necessarily mean that you are mentally ill. You may be experiencing significant stress at a particular time and turn to self-harm as a way of coping with this. Every one of us has a state of 'mental health', just as we all have a state of 'physical health'. There are times when we will all feel stressed, overwhelmed and unhappy – refer back to earlier sessions that covered these topics. Our mental health is not fixed and we can all experience times whenwe are feeling well and times when we are not – and we may need help. The charity, Mind, have found that, in a year 1 in 4 people will experience some form of mental health problem. So, anyone can be affected. By itself self-harm indicates that someone is experiencing mental or emotional distress, not necessarily that they are mentally ill.
The only form of self-harm is cutting	Myth	This statement is a myth. Self-harm includes a large number of behaviours that are used as an attempt to cope with, or relieve, emotional distress. Cutting is one type of behaviour, but there are many, many others. However someone harms themselves, the focus needs to be on: Tending to any wounds/injuries Addressing the REASON for the self-harm, what is causing the emotional distress.

Worksheet 1.22
Amie's Story

Activity 1.9

Amie's Story

Amie is a 15-year-old girl who has been worried and distracted for the past few weeks. You have seen her arguing with people who are usually her friends over small things. She has now started sitting by herself and removing herself from her friends.

You know that Amie has seen her step-dad hitting her mum. You know that Amie was in an abusive relationship in the past.

You know that Amie used to self-harm by cutting herself and sometimes by banging her head. You think that she is self-harming again.

You are worried about Amie. What would you do?

Activity 1.10
Self-Harm 2

Aims

* For the students to feel safe & confident to participate in the session
* To explore the thoughts and feelings of someone who might engage in self-harming
* To understand personal circumstances that might trigger self-harming
* To develop a plan to support the students during circumstances that might trigger self-harming

Group Rules 2 mins

Materials: Worksheet 1.1 'Visual Timetable' (p. 27); Group Rules Chart created in Activity 1.1.

Using Worksheet 1.1 and the Group Rules Chart, remind the group of the structure of each session and of the rules that were agreed in Activity 1.1. Ask if anyone would like to add a rule, or have a rule explained again.

Talk Time 5 mins

Materials: Post-it notes.

Ask the students: 'When might someone self-harm?'

Students have the opportunity to discuss their answers, write them on post-its, or to reflect on their responses without sharing with the group.

Ice-Breaker 5 mins

Materials: Worksheets 1.23 'Mindfulness Colouring' (p. 97), 1.24 'Mindfulness Sudoku' (p. 98) & 1.25 'Mindfulness Doodling' (p. 99); coloured pens/pencils.

Let the students choose the worksheet they wish to complete; as they work, suggest that they reflect on how they are feeling. You may need to prompt them with words such as 'relaxed', 'calm', 'deep in thought', 'happy'.

Core Activity 1: Letter from Sally   15 mins

Materials: Worksheet 1.26 'A Letter from Sally' (p. 100) (one each).

> Attention: This activity involves a sensitive letter that could be distressing for some students – it is important to be mindful of this.

Ask the students to read Sally's letter on Worksheet 1.26 and discuss some of the key issues, particularly in the light of previous activities in *The ASD Girls' Wellbeing Toolkit*. Key questions for the discussion:

- How do you think that Sally is feeling?
- What underlying issues are going on in her life?
- Do you think that she is attention-seeking?
- Could she be suicidal?
- If you asked Sally about the marks on her wrists, do you think she would tell you?
- If you asked Sally about her parents splitting up, do you think she would like to talk about that?

Review what has been covered in previous sessions. Everyone goes through difficult times and has different ways of coping. Self-harm is a way of coping with pressure people feel inside. Often they prefer to talk about whatever is causing the pain than about the injury. Sometimes someone may feel very low and be thinking about suicide. If you think someone may be suicidal, **don't ignore it** – ask them how they are feeling. Remember, if you are worried, tell someone!

Core Activity 2: Keeping Safe   15 mins

Materials: Worksheet 1.27 'My Safety Plan' (p. 101); pens/pencils.

For young people who struggle with thoughts around self-harm, it can be very helpful to have a plan that is created by the student themselves, with a trusted adult (in this case, you, as facilitator). This plan can be very empowering and gives the young person clear, personal guidance for staying safe if they feel overwhelmed or distressed.

> This activity is quite a personal activity and so it is important to be clear with the students that they will be completing their safety plans individually and will not be required to share their plans with the rest of the group.

The safety plan on Worksheet 1.27 includes the option that it may be jointly signed by the young person and the facilitator (or another trusted adult). A list of alternative coping methods is also

Activity 1.10

included on the second page; this can be used as a prompt when completing the safety plan, but it is not exhaustive and may be added to.

This safety plan has been adapted from *the Brent Adolescent Team Self-Harm and Safety Plan* produced by the Central and North West London NHS Foundation Trust (CAMHS & Me).

Reflections & Feedback   5 mins

Materials: Facilitator Guide 1 'Reflections & Feedback' (p. 262).

Ask the students to focus on the questions on the facilitator guide.

Target-Setting   5 mins

Materials: Worksheet 1.4 'My Targets' (p. 30) (one each); pens.

Use Worksheet 1.4 to support each student in setting their weekly targets. They can do this in pairs and support each other to identify what they would like to work on during the coming week. Allow a little time for reflection on the achievement (or otherwise) of the previous week's targets.

Compliments to Close   5 mins

Materials: Each individual's 'Golden Scroll' & a gold permanent marker each; Facilitator's Guide 2 'The Golden Scroll' (p. 263).

The guide will support you in directing the group as they add positive comments to their Golden Scrolls.

Relaxation   10 mins

Materials: Facilitator Guide 3 'Guided Relaxation' (p. 264).

Use the script on the facilitator guide to support the students in deep relaxation.

Worksheet 1.23

Activity 1.10

Mindfulness Colouring

Worksheet 1.24

Mindfulness Sudoku

Activity 1.10

	8						2	
				8	4		9	
		6	3	2			1	
	9	7					8	
8			9		3			2
	1					9	5	
	7			4	5	8		
	3		7	1				
		8					4	

Worksheet 1.25
Mindfulness Doodling

Activity 1.10

Worksheet 1.26

A Letter from Sally

Activity 1.10

Dear you,

I always thought it was just mad people who cut themselves, but I've been cutting myself for nearly a year and it's getting worse and I really need help.

I'm 16 and I just can't cope. My mum and dad split up two years ago and I still cry myself to sleep. I get so bitter and angry with them both, it's so selfish. They don't think of anyone but themselves. Because I am miserable I don't have any friends and I just eat and eat but I don't care. Nobody else cares what I look like so why should I? Sometimes I feel like my whole body is under pressure and that it's going to explode. I am angry and I don't know what to do.

I started cutting by accident. I found a razor blade in the bathroom and I took it into my bedroom and started to slash a photograph of Helen, she used to be Mum's best friend til she ran off with my dad. I cut my finger and the blood started to ooze - it was almost as though some of the anger oozed away with it.

I don't cut deep, just into the skin so the blood shows and runs along the grooves. I usually cut my arms, so I have to wear long sleeved shirts so people can't see. Sometimes I cut the top of my legs.

I'm scared someone will really notice my wrists but the pain and blood really helps me to take my mind off of things. It is hard to describe what it feels like.

I know I have to stop it but I don't know how. Please help me, there's nobody I can talk to and it sometimes feels like no-one would notice if I just died.

Source: Samaritans Lesson B2 Understanding Self-Injury
This letter is based on letters sent to the Samaritans' correspondence branch

Worksheet 1.27
My Safety Plan

Activity 1.10

1. What makes me want to harm myself? (It might be certain feelings, places, people, or thoughts/memories.)
   _____

2. What else helps me to cope, other than harming myself?
   _____

3. What would I tell a close friend to do if they were feeling this way?
   _____

4. What could others do that could help?
   _____

5. If I feel like harming myself I will do one of the following (try to get to at least 6, aim to get to 8):
   1. _____
   2. _____
   3. _____
   4. _____
   5. _____
   6. _____
   7. _____
   8. _____

6. If the plan doesn't work, and I still feel like harming myself, I will do at least one of the following:

   - Talk to _____ [name of member of school staff]
   - Call Childline on 0800 1111
   - Call Samaritans on 116 123

   Signed _____ [Student]   Date: _____

   Signed _____ [Member of staff]   Date: _____

page 1 of 2

Worksheet 1.27
My Safety Plan

Activity 1.10

Alternative Coping Methods

This is a list of some possible alternative coping methods. This list has been created with the suggestions of young people who have self-harmed and what they found helpful. These are suggestions and there are lots more ideas to try. Remember that there is not 'only one' coping method; young people find that different things help at different times. Some don't work at first, but do work later.

- Talk to someone you feel comfortable and safe with OR call someone you trust OR call a helpline.
- Do something you like, for example, drawing, singing, dancing.
- Get some sleep.
- Cuddle someone you trust.
- Cuddle a toy.
- Cuddle a pet.
- Do some kind of exercise: go for a walk, go to the gym, go swimming, dance.
- Distract yourself by watching TV or YouTube.
- Tidy/clean your room.
- Listen to some music that puts you in a good mood/relaxes you/makes you want to dance.
- Hit/punch pillows, or scream into a pillow to release your anger.
- Hold ice cubes in your hand to cause numbness.
- Put an elastic band round your wrist and ping it.
- Give yourself some harmless pain, for example, have a cold shower.
- Pamper yourself, for example, paint your nails or have a bath.
- Think about something that relaxes you.
- Do some relaxation techniques – relax your mind and focus on something calming/happy.
- Keep a journal of how you are feeling (positive and negative) so that you can start to identify what triggers self-harm and what supports you.

Part 2
Relationships & Communication Skills

1 Non-Verbal Communication
Non-Verbal Communication
Photo Stories

2 Verbal Communication
What is Assertiveness?
My Scripts

3 Relationships 1
Speak & Guess Cards
Other People

4 Relationships 2
Beliefs about Relationships
Good Partners versus Toxic Partners

5 Relationships 3
Challenging Controlling Behaviour
The Effects of Kindness

6 Sexual Behaviours
Exploitation
Sources of Support

7 Online Behaviours
Online Grooming
Online Grooming Case Study

8 Media & Other Influences 1
Online Images
Sexting

9 Media & Other Influences 2
Who Are You Talking To?
Safe Profiles

10 Risk-Taking
Saying 'No'
Risk

Activity 2.1
Non-Verbal Communication

Aims

* For the students to feel safe & confident to participate in the session
* To experiment with different forms of non-verbal communication
* To consider the messages that can be received through non-verbal communication
* To begin to decipher non-verbal communication techniques

Group Rules — 2 mins

Materials: Worksheet 1.1 'Visual Timetable' (p. 27); Group Rules Chart created in Activity 1.1.

Using Worksheet 1.1 and the Group Rules Chart, remind the group of the structure of each session and of the rules that were agreed in Activity 1.1.

Talk Time — 5 mins

Materials: Post-it notes.

Ask the students: 'What is non-verbal communication?'

Students have the opportunity to discuss their answers, write them on post-its, or to reflect on their responses without sharing with the group.

Ice-Breaker — 5 mins

Materials: Worksheet 2.1 'More than Words' (p. 107).

Communication is a dynamic process that happens within a particular context (i.e., it is more than the transfer of words/information), so it is worth considering how this process unfolds. This activity should raise awareness of the complexity of communication and is concerned with the role of tone of voice and non-verbal signals of mood.

In the first part of the activity the group focuses on the phrase: 'I didn't say she took the phone.' Cut up the slips on Worksheet 2.1 and give one to each group member. Each person takes a turn to say the phrase, but with different emphasis.

Discuss as a whole group how emphasis alters meaning. Were people surprised at how much it can alter meaning? Can anyone think of any other examples of emphasis or tone of voice affecting meaning? Why might it be useful to reflect on this and raise our awareness of it?

Core Activity 1: Non-Verbal Communication   20 mins

Materials: Computer with audio, safe internet access, flip chart & paper, flip-chart pen.

In this activity the group will be developing their non-verbal communication skills by analysing the body language, gesture and facial expressions of other people and reflecting on their own non-verbal communication.

Watch the video clip below in advance to check for suitability. It is a clip from the TV show *Friends* ('Bracelet Buddies'); if there is another clip more appropriate to the needs and interests of your group, by all means substitute it. Make sure you select a clip using both immediately obvious and more complex non-verbal communication.

1 Show the video clip to the group and ask them to discuss what is going on: https://www.youtube.com/watch?v=tj219mX6Bx8&index=5&list=PL234F9D21D1664C89

2 Now brainstorm from memory all the types of non-verbal communication that people noticed in the clip, listing them on a flip chart.

3 Then watch the clip again and add to the list, stopping and starting the clip as needed.

4 Discuss how easy or hard this activity was and why it might be useful to develop skill in reading non-verbal communication.

5 Suggest that we can improve our communication skills through practice and reflection, just as we do other skills (e.g. reading, diving).

6 Discuss the idea that many psychologists believe that non-verbal communication is crucial to all communication and can be easier to read than verbal communication, because people are generally unaware of it. For example, emotions often 'leak' out non-verbally, when the verbal message is something different, for example: when a person says they are happy, but their body language saying the opposite. How might it be helpful to get better at noticing people's 'emotional leakage'?

Core Activity 2: Photo Stories 10 mins

Materials: Worksheet 2.2 'Photo Stories' (p. 108); paper & pens.

In pairs, ask the group to reflect on Worksheet 2.2, thinking about the messages and 'hidden messages' in people's communication. They do not need to write on the sheet, just discuss it and jot down any ideas if they would like to. Take care to point out that we should be careful about making assumptions regarding how people feel and what they think: we can only give it our best guess!

Reflections & Feedback 5 mins

Materials: Facilitator Guide 1 'Reflections & Feedback' (p. 262).

Ask the students to focus on the questions on the facilitator guide.

Target-Setting 5 mins

Materials: Worksheet 1.4 'My Targets' (p. 30) (one each); pens.

Use Worksheet 1.4 to support each student in setting their weekly targets. They can do this in pairs and support each other to identify what they would like to work on during the coming week. Allow a little time for reflection on the achievement (or otherwise) of the previous week's targets.

Compliments to Close 5 mins

Materials: Each individual's 'Golden Scroll' & a gold permanent marker each; Facilitator's Guide 2 'The Golden Scroll' (p. 263).

The guide will support you in directing the group as they add positive comments to their Golden Scrolls.

Relaxation 10 mins

Materials: Facilitator Guide 3 'Guided Relaxation' (p. 264).

Use the script on the facilitator guide to support the students in deep relaxation.

Activity 2.1

106 P This page may be photocopied for instructional use only. *The ASD Girls' Wellbeing Toolkit* © Tina Rae & Amy Such 2019

Worksheet 2.1
More than Words

Activity 2.1

'**I** didn't say she took the phone.'

'I **didn't** say she took the phone.'

'I didn't **say** she took the phone.'

'I didn't say **she** took the phone.'

'I didn't say she **took** the phone.'

'I didn't say she took **the** phone.'

'I didn't say she took the **phone**.'

Worksheet 2.2
Photo Stories

Activity 2.1

Notes

page 1 of 3

108 — This page may be photocopied for instructional use only. *The ASD Girls' Wellbeing Toolkit* © Tina Rae & Amy Such 2019

Worksheet 2.2
Photo Stories

Activity 2.1

Notes

page 2 of 3

This page may be photocopied for instructional use only. *The ASD Girls' Wellbeing Toolkit* © Tina Rae & Amy Such 2019

Worksheet 2.2
Photo Stories

Activity 2.1

Notes

page 3 of 3

Activity 2.2
Verbal Communication

Aims

* For the students to feel safe & confident to participate in the session
* To practise using scripted responses
* To be able to define passive, aggressive and assertive responses to social situations
* To compare the use of non-verbal and verbal responses

Group Rules — 2 mins

Materials: Worksheet 1.1 'Visual Timetable' (p. 27); Group Rules Chart created in Activity 1.1.

Using Worksheet 1.1 and the Group Rules Chart, remind the group of the structure of each session and of the rules that were agreed in Activity 1.1.

Talk Time — 5 mins

Materials: Post-it notes.

Ask the students: 'When is verbal communication difficult?'

Students have the opportunity to discuss their answers, write them on post-its, or to reflect on their responses without sharing with the group.

Ice-Breaker — 5 mins

Materials: Worksheet 2.3 'Response Scripts' (p.115).

This activity is about thinking about (and possibly trying to use) prepared responses, including scripts. A 'script' can be thought of as a planned verbal response, backed up with non-verbal signals. Examples of response scripts that might serve the purpose of communicating 'go away', because they offer a response without engaging directly, include: 'I understand', 'Right', or 'Okay'.

Before you begin the activity, make sure the students understand what response scripts are and that they are not generally appropriate when we are in danger. Nor do scripts acknowledge the validity of the other person's comments or actions. They are just a tool to bear in mind when communicating with others in situations of **low** threat.

1   Start by discussing when it might be helpful to use planned verbal and non-verbal responses and when it might not.

2   Ask students in small groups (pairs or threes) to work through Worksheet 3.2, coming up with some response scripts that would be happy to use to communicate various messages.

3   They can try these out if they feel comfortable or curious to do so.

Core Activity 1: What is Assertiveness? 20 mins

Materials: One copy each of Worksheet 2.4 'What is Assertiveness?' (p. 116) (printed on A3 paper), Worksheet 2.5 'The Assertiveness Scale' (p. 117) & Worksheet 2.6 'Assertiveness Skills' (p. 118) (one each). Computer with audio, safe internet access, flip chart & paper, flip-chart pen, highlighter pens.

Students are introduced to the concept of assertiveness and begin to recognise (by use of video clips) what assertive, aggressive and passive behaviour and language look like.

1   First use Worksheet 2.4 to define assertiveness and introduce the following key points:

- Assertiveness is about identifying how you feel and what you want and communicating it in a firm, calm and non-confrontational way. It is not about winning; it is about communicating. Self-esteem and self-confidence are required to practise assertiveness, because they help us identify and state how we feel and what we want, and to feel that we deserve to do so. Thus, this activity might draw on things that have already been discussed in the ASD Girls' Wellbeing Toolkit sessions, because having a positive view of yourself is the first step towards asserting yourself.

- Assertiveness can be positioned on a scale between passivity and aggression. It is best understood as a set of skills that can be learned through practice. As with learning any skill, this requires work. Here are some basic definitions:
    * **Aggressive:** When you consider your feelings and needs above those of others and act to meet them – to 'win'
    * **Assertive:** When you consider your feelings and needs and those of others.
    * **Passive:** When you consider the needs of others above your own needs and avoid conflict at any cost.

- It is important to mention that aggression and passivity are both normal (and sometimes adaptive) responses to experiencing overwhelming fear or terror. In certain contexts, aggressive and passive behaviour can help us survive. This programme is not about analysing or criticising past responses, many of which have helped people to survive traumatic experiences. It is about moving forwards into a new stage of our lives and developing skills to help us to do so.

2   Then, when you feel the group have understood what assertiveness is, show this video clip from *Back to the Future* on YouTube:

   https://www.youtube.com/watch?v=fLvd7IAU35o

3   Discuss:

   * What do people think about these behaviours/communication styles?
   * Are they passive, aggressive, assertive? Why?
   * Is the behaviour of Biff ever a good idea?
   * What about McFly's communication? Why/why not?

4   Consolidate using this one minute clip of the three types of behaviour:

   https://www.youtube.com/watch?v=o6LcPfnwGec

5   Now use The Assertiveness Scale on Worksheet 2.5 to talk through what assertiveness is and recap the definitions above. It is important that everyone understands that assertiveness can be learnt and can be a useful life skill. Anyone can learn it, but (as discussed) they have to believe that they are worth it, because it involves respecting yourself and believing in your right to: have feelings, express feelings, express preferences, and say 'no'.

6   Now have a look at Worksheet 2.6. Ask the students to highlight any skills they feel they have. During the discussion, they might like to give examples of when they have used these skills. How might they learn additional skills?

Core Activity 2: My Scripts   15 mins

Materials: Worksheet 2.7 'Communication Scripts' (p. 119); flip chart & paper, flip-chart pen (or whiteboard & dry-wipe pen), scissors; one jar/box/other container per group of three people.

This activity is about the students experimenting with their own assertiveness and what they feel comfortable with/would like to try out in their own lives. Start by practising some non-verbal communication, working in groups of three.

Each group has a container holding all of the 6 statements on the worksheet (cut, fold and insert the slips in the containers in advance of the session). Then write the 6 statements on the flip chart so that everyone can see them.

1   One member of the group takes a slip and tries to communicate what is on it non-verbally (no words allowed!) The other two members of the group try to guess which slip the

participant has. Students now swap roles until all 6 statements have been expressed non-verbally. This should remind everyone of how important non-verbal communication is, and also of the power of language.

2   Next, repeat the activity verbally. The participant takes a slip and chooses whether to use a passive voice, aggressive voice, or assertive voice. The other two group members need to guess which voice they have chosen to use. Encourage discussion of what assertive communication looks like, for example: open body language, calm but firm voice, eye contact but not too much.

3   Finally, discuss how prepared scripts might be helpful, for example: can they help us to say 'no' to things we do not want?

Reflections & Feedback   5 mins

Materials: Facilitator Guide 1 'Reflections & Feedback' (p. 262).

Ask the students to focus on the questions on the facilitator guide.

Target-Setting   5 mins

Materials: Worksheet 1.4 'My Targets' (p. 30) (one each); pens.

Use Worksheet 1.4 to support each student in setting their weekly targets. They can do this in pairs and support each other to identify what they would like to work on during the coming week. Allow a little time for reflection on the achievement (or otherwise) of the previous week's targets.

Compliments to Close   5 mins

Materials: Each individual's 'Golden Scroll' & a gold permanent marker each; Facilitator's Guide 2 'The Golden Scroll' (p. 263).

The guide will support you in directing the group as they add positive comments to their Golden Scrolls.

Relaxation   10 mins

Materials: Facilitator Guide 3 'Guided Relaxation' (p. 264).

Use the script on the facilitator guide to support the students in deep relaxation.

Worksheet 2.3
Response Scripts

Activity 2.2

Message you want to give	Possible Script / Ideas	Non-verbal signals
What you have said has upset me.		
I want you to stop talking to me.		
I am interested in what you are saying.		
I need you to listen to me.		

Worksheet 2.4

What is Assertiveness?

Activity 2.2

Assertiveness: Key Points

1. Assertiveness is about identifying how you feel and what you want, and communicating it in a firm, calm and non-confrontational way. It is not about winning; it is about communicating. Self-esteem and self-confidence are required to practise assertiveness, because they help us identify and state how we feel and what we want, and to feel that we deserve to do so. Thus, this activity might draw on things that have already been discussed during ASD Girls' Wellbeing Toolkit sessions, because having a positive view of yourself is the first step towards asserting yourself.

2. Assertiveness can be positioned on a scale between passivity and aggression. It is best understood as a set of skills that can be learned through practice. As with learning any skill, this requires work. Here are some basic definitions:

    * **Aggressive:** When you consider your feelings and needs above those of others and act to meet them – to 'win'

    * **Assertive:** When you consider your feelings and needs and those of others.

    * **Passive:** When you consider the needs of others above your own needs and avoid conflict at any cost.

3. It is important to realise that aggression and passivity are both normal (and sometimes adaptive) responses to experiencing overwhelming fear or terror. In certain contexts, aggressive and passive behaviour can help us survive. The ASD Girls' Toolkit is not about analysing or criticising past responses, many of which have helped people to survive traumatic experiences. It is about moving forwards into a new stage of our lives and developing skills to help us to do so.

Worksheet 2.5
The Assertiveness Scale

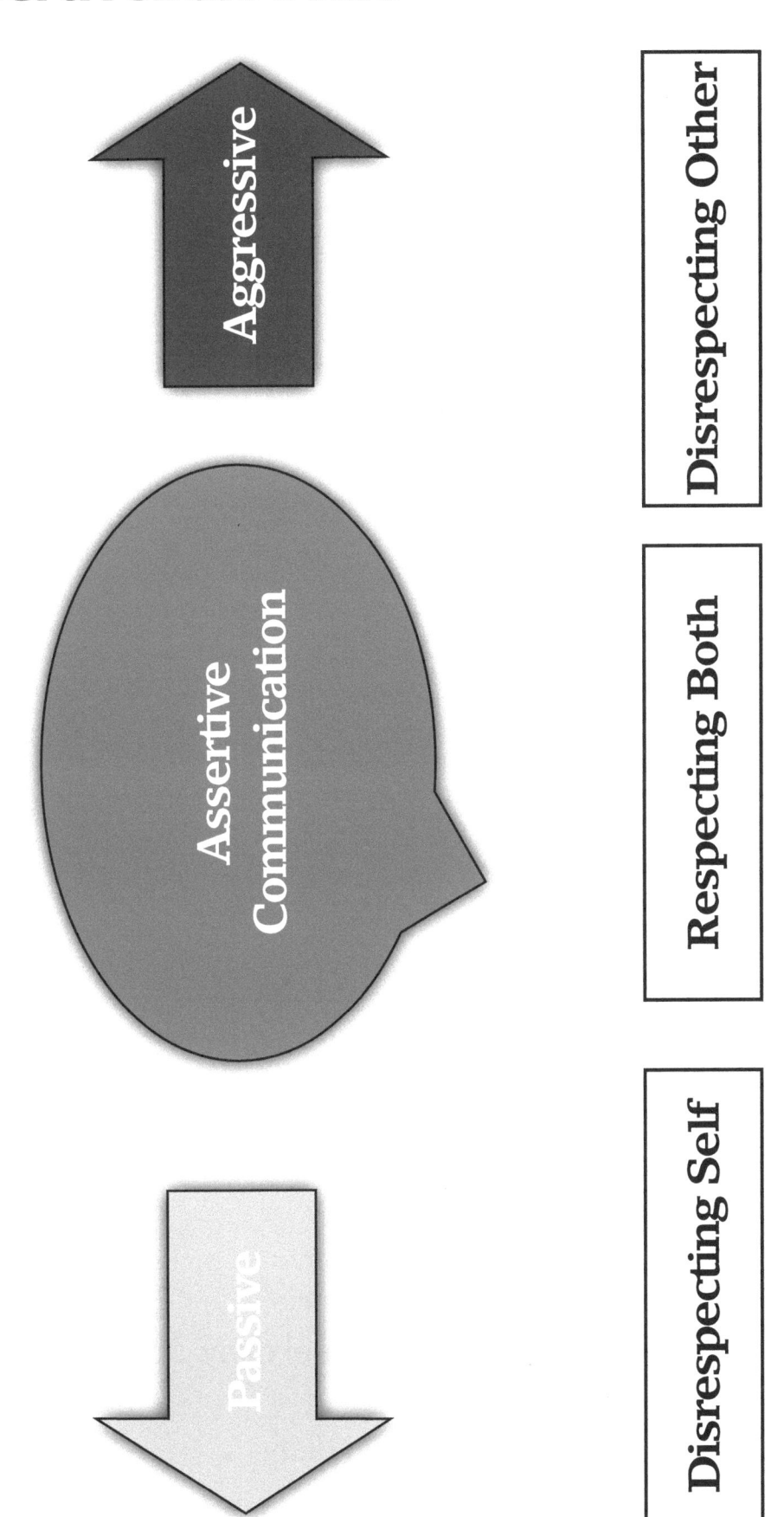

Activity 2.2

Aggressive — Disrespecting Other

Assertive Communication — Respecting Both

Passive — Disrespecting Self

Worksheet 2.6
Assertiveness Skills

Activity 2.2

- ✓ I value myself and my rights

- ✓ I value the rights and needs of others

- ✓ I believe I should be treated with respect and dignity

- ✓ I believe others should be treated with respect and dignity

- ✓ I believe I have the right to say 'no'

- ✓ I can say 'no' when I need to

- ✓ I can identify how I feel

- ✓ I can say how I feel calmly and clearly out loud, including negative feelings

- ✓ I can identify what I want

- ✓ I can say what I want calmly and clearly out loud

- ✓ I believe people are responsible for their own behaviour

- ✓ I think it is okay to make a mistake

- ✓ I can receive a compliment and feel okay

- ✓ I can receive a criticism and feel okay

Worksheet 2.7
Communication Slips

Activity 2.2

Go away and leave me alone.	Yes, please.
No.	I don't know what you mean.
Can you repeat that?	How interesting.

Activity 2.3
Relationships 1

Aims

- For the students to feel safe & confident to participate in the session
- To continue practising reading non-verbal communication, with the introduction of different emotional responses
- To explore the difference between what people say and what they think
- To explore social anxiety and develop coping strategies for social situations

Group Rules — 2 mins

Materials: Worksheet 1.1 'Visual Timetable' (p. 27); Group Rules Chart created in Activity 1.1.

Using Worksheet 1.1 and the Group Rules Chart, remind the group of the structure of each session and of the rules that were agreed in Activity 1.1.

Talk Time — 5 mins

Materials: Post-it notes.

Ask the students: 'What social situations make you feel anxious?'

Students have the opportunity to discuss their answers, write them on post-its, or to reflect on their responses without sharing with the group.

Ice-Breaker — 5 mins

Materials: Worksheets 2.8 'Name the Emotion' (p. 124) & 2.9 'Intensity of Feeling' (p. 125) (one for each pair); pens.

This activity is about recognising and communicating emotion without using words.

First discuss why people may wish to show how they feel, and why sometimes they may not.

Then practise naming emotions. This is not a test and students should be reassured that everyone is different in the way they recognise and express emotion.

There is some evidence that emotion recognition and developing a vocabulary around emotion can support communication and wellbeing. An important part of this is recognition that our emotions matter.

Students should work in pairs to give a name to each emotion on Worksheet 2.8. They can come up with names on their own, or may like to use the chart on Worksheet 2.9 to give them some ideas. They should be supported not to worry about 'getting the right answer'.

Open up some discussion about how they made their decisions, based only on faces:

- What were they looking for?
- Was this easy/hard?
- What more information would they like to be more confident they were picking the 'right' emotion?

Core Activity 1: Speak & Guess   15 mins

Materials: Worksheet 2.10 'Speak & Guess Cards' (p. 126) (one set per pair, cut into separate slips); envelopes (one per pair).

This activity builds on the skills developed in 'Photo Stories' (Activity 2.1), which focused on non-verbal communication. Using the cards on Worksheet 2.10, students are encouraged to guess what someone might be thinking, although they may be saying something different. Provide some context by explaining that this activity is based on a school trip to Alton Towers.

The students work in pairs, each pair with a set of the 'Speak & Guess Cards' (cut up in advance). Each one of the pair takes it in turns to be the speaker and the guesser. The speaker picks a card and spends about a minute thinking about the 'in your head' prompt. They then say the phrase with this in mind. The guesser guesses what was in their head. They then discuss.

> Attention. Remind everyone that this is a potentially challenging exercise. If they are not happy doing it (or want to stop part way through) that is fine. It can be difficult and uncomfortable to imagine being someone else. Some pairs may wish to simply discuss each slip rather than play 'speak and guess' and that is also fine.

Discuss how easy or hard it was to guess what was going on in the other person's head:

- What kind of things gave us clues?
- When you were the actor was it easy to 'act' the different emotions and thoughts? What helped you do this?
- What was hard?

Discuss what might be the point of doing these kinds of exercises? It can sometimes be helpful to consciously 'act' more confident than you feel. Discuss when this might be a good/bad idea. Introduce the psychological concept of 'acting as if'. This is when we pretend to be more confident than we feel. Talk over the advantages and disadvantages of this approach and get people's ideas.

Core Activity 2: Other People   15 mins

Materials: Worksheet 2.11 'Feeling Positive with Others' (p. 127) (one each); pens.

This activity looks at social anxiety, what it is and how it can be addressed in positive ways. The young people may be familiar with the term 'social anxiety', but some may not know it.

The starting point of the session can be a question: What is social anxiety? Once the group have shared their ideas, the following key information can also be shared:

- Everyone feels anxious in some social situations. This is normal.
- Social anxiety is when people feel very anxious/self-conscious in normal social situations. In severe cases, people feel anxious almost all the time when in social situations. In more mild cases, people may only feel anxious in certain social situations, for example, with new people or when speaking in public.
- Social anxiety is a common issue and many people experience it at some point in their lives.

Worksheet 2.11 allows the young people to think about their anxieties in social situations and what helps them. Inform the students that this is an individual activity and they will not need to share their responses with the rest of the group.

Reflections & Feedback   5 mins

Materials: Facilitator Guide 1 'Reflections & Feedback' (p. 262).

Ask the students to focus on the questions on the facilitator guide.

Target-Setting   5 mins

Materials: Worksheet 1.4 'My Targets' (p. 30) (one each); pens.

Use Worksheet 1.4 to support each student in setting their weekly targets. They can do this in pairs and support each other to identify what they would like to work on during the coming week. Allow a little time for reflection on the achievement (or otherwise) of the previous week's targets.

Compliments to Close   5 mins

Materials: Each individual's 'Golden Scroll' & a gold permanent marker each; Facilitator's Guide 2 'The Golden Scroll' (p. 263).

The guide will support you in directing the group as they add positive comments to their Golden Scrolls.

Relaxation   10 mins

Materials: Facilitator Guide 3 'Guided Relaxation' (p. 264).

Use the script on the facilitator guide to support the students in deep relaxation.

Worksheet 2.8
Name the Emotion

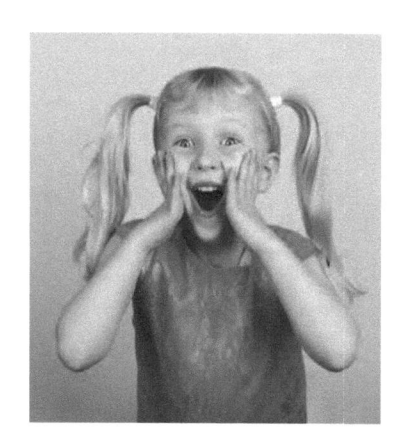

Activity 2.3

Worksheet 2.9
Intensity of Feeling

Activity 2.3

	Happy	Sad	Angry	Confused	Afraid	Weak	Strong	Guilty
High	Elated	Depressed	Furious	Bewildered	Terrified	Helpless	Powerful	Sorrowful
	Excited	Disappointed	Enraged	Trapped	Horrified	Hopeless	Aggressive	Remorseful
	Overjoyed	Alone	Outraged	Troubled	Scared stiff	Beat	Gung ho	Ashamed
	Thrilled	Hurt	Aggravated	Desperate	Petrified	Overwhelmed	Potent	Unworthy
	Exuberant	Left out	Irate	Lost	Fearful	Impotent	Super	Worthless
	Ecstatic	Dejected	Seething		Panicky	Small	Forceful	
	Fired up	Hopeless				Exhausted	Proud	
	Delighted	Sorrowful				Drained	Determined	
Medium	Cheerful	Heartbroken	Upset	Disorganised	Scared	Dependant	Energetic	Sorry
	Up	Down	Mad	Foggy	Frightened	Incapable	Capable	Lowdown
	Good	Upset	Annoyed	Misplaced	Threatened	Lifeless	Confident	Sneaky
	Relieved	Distressed	Frustrated	Disoriented	Insecure	Tired	Persuasive	
	Satisfied	Regretful	Agitated	Mixed up	Uneasy	Rundown	Sure	
	Contented		Hot		Shocked	Lazy		
			Disgusted			Insecure		
						Shy		
Mild	Glad	Unhappy	Perturbed	Unsure	Apprehensive	Unsatisfied	Secure	Embarrassed
	Content	Moody	Uptight	Puzzled	Nervous	Under par	Durable	
	Satisfied	Blue	Dismayed	Bothered	Worried	Shaky	Adequate	
	Pleasant	Sorry	Put out	Uncomfortable	Timid	Unsure	Able	
	Fine	Lost	Irritated	Undecided	Unsure	Soft	Capable	
	Mellow	Bad	Touchy	Baffled	Anxious	Lethargic		
	Pleased	Dissatisfied		Perplexed		Inadequate		

Worksheet 2.10
Speak & Guess Cards

Activity 2.3

What you say: I don't want to go to Alton Towers	**In your head:** Happy
What you say: I really enjoyed it.	**In your head:** I really didn't enjoy it, I was scared the whole time.
What you say: OK, I would like to sit with you on the coach.	**In your head:** I never want to see you again, but I don't want you to know.
What you say: How are you?	**In your head:** Worry and anxiety
What you say: I can't wait to go on that roller coaster	**In your head:** Keep calm. Everything is fine. I can do this.

Worksheet 2.11
Feeling Positive with Others

Activity 2.3

What social situations make you feel anxious? Tick those that apply to you and add others in the blank spaces if you want.

Talking on the phone to a friend	Talking on the phone to someone you don't know	Being the centre of attention
Being out with your friends	Making eye contact	Going to a crowded place
Going on a date	Spending time with a close friend	Meeting authority figures
Meeting new people	Going to the supermarket	Giving a speech

Imagine yourself in a social situation that makes you worried, for example, meeting new people. What are you worried about? (Again, tick those that apply and add others in the blanks spaces.)

Not knowing what to say	Not knowing what to do	How I look	That people won't like me	That I will look stupid
That I will embarrass myself				

page 1 of 2

Worksheet 2.11
Feeling Positive with Others

Activity 2.3

It is common when we feel anxious about a social situation to avoid it. But if we keep avoiding things it makes it even harder to do them. For example, if you are uncomfortable speaking on the phone, then you might not answer your phone and then it makes it more difficult to answer your phone next time.

Think of someone you trust [friend/family member/teacher etc.]

_____

What would they say if you told them about your worry?

_____

_____

Take a moment to imagine what would happen if you woke up tomorrow morning and your anxiety had gone! You are not anxious in these social situations anymore. What would be different in your life? Give examples and make them as specific as you can.

1 _____

_____

2 _____

_____

3 _____

_____

Activity 2.4
Relationships 2

Aims

* For the students to feel safe & confident to participate in the session
* To continue practising fundamental communication skills
* To explore beliefs that surround relationships
* To discuss characteristics that you would find in a suitable partner

Group Rules   2 mins

Materials: Worksheet 1.1 'Visual Timetable' (p. 27); Group Rules Chart created in Activity 1.1.

Using Worksheet 1.1 and the Group Rules Chart, remind the group of the structure of each session and of the rules that were agreed in Activity 1.1.

Talk Time   5 mins

Materials: Post-it notes.

Ask the students: 'Why do people have romantic relationships?'

Students have the opportunity to discuss their answers, write them on post-its, or to reflect on their responses without sharing with the group.

Ice-Breaker   5 mins

Materials: Beach ball.

This activity is about the idea of 'attunement'. Attunement is when two people communicate really well – they are 'in tune' with each other, really paying attention to each other and 'receiving' each other's communication, including emotion. Today we are going to have a go at 'tuning in' to another person.

To start, the whole group should participate in a game such as 'Beach Ball Questions'. Begin by choosing a topic (e.g., famous people, places, animals, food). A ball is thrown around the room and when each person catches it they say something connected with the topic, change the topic, or say 'pass'. Remind the group to attempt to tune into what their fellow students are saying.

Core Activity 1: Beliefs about Relationships   10 mins

Materials: Worksheet 2.12 'Relationship Rules' (p. 132).

Relationships are much more than just romantic or sexual. This activity supports the students to think about their relationships – romantic, family, with friends and with others. This is an incredibly sensitive and difficult topic, and it is essential to give the young people time to reflect on their previous experiences and how this might inform beliefs that they have about relationships.

The group should consider each statement listed on Worksheet 2.12 and discuss whether they agree or disagree, and why. These statements act as prompts to encourage deeper discussion about why people hold different beliefs about relationships. The discussion should be nuanced, with some feeling that they agree or disagree with statements sometimes, or under certain conditions.

Core Activity 2: Good Partner versus Toxic Partner

Materials: Worksheet 2.13 'People Outlines' (p. 133) (two copies each); small post-it notes, A4 paper, pens.

This activity is developed from Moran's (2006) 'Drawing the Ideal Self', a technique used by psychologists, social workers, therapists and other professionals to explore and understand ways that a child or young person sees themselves. This builds on the theory and philosophy of Personal Construct Psychology (Kelly, 1955).

Each person is given a copy of Worksheet 2.13 showing three human outlines – male, female and gender neutral – and is asked to select whichever image feels most relevant to them if picking a partner. Alternatively, the students can just use a blank piece of paper. Using small post-it notes, or by writing inside the outline, the group are asked to identify the characteristics of a toxic partner. Discuss how they would react to a situation in which their partner proved toxic:

- What would they do?
- What would they say?
- How would they behave?
- What qualities would be toxic?

Talk about how you might recognise someone like this. Perhaps they act cruelly, saying unkind things, or perhaps they embarrass you in public/in front of your friends?

Repeat the above activity for a good partner.

Explain that a trusting, equal and respectful relationship is not just what you might find with a 'perfect' partner, but is what everyone deserves. They can also discuss what a 'perfect' or 'ideal' partner would be like.

During the discussion, you might wish to include reflections on key relationships from TV or the media, exploring whether or not they are positive.

Reflections & Feedback   5 mins

Materials: Facilitator Guide 1 'Reflections & Feedback' (p. 262).

Ask the students to focus on the questions on the facilitator guide.

Target-Setting   5 mins

Materials: Worksheet 1.4 'My Targets' (p. 30) (one each); pens.

Use Worksheet 1.4 to support each student in setting their weekly targets. They can do this in pairs and support each other to identify what they would like to work on during the coming week. Allow a little time for reflection on the achievement (or otherwise) of the previous week's targets.

Compliments to Close   5 mins

Materials: Each individual's 'Golden Scroll' & a gold permanent marker each; Facilitator's Guide 2 'The Golden Scroll' (p. 263).

The guide will support you in directing the group as they add positive comments to their Golden Scrolls.

Relaxation   10 mins

Materials: Facilitator Guide 3 'Guided Relaxation' (p. 264).

Use the script on the facilitator guide to support the students in deep relaxation.

Activity 2.4

Worksheet 2.12
Relationship Rules

Activity 2.4

It is normal to check your partner's phone	A man shouldn't have to wear a condom if they don't want to
It is okay to flirt with your friend's partner	Being jealous shows how much he loves me
You should only have sex with someone you love	If someone is your boyfriend/girlfriend then you should be having sex with them
If my partner doesn't want me to see some of my friends, then I should stop seeing them	When you are in love you never argue
Cheating is okay	You should never break your promises
You can't trust anyone	Friends should always be there for each other
Parents always protect their children	When you are in a relationship, your partner is more important than your other relationships with friends/family
There are different rules for men and women in relationships	It is good to trust people
Violence is always unacceptable in a relationship	It is better to be in a relationship than to be single

Worksheet 2.13
People Outlines

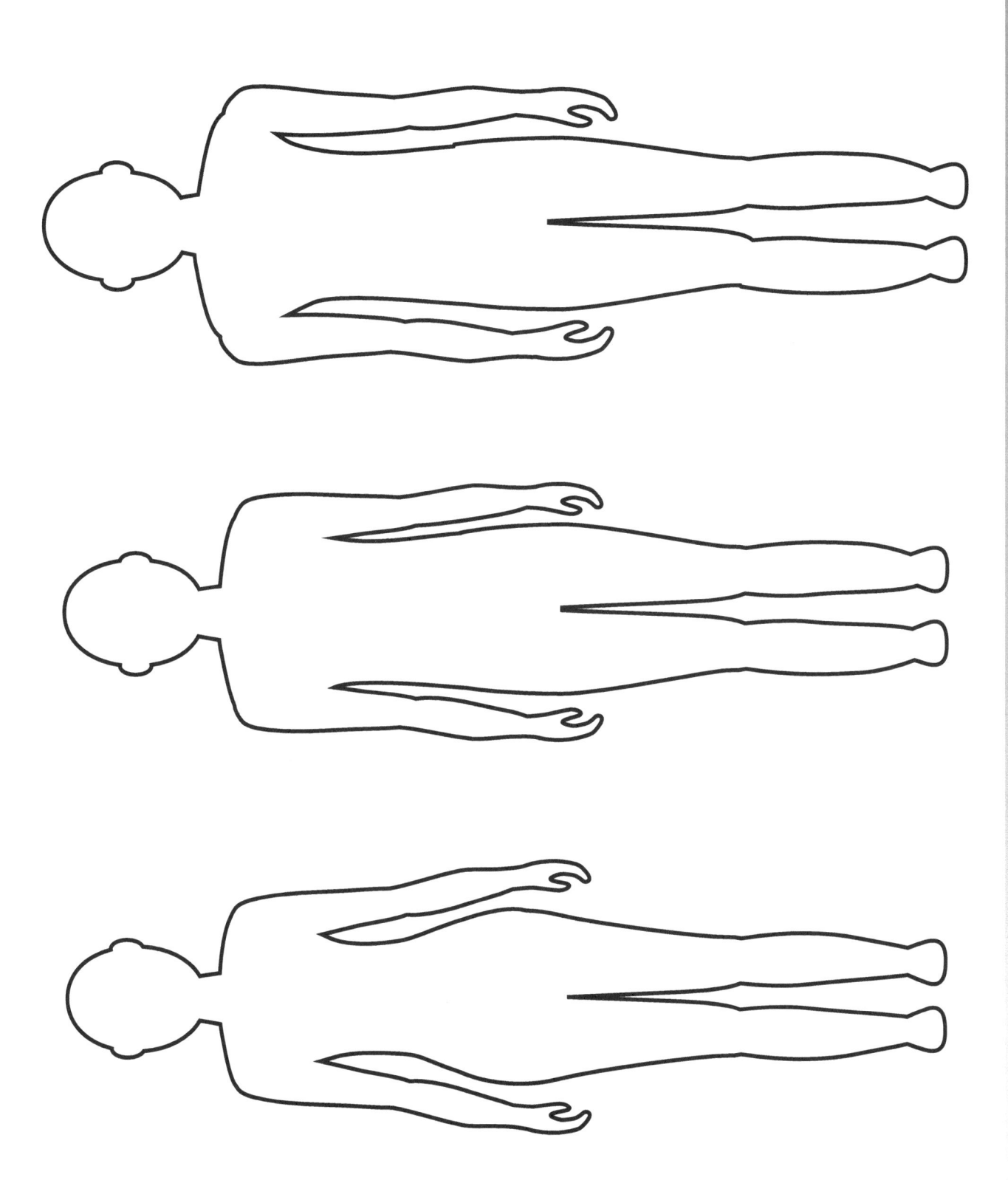

Activity 2.4

Worksheet 2.13

This page may be photocopied for instructional use only. *The ASD Girls' Wellbeing Toolkit* © Tina Rae & Amy Such 2019

133

Activity 2.5
Relationships 3

Aims

* For the students to feel safe & confident to participate in the session
* To be able to describe different types of abuse and give an example of each
* To consider how different types of abuse present in real life
* To practise implementing Positive Psychology as a support mechanism

Group Rules   2 mins

Materials: Worksheet 1.1 'Visual Timetable' (p. 27); Group Rules Chart created in Activity 1.1.

Using Worksheet 1.1 and the Group Rules Chart, remind the group of the structure of each session and of the rules that were agreed in Activity 1.1.

Talk Time   5 mins

Materials: Post-it notes.

Ask the students: 'Why might someone stay in an abusive relationship?'

Students have the opportunity to discuss their answers, write them on post-its, or to reflect on their responses without sharing with the group.

Ice-Breaker   5 mins

Materials: Worksheet 2.14 'What Type of Abuse is This?' (p. 138); pens.

The aim of this activity is to support the young people to develop their understanding of some of the complexities of different types of abuse that can be identified in relationships. They are further supported to discuss some of the nuances of these situations and reflect on the relationships from different perspectives.

The students should be instructed to complete the activity independently, using arrows to link the scenarios to the different types of abuse given on Worksheet 2.14.

Correct answers:

1. Physical abuse
2. Sexual abuse
3. Emotional abuse
4. Isolation
5. Financial abuse
6. Threats

Then each scenario is discussed in detail. The key question when talking about each type of abuse is:

- How this would make someone feel?
- Were there any behaviours that surprised the group?
- Are there any that they would not have really considered as abuse?

Core Activity 1: Challenging Controlling Behaviour   25 mins

Materials: Worksheet 2.15 'Ayisha & Naomi's Stories' (p. 139).

The focus here is on developing a picture of what the features are of a healthy and respectful relationship. A recent report from Girlguiding UK provides an insight into girls' understanding of relationships.

> Although most felt they could recognise different types of controlling behaviour in theory… they were quick to make excuses for the controlling behaviour. They readily imagined situations where it might be acceptable or even their fault. Some even found this behaviour endearing.
> (Care versus Control: Healthy Relationships, 2013)

While most girls and young women felt that violence, threats, sexual coercion and abusive relationships are unacceptable in theory, some struggled to identify these factors in real-life scenarios and some girls were less clear about more subtle forms of abuse and controlling behaviours. A key issue identified by this research was that controlling behaviour was interpreted by some as jealousy and this was seen as proof of genuine care and concern. It is important to note that this research was conducted on a broad sample of girls and young women, consequently, we may well expect that this to be more significant with vulnerable young people.

Share Ayisha and Naomi's stories on Worksheet 2.15. Ask the group to consider these stories, thinking about the following:

- What advice would you give Ayisha if you were her friend?
- What/who might help Ayisha?
- Are there different kinds of abuse happening in this story?
- How does Ayisha feel at the moment?
- What advice would you give Naomi if you were her friend?
- What/who might help Naomi?
- Are there different kinds of abuse happening in this story?
- How does Naomi feel at the moment?

The final discussion can focus on what the group hope for Ayisha and Naomi – how can they be supported to change the situations that they are in?

Core Activity 2: The Effects of Kindness   5 mins

Materials: Worksheets 2.16 'Random Acts of Kindness' (p. 140) & 2.17 Random Acts of Kindness Diary' (p. 141) (one each).

When we have experienced people being 'kind' to us in an abusive or coercive way (e.g., buying us gifts to try to get our loyalty/friendship/favour), it can sometimes become difficult to distinguish these 'kindnesses' from acts of kindness that are genuine and intended to make us feel good about ourselves and generally happier in our lives.

You can ask the group to identify times when they have been on the receiving end of kindness or generosity for the wrong reason and then focus on the opposite of this.

What are genuine acts of kindness and why are these so important? Move the focus from the negative to the positive here and also away from the self. Positive Psychologists (e.g., Seligman, 2011) tell us that there are enormous benefits for our own wellbeing in doing good things for others.

Doing things to help others is not only good for the recipients – it has a positive payback for our happiness and health too. When people experience kindness it also makes them kinder as a result – so kindness is contagious! As the saying goes: 'If you want to feel good, do good'.

Suggest to the group that they could attempt to perform one act of kindness every day. This could be a compliment, a helping hand, a hug, a gift, or something else. The act may be large or small and the recipient may not even be aware of it. Refer to Worksheet 2.16 for inspiration.

Ideally your acts of kindness should be beyond the kind things you already do on a regular basis. And of course, the acts mustn't put you or others in danger!

Try to do one extra kind act each day for a week. Use Worksheet 2.17 to keep a record of your acts of kindness. You can also note down how you felt about doing them and whether you found them easy or difficult.

Reflections & Feedback — 5 mins

Materials: Facilitator Guide 1 'Reflections & Feedback' (p. 262).

Ask the students to focus on the questions on the facilitator guide.

Target-Setting — 5 mins

Materials: Worksheet 1.4 'My Targets' (p. 30) (one each); pens.

Use Worksheet 1.4 to support each student in setting their weekly targets. They can do this in pairs and support each other to identify what they would like to work on during the coming week. Allow a little time for reflection on the achievement (or otherwise) of the previous week's targets.

Compliments to Close — 5 mins

Materials: Each individual's 'Golden Scroll' & a gold permanent marker each; Facilitator's Guide 2 'The Golden Scroll' (p. 263).

The guide will support you in directing the group as they add positive comments to their Golden Scrolls.

Relaxation — 10 mins

Materials: Facilitator Guide 3 'Guided Relaxation' (p. 264).

Use the script on the facilitator guide to support the students in deep relaxation.

Worksheet 2.14
What Type of Abuse is This?

Activity 2.5

1 Hitting, pushing, punching, kicking, biting, slapping, hair-pulling, throwing or smashing things, punching the wall, smashing the windows, burning, strangling, stabbing, murder

2 Making someone do sexual things that they don't want to do, or raping them; calling the person a slag/slut, or telling them that they are frigid; not allowing the person to dress in the way they want to, or only in a certain way.

3 Constantly putting someone down, making them feel bad about themselves; insulting them by calling them fat, ugly, or stupid; always lying to them; ignoring them; withholding affection; threatening to leave, or to throw them out; threatening to commit suicide if they leave; checking up on where they are and what they are doing; timing a person when they are out, making them explain every movement.

4 Stopping someone from seeing friends and family; not allowing the person to have visitors; stopping them from going to school or college, or having a job; not allowing the person to talk to their friends or family on the phone; going everywhere with them.

5 Taking a person's money; making a person ask for money; not allowing them to work and earn money; making a person give them all their money; making all the decisions about how to spend money

6 Making the person afraid by using looks and gestures; saying they will hurt or kill them, someone precious to them, or their pet; threatening to smash things; threatening to tell other people how stupid they are

- Financial Abuse
- Threats
- Sexual Abuse
- Physical Abuse
- Emotional Abuse
- Isolation

Worksheet 2.15
Ayisha & Naomi's Stories

Activity 2.5

Ayisha's Story

I am quite a scatter-brained person and my boyfriend always told me that he was the only one who would put up with it. He told me he loved me and that he was the only person I needed in my life.

He was really possessive and jealous. I couldn't go anywhere without him. He would kick up a fuss even when I was meeting up with my friends from school. I lost all my confidence and I lost most of my friends as well – they couldn't put up with his temper and they couldn't understand why I put up with him. I wanted to finish with him, but he said he would hurt me or kill himself if I ever left him.

He would get really angry and sometimes hit me if I got dressed up to go anywhere, saying I had too much make-up on, or my skirt was too short. One day he snatched my phone off me and threw it at me, because he overheard me telling a friend that I had walked home from school with a couple of lads from Year 10. Just little things would set him off. I learnt to see the warning signs and how to say the right things to get around him and his temper. I never tried to wind him up or fight back. I shut myself off from everybody and tried to pretend that everything was OK.

Naomi's Story

My boyfriend wanted to spend all of his free time with me. He said he loved me. I thought I loved him too and so I did spend most of my time with him.

All he wanted to do was stay at home and watch movies, so we never went out. I hadn't seen my friends for weeks and they asked me to go out with them for a pizza and to the pictures one night. I told him he could come too. He didn't want to go and he didn't want me to go either, but I did. He followed me to the pizza place and he saw a couple of lads come over and start chatting up a couple of my mates. He went absolutely mad. He came storming over, saying I was trying to pick this lad up and he called me a slag. He yelled at me to leave and began swearing at me. I was really embarrassed and, when I asked him not to swear at me, he stormed off outside saying I would be sorry later.

I followed him outside and saw him punching the wall and I just knew that if I went off with him I would get hit next. I was really shocked and frightened, but I told him that I was staying with my friends. He began swearing at me again calling me 'a lying bitch' and lots of other horrible names. That's when I knew that he never really loved me, so I finished with him right then and there and went back to my friends. I was scared and crying, but I knew that he would have hurt me, either that night or some other time in the future, if I stayed with him.

(From *Expect Respect: A Toolkit for addressing teenage relationship abuse*, Home Office & Women's Aid)

Worksheet 2.16
Random Acts of Kindness

Activity 2.5

- Give up your seat
- Hold a door open for someone
- Give a (sincere) compliment
- Make someone laugh
- Give someone a hug
- Take time to really listen to someone
- Make someone new feel welcome
- Let one car in on every journey
- Give directions to someone who's lost
- Have a conversation with a stranger
- Pick up litter as you walk
- Let someone in front of you in the supermarket queue
- Tell someone they mean a lot to you
- Let someone have your parking spot
- Read a story with a child
- Offer your change to someone struggling to find the right amount
- Treat a loved one to breakfast in bed
- Buy cakes or fruit for your colleagues
- Invite your neighbour round for a drink and a chat
- Offer to help with someone's shopping
- Tell someone if you notice they're doing a good job
- Pass on a book you've enjoyed
- Say sorry (you know who to)
- Forgive someone for what they've done
- Visit a sick friend, relative or neighbour
- Buy an unexpected gift for someone
- Bake something for a neighbour
- Pay for someone in the queue behind
- Do a chore that you don't normally do
- Help out someone in need
- Offer to look after a friend's children
- Offer to mow your neighbour's lawn
- Donate your old things to charity
- Give food to a homeless person and take time to talk with them
- Visit someone who may be lonely
- Give blood
- Get back in contact with someone you've lost touch with
- Organise a fundraising event
- Volunteer your time for a charity
- Plan a street party

Worksheet 2.17

Random Acts of Kindness Diary

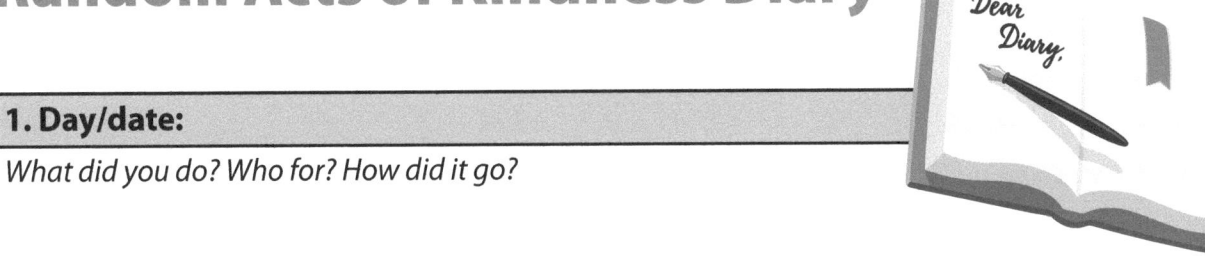

Activity 2.5

1. Day/date:

What did you do? Who for? How did it go?

2. Day/date:

What did you do? Who for? How did it go?

3. Day/date:

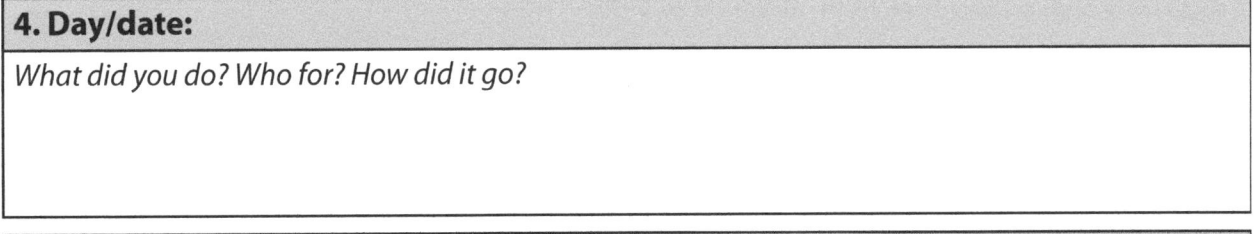

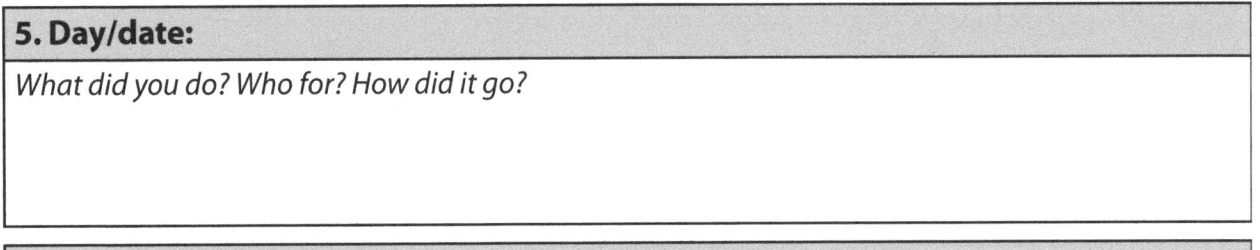

What did you do? Who for? How did it go?

4. Day/date:

What did you do? Who for? How did it go?

5. Day/date:

What did you do? Who for? How did it go?

6. Day/date:

What did you do? Who for? How did it go?

7. Day/date:

What did you do? Who for? How did it go?

Activity 2.6
Sexual Behaviours

Aims

- For the students to feel safe & confident to participate in the session
- To be able to define the term 'Child Sexual Exploitation'
- To recognise warning signs of CSE
- To know where to go to for support if they believe they or someone they know might be involved with CSE

Group Rules — 2 mins

Materials: Worksheet 1.1 'Visual Timetable' (p. 27); Group Rules Chart created in Activity 1.1.

Using Worksheet 1.1 and the Group Rules Chart, remind the group of the structure of each session and of the rules that were agreed in Activity 1.1.

Talk Time — 5 mins

Materials: Post-it notes.

Ask the students: 'Who might you talk to if you were worried about what someone was asking you to do?'

Students have the opportunity to discuss their answers, write them on post-its, or to reflect on their responses without sharing with the group.

Ice-Breaker — 5 mins

Materials: flip chart & paper, flip-chart pen (or whiteboard & dry-wipe pen)

The group are presented with the term 'child sexual exploitation (CSE)' and asked to contribute ideas around what the phrase means. You should note down the group's ideas on a flip chart or whiteboard.

Inform the students that the NSPCC's definition of CSE is:

> Children in exploitative situations and relationships receive something such as gifts, money or affection as a result of performing sexual activities or others performing sexual activities on them.

Students should be made aware that CSE can occur online and is not only a face-to-face interaction.

Core Activity 1: Exploitation — 20 mins

Materials: Worksheet 2.18 'CSE Case Studies' (p. 145) (one each).

For this activity, explain that you will be looking at a range of case studies relating to individuals who have been the victims of CSE. It might be useful to give each student their own copy of each case study so they are able to recap the text on Worksheet 2.18.

Select one/two case studies that seem most relevant to the group of students you are working with.

After reading through the case studies, the group can focus on a series of key questions as follows:

- Why did this all happen?
- How did it start?
- Why or how was the victim vulnerable in the first place?
- Who was in control?
- What do you think the abuser was thinking and feeling?
- What was the victim thinking and feeling?
- What would you do if you were in their shoes now?
- What advice would you give them?
- How could the victim take back control here? Is this possible?
- What are the sources of support?

Core Activity 2: Sources of Support — 10 mins

Materials: A3 & A4 paper, coloured pencils/pens, scissors, glue, a variety of collage materials, safe access to the internet.

Make a poster to display around school that will help other students identify situations where they might be being exploited and inform them of where they can get help.

Students might like to use resources such as:

* NSPCC website: https://www.nspcc.org.uk/preventing-abuse/child-abuse-and-neglect/child-sexual-exploitation/
* The Children's Society website: https://www.childrenssociety.org.uk/what-is-child-sexual-exploitation
* Barnardo's website: https://www.barnardos.org.uk/what_we_do/our_work/sexual_exploitation/about-cse.htm

Reflections & Feedback — 5 mins

Materials: Facilitator Guide 1 'Reflections & Feedback' (p. 262).

Ask the students to focus on the questions on the facilitator guide.

Target-Setting — 5 mins

Materials: Worksheet 1.4 'My Targets' (p. 30) (one each); pens.

Use Worksheet 1.4 to support each student in setting their weekly targets. They can do this in pairs and support each other to identify what they would like to work on during the coming week. Allow a little time for reflection on the achievement (or otherwise) of the previous week's targets.

Compliments to Close — 5 mins

Materials: Each individual's 'Golden Scroll' & a gold permanent marker each; Facilitator's Guide 2 'The Golden Scroll' (p. 263).

The guide will support you in directing the group as they add positive comments to their Golden Scrolls.

Relaxation — 10 mins

Materials: Facilitator Guide 3 'Guided Relaxation' (p. 264).

Use the script on the facilitator guide to support the students in deep relaxation.

Worksheet 2.18
CSE Case Studies

Activity 2.6

Anna's Story

John told me he was 23, but the police told me later he was 44.

We became friends because he used to buy us all cigarettes and drinks and that. He let us go round his flat to hang out. We knew he was trying to get with us, but we just led him on to get stuff out of him.

One night, he tried to touch me and kiss my mate and we panicked. It kicked off and we had a massive row in the car when we made him take us home.

I thought I was in control of the situation, but when he got angry, I realised I wasn't.

I called the police later that night. My friend didn't want to. Said we would get in trouble, but I was scared by how angry he'd got. I was worried what my dad would say too, but I didn't know what else to do.

During their investigation, the police discovered that John had 'befriended' several other girls, and made illegal sexual advances to them. John was found guilty and sent to prison for five years.

Damon's story

I met Joe when I was 11. He worked at the stables I used to hang around at.

I really wanted to ride horses, like I used to see on the films I'd watch on a Sunday afternoon. Joe let me do that. He was also the first person that bought me cigarettes and I thought smoking was really cool, but did not want my mum and dad finding out.

I got on with my parents and sister well, but Joe let me sort of do what I wanted.

I suppose I wanted to grow up quick and Joe made me feel like an adult. But I wasn't an adult, I was a kid – you know, I still find that hard to accept, because I've realised just how much of a good job at manipulating and brainwashing me into thinking I was his equal he did.

He showed me pornographic magazines to start with and then it went on from there. He'd do truth/dare with me and it always seemed to end up with him touching me and doing stuff.

page 1 of 4

Worksheet 2.18
CSE Case Studies

Activity 2.6

But I'd kind of try and forget about it because he would buy me records, cigs, food, trainers, magazines and let me ride the horses whenever I wanted to. It was like they were mine. It really messed my head up later in life.

I blamed myself for taking the items off him. It was like he'd bought me.

I kept all this quiet for about 15 years, mainly because I didn't want to admit to myself what had happened, never mind admitting to anyone else. I was ashamed, felt guilty and just hated myself for it all.

But I found someone to talk to, someone like me that helped me challenge my own thinking. I got so much from talking to him, and then others until I found myself realising that this wasn't my fault.

I missed out on a good education when I was younger because of what was going on for me, so getting one now is really important and I think I'm doing pretty well for myself now. I have a degree I worked really hard for a good job, and I can finally talk about what happened.

I'm not ashamed anymore because I know I have nothing to be ashamed about – I did nothing wrong.

Jade's story

When I was 6, my dad was taken away from our house. My mum was an alcoholic with depression, and I know she took drugs too.

My brothers and sisters were sent to live with other members of our family and I have never been home since. I was moved around a lot and stayed with different people. When I was 15 I stopped seeing my mum completely and was taken into care.

I was always in trouble – running away, drinking, and taking drugs. I stole things too so I could get money. Me and my mates would ask random blokes to buy us cigarettes or vodka. Whatever we could get.

I started to hurt myself. I hated my life. I would cut my arms or take lots of painkillers.

Me and my mates hung around with blokes that were older than us and I slept with some of them, even though I didn't really want to. Even though I was only

Worksheet 2.18
CSE Case Studies

Activity 2.6

15, groups of older blokes would still try and get me and my mates to go back to hotel rooms with them. If they bought us drinks, then we would a lot of the time. When I was drunk I never really thought about what I was doing.

I told the police about a guy who attacked me once. I got a lot of stick from my mates and other guys for doing this.

A social worker is helping me now. I actually really like her. She answers her phone to me, even when I ring really early or late.

My criminal record means that I can't become a police officer or social worker like I wanted. But I am trying hard at college now and have done some volunteering for young people.

I want other young girls to know that they need to be careful. What happened to me could easily happen to you.

Dipika's story

I was good at sport at school. And my family was what you would call 'normal'.

I met Nick on the internet and thought he was in his mid-twenties. We got on really well and agreed to meet up. As soon as I saw him, I knew something was wrong – he looked about fifty!

I'd invited him to my house when my parents were out and it was clear he was expecting sex or something.

I felt like I'd led him on and didn't know how to say no, so I agreed to have sex with him.

I immediately regretted it and told him I didn't want to see or speak to him anymore. But he wouldn't leave me alone and kept trying to get in touch. I didn't know what to do, so I told a family friend and the police got involved.

The police identified the man as a local business man. When they seized his computer they discovered that he had been chatting to other under-age young people, telling them he liked 'young girls'. He frequently tried to meet up with the people he chatted with, for the explicit purposes of having sex with them, even though he knew they were not yet 16.

Worksheet 2.18
CSE Case Studies

Activity 2.6

Paige's story

My mum and dad drank a lot and took drugs. My dad used to hit Mum and me sometimes. We kept kicking him out and moving house, but he always managed to find us and start causing problems again.

When I was 12 a boy at my school tried to get me to have sex with him and hurt me. I told people about it, but then I got scared and didn't want anything to happen about it. So he got away with it.

At 13 I got a new boyfriend who was a lot older than me. We had sex. He said he loved me.

I started cutting myself, not eating, and I took lots of my mum's medicines for her depression. Eventually social services took me to a hospital and I stayed there for few months. I used to run away from there a lot, meeting up with mates and that. I had sex with some of them sometimes, or friends of theirs. A lot of them were older than me.

I smoked a lot of weed and drank as much as I could to get off my head.

Sometimes when I woke up, I didn't know where I was or who I was with, even though we had just had sex.

One man threatened to hurt my friends if I didn't have sex with him. He told the police he thought I was 16, but he knew I wasn't.

Paige was referred to a specialist child sexual exploitation team. They earned her trust and helped her move to a new area, away from the threats and bad influences. She told them what happened to her and they were able to identify and prosecute the people who committed offences against her and her friends.

Activity 2.7
Online Behaviours

Aims

* For the students to feel safe & confident to participate in the session
* To be able to define the term 'grooming'
* To recognise warning signs of grooming
* To know where to go to for support if they believe they or someone they know might be being groomed

Group Rules — 2 mins

Materials: Worksheet 1.1 'Visual Timetable' (p. 27); Group Rules Chart created in Activity 1.1.

Using Worksheet 1.1 and the Group Rules Chart, remind the group of the structure of each session and of the rules that were agreed in Activity 1.1.

Talk Time — 5 mins

Materials: Post-it notes.

Ask the students: 'When is it appropriate to give someone a gift?'

Students have the opportunity to discuss their answers, write them on post-its, or to reflect on their responses without sharing with the group.

Ice-Breaker — 5 mins

Materials: Worksheet 2.19 'Venn Diagram' (p. 153) (one each); small post-its.

Ask the students to list all the social media platforms they can think of that allow them to interact with people they know as well as strangers.

They should be encouraged to write each platform on a small post-it note, which can then be stuck onto the Venn diagram on the worksheet, categorised by platforms that allow public discussion, private discussion and both.

This page may be photocopied for instructional use only. *The ASD Girls' Wellbeing Toolkit* © Tina Rae & Amy Such 2019

Core Activity 1: Online Grooming — 15 mins

Materials: Worksheet 2.20 'Predator Tactics' (p. 154) (one each).

This activity explores online grooming. Many of the girls in the group will have experienced grooming. How does online grooming work? Normally an abuser will make initial contact with children via a chat room, social network or other place in which young people commonly meet and chat. The predator will usually pose as another young person of the same age and try to establish a rapport.

Over time the predator will try to build up trust with their victim using gifts, compliments and simply by 'being there' to listen to their problems. Over time, online conversations will become more sexualised and the child will be encouraged to share intimate details and photographs of themselves. Often predators will then try and arrange a meeting 'in real life' to escalate the abuse.

Groomers design what they say as they go along, tailoring their flattery or offers as they learn about the victim. On Worksheet 2.20 are some tactics young people should watch out for. Ask the students to discuss each of the tactics in term, considering what risk each tactic presents to the young person. Included in this, you might like to contemplate what motivation the predator may have behind each comment.

- **'Let's go private'** (leave the public chatroom and create a private chat, or move to instant-messaging or phone texting)
- **'Where's your computer in the house?'** (to see if parents might be around)
- **'Who's your favourite band/designer/film?'** (questions like these tell the groomer more about you so they know what gifts to offer – e.g., concert tickets; Webcam, software, clothes, CDs)
- **'I know someone who can get you a modelling job'** (flattery, they think, will get them everywhere)
- **'I know a way you can earn money fast'** (playing to a young person's need for money)
- **'You seem sad; tell me what's bothering you'** (the sympathy angle)
- **'What's your phone number?'** (asking for personal information of any kind usually happens at a later stage, after the target is feeling comfortable with the groomer, but young people should nevert give out personal details online)
- **'If you don't … [do what I ask], I'll … [tell your parents OR share your photos in a photo blog/webcam directory/file-sharing network]'** (intimidation – used as the groomer learns more and more about the target)
- **'You are the love of my life'** (this may be the message all young people wish to hear at some point)

Core Activity 2: Online Grooming Case Study 15 mins

Materials: Worksheet 2.21 'Online Grooming Case Study' (p. 155) (one each); A3 & A4 paper, coloured pencils/pens, scissors, glue, a variety of collage materials, safe access to the internet.

Consider Kayleigh's story, showing the short video clip below. Ask for responses to this. Do they think this should be shown to all teenage girls and perhaps those who are younger? What would they do?

https://youtu.be/WsbYHI-rZOE

> Attention: If it does not feel appropriate to show the video, you may wish to read the story below, using Worksheet 2.21 as a visual aid. This sheet can also be used in addition to the video.

Kayleigh's 'Love' Story

Kayleigh Haywood began speaking to Luke Harlow, a man she had never met, on 31 October 2015. Over the course of 13 days they exchanged 2643 messages. He told the 15-year-old many things a young teenage girl wants to hear. He told her that she was special, beautiful and that he cared for her. Harlow was grooming Kayleigh, along with two other young girls he had also been speaking to. However, it was Kayleigh that finally agreed to his requests to spend the night of Friday 13 November 2015 at his house. She spent the next day with him too, and in the early hours of Sunday 15 November, having been held against her will by Harlow and by his next door neighbour Stephen Beadman, Kayleigh was raped and murdered by Beadman. With the support of Kayleigh's family, Leicestershire Police has made a film about aspects of the last two weeks of her life. *Kayleigh's Love Story* is a warning to young people, both girls and boys, about the dangers of speaking to people they do not know online. The film highlights just how quick and easy it can be for children to be groomed online without their parents or those around them knowing it is even happening. The purpose of this is to protect children now and in the future, and to prevent another family losing a child in this way.

Reflections & Feedback 5 mins

Materials: Facilitator Guide 1 'Reflections & Feedback' (p. 262).

Ask the students to focus on the questions on the facilitator guide.

Target-Setting 5 mins

Materials: Worksheet 1.4 'My Targets' (p. 30) (one each); pens.

Use Worksheet 1.4 to support each student in setting their weekly targets. They can do this in pairs and support each other to identify what they would like to work on during the coming week. Allow a little time for reflection on the achievement (or otherwise) of the previous week's targets.

Compliments to Close 5 mins

Materials: Each individual's 'Golden Scroll' & a gold permanent marker each; Facilitator's Guide 2 'The Golden Scroll' (p. 263).

The guide will support you in directing the group as they add positive comments to their Golden Scrolls.

Relaxation 10 mins

Materials: Facilitator Guide 3 'Guided Relaxation' (p. 264).

Use the script on the facilitator guide to support the students in deep relaxation.

Worksheet 2.19
Venn Diagram

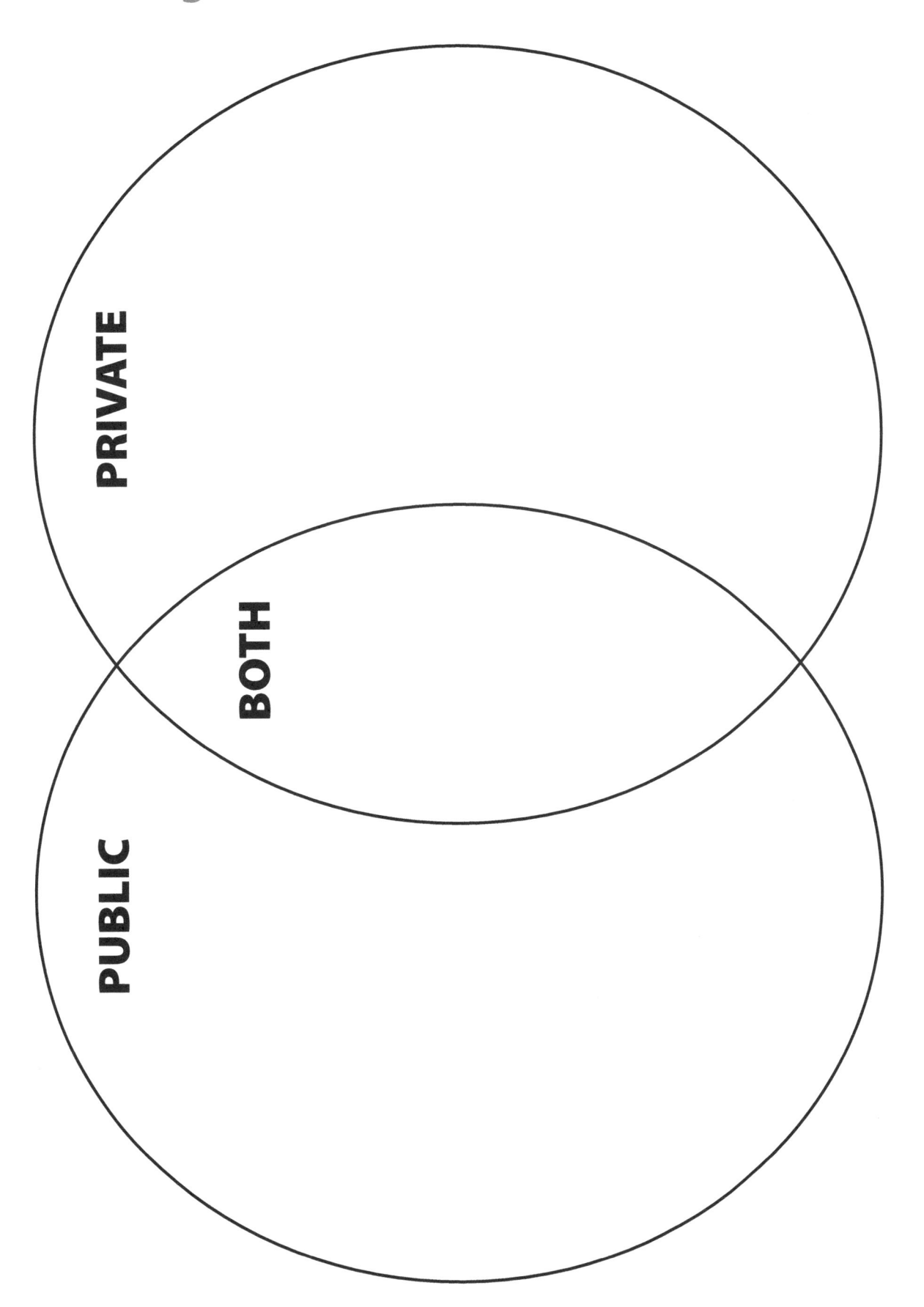

Activity 2.7

PRIVATE

BOTH

PUBLIC

Worksheet 2.20
Predator Tactics

Activity 2.7

The predator says …	The predator thinks …	The young person is at risk of …
Let's go private		
Where's your computer in the house?		
Who's your favourite band/designer/film?		
I know someone who can get you a modelling job		
I know a way you can earn money fast		
You seem sad; tell me what's bothering you		
What's your phone number?		
If you don't … [do what I ask], I'll … [tell your parents OR share your photos in a photo blog/webcam directory/file-sharing network		
You are the love of my life		

Worksheet 2.21

Activity 2.7

Online Grooming Case Study

Kayleigh Haywood, aged 15

Luke Harlow, aged 27

Convicted of:
- Grooming
- Sexual activity with a child
- False imprisonment

Sentence: 12 years

Stephen Beadman, aged 29

Convicted of:
- Rape
- Murder

Sentence: Life
(Minimum 35 years)

Activity 2.8

The Media & Other Influences 1

Aims

- For the students to feel safe & confident to participate in the session
- To understand how images online can be generated
- To understand the psychological impact of 'fake' images on young people
- To be able to recite the law on 'sexting'

Group Rules — 2 mins

Materials: Worksheet 1.1 'Visual Timetable' (p. 27); Group Rules Chart created in Activity 1.1.

Using Worksheet 1.1 and the Group Rules Chart, remind the group of the structure of each session and of the rules that were agreed in Activity 1.1.

Talk Time — 5 mins

Materials: Post-it notes.

Ask the students: 'What helps people feel good about how they look?'

Students have the opportunity to discuss their answers, write them on post-its, or to reflect on their responses without sharing with the group.

Ice-Breaker — 5 mins

Materials: Worksheet 2.22 'Social Media Images' (p. 159) (one each).

Ask students to look at the images of young men and women displayed on the worksheet. Ask them to discuss their initial thoughts in pairs and feed back to the group.

- What do you think?
- How do these images make you feel?
- Is there a 'perfect' body there?
- What makes the 'perfect' body image?

Core Activity 1: Online Images   10 mins

Materials: Worksheet 2.23 'Online Images: Fact or Fiction?' (p. 160) (one each); pens.

Provide each student with a copy of the first page of the worksheet. Keep the final answers page for yourself. Encourage the students to initially work through the sheet independently.

Following completion of the quiz, provide students with the correct answers and pose the question: What impact do you think online images could have on someone's mental health and wellbeing?

Core Activity 2: Sexting   20 mins

Materials: Worksheets 2.24 'Young People & Pornography' (p. 162) & 2.25 'Sexting Facts' (p. 165) (one each).

Read the article on the Worksheet 2.24, and then ask the group to work in pairs and complete the brainstorm on Worksheet 2.25. Areas to cover should include:

- Why might someone send a 'sext'?
- Is all 'sexting' dangerous?
- What is the law on 'sexting'?
- What would your advice be to someone who feels under pressure to send a 'sext'?

Next, encourage the students to share their ideas as a group.

It is important that you are aware of the law surrounding 'sexting'. The NSCPP advice:

> Sexting can be seen as harmless, but creating or sharing explicit images of a child is illegal, even if the person doing it is a child. A young person is breaking the law if they:
>
> - take an explicit photo or video of themselves or a friend
>
> - share an explicit image or video of a child, even if it's shared between children of the same age
>
> - possess, download or store an explicit image or video of a child, even if the child gave their permission for it to be created.
>
> However, as of January 2016 in England and Wales, if a young person is found creating or sharing images, the police can choose to record that a crime has been committed but that taking formal action isn't in the public interest.

Activity 2.8

Crimes recorded this way are unlikely to appear on future records or checks, unless the young person has been involved in other similar activities which may indicate that they're a risk.

Reflections & Feedback — 5 mins

Materials: Facilitator Guide 1 'Reflections & Feedback' (p. 262).

Ask the students to focus on the questions on the facilitator guide.

Target-Setting — 5 mins

Materials: Worksheet 1.4 'My Targets' (p. 30) (one each); pens.

Use Worksheet 1.4 to support each student in setting their weekly targets. They can do this in pairs and support each other to identify what they would like to work on during the coming week. Allow a little time for reflection on the achievement (or otherwise) of the previous week's targets.

Compliments to Close — 5 mins

Materials: Each individual's 'Golden Scroll' & a gold permanent marker each; Facilitator's Guide 2, 'The Golden Scroll' (p. 263).

The guide will support you in directing the group as they add positive comments to their Golden Scrolls.

Relaxation — 10 mins

Materials: Facilitator Guide 3 'Guided Relaxation' (p. 264).

Use the script on the facilitator guide to support the students in deep relaxation.

Worksheet 2.22
Social Media Images

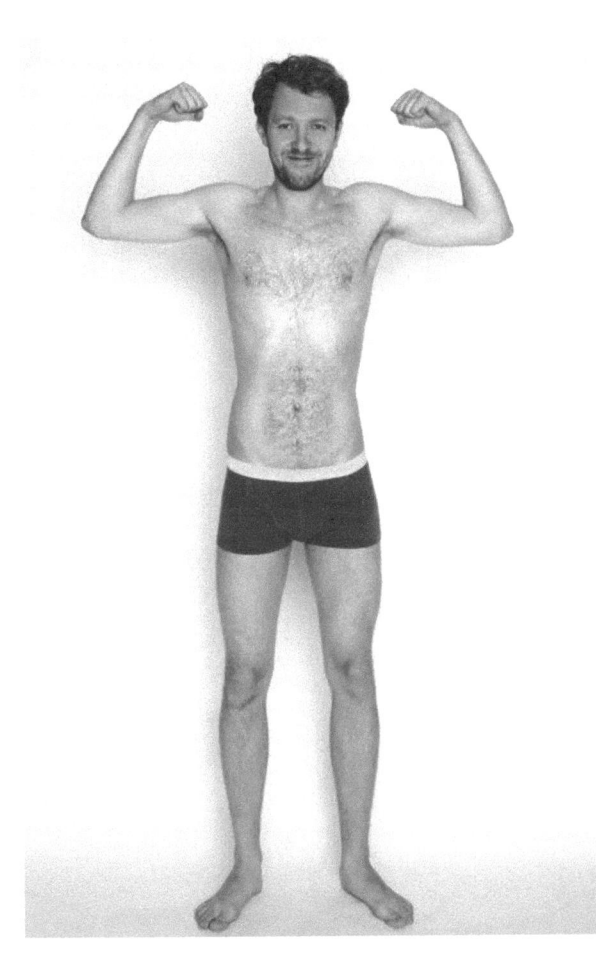

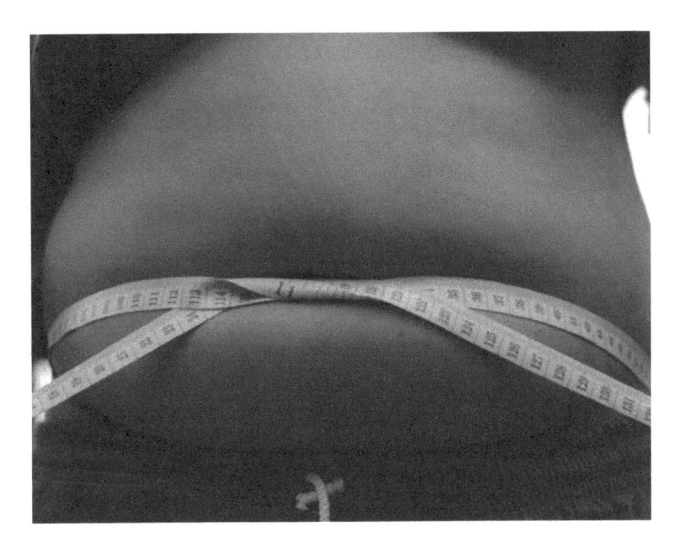

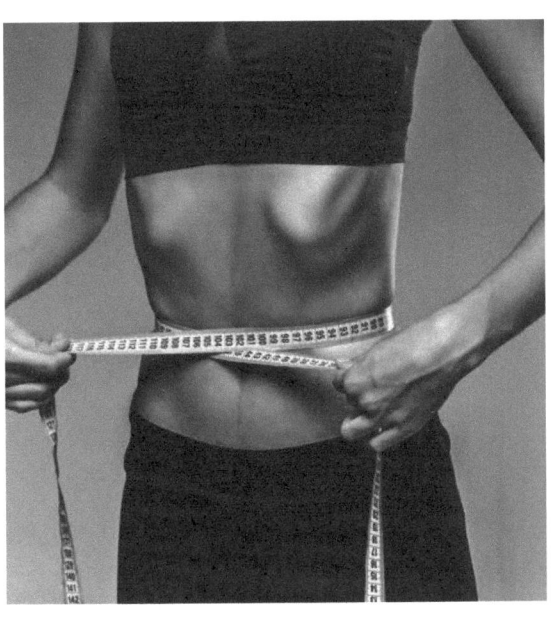

Activity 2.8

Worksheet 2.23

Activity 2.8

Online Images: Fact or Fiction?

1. Posting pictures of you looking good when you're feeling lonely will make you feel better about your life.

   Fiction ☐   Fact ☐

2. 80% of teenagers is the US use Snapchat at least once a month and 79% of teenagers use Instagram at least once a month.

   Fiction ☐   Fact ☐

3. Once you post a picture online, it will remain in cyberspace forever and will always link back to your digital footprint (even if you delete it).

   Fiction ☐   Fact ☐

4. The more 'likes' a picture gets, the more popular you are.

   Fiction ☐   Fact ☐

5. It is possible to be addicted to social media.

   Fiction ☐   Fact ☐

6. In order to post a picture of a celebrity online, it must go through a number of authentication checks to ensure the picture is a true representation of that person.

   Fiction ☐   Fact ☐

7. Sharing cute images of cats has been found to increase the happiness of those who see them.

   Fiction ☐   Fact ☐

8. Over 50% of 11- to 15-year-old girls read fashion and beauty magazines.

   Fiction ☐   Fact ☐

page 1 of 2

Worksheet 2.23
Online Images: Fact or Fiction?

Activity 2.8

Answers for Facilitators

1. Posting pictures of you looking good when you're feeling lonely will make you feel better about your life – **FICTION**. *Time* magazine reported that browsing social media when you're feeling lonely can make you feel worse, since looking at other people's successes may make you feel envious and dissatisfied with your life.

2. 80% of teenagers in the US use Snapchat at least once a month and 79% of teenagers use Instagram at least once a month – **FACT**. To have a Snapchat or Instagram account you must be at least 13 years old. You should never contact anyone you do not know in person via social media and it's always a good idea to share your accounts with your parents.

3. Once you post a picture online, it will remain in cyberspace forever and will always link back to your digital footprint (even if you delete it) – **FACT**. Given how cheap it is to store online data, very little is ever permanently deleted. Most computer experts would say that information is only truly deleted when the drive on which it is stored is physically destroyed.

4. The more 'likes' a picture gets, the more popular you are – **FICTION**.

5. It is possible to be addicted to social media – **FACT**. Social media sites are designed to draw people into them and social media addictions can have damaging effects on careers, quality of life and relationships. The inability to quit social media even has a name: 'social media reversion'.

6. In order to post a picture of a celebrity online, it must go through a number of authentication checks to ensure the picture is a true representation of that person – **FICTION**.

7. Sharing cute images of cats has been found to increase the happiness of those who see them – **FACT**. Research published in the journal *Computers in Human Behaviour* found that watching cat videos can boost energy levels and increase happiness!

8. Over 50% of 11- to 15-year-old girls read fashion and beauty magazines – **FACT**. Seeing body images of celebrities and models can reduce your self-esteem and increase anxiety in the short-term, but there is very little evidence currently available to suggest that fashion magazines can have a long-term effect on self-esteem and anxiety.

Worksheet 2.24
Young People & Pornography

Activity 2.8

Pornography: Young children and teens who send sex images risk mental problems

Ministers should impose controls on adult web content from sites based in Britain or overseas, said a poll.

Mail Online
16 March 2016 • 12:59PM

Cyberbullying and 'sexting' could be placing whole generations of children and young adults at greater risk of depression and other psychological problems, a leading psychiatrist has warned.

Dr Natasha Bijlani, a consultant psychiatrist at the Priory Hospital, said online pressures – particularly over sex and nudity – could even drive an upturn in the number of young people who go on to self-harm.

Mental harm caused in childhood can emerge in adulthood

She added that the full impact of internet abuse and sexting – when intimate photographs are swapped between users – may not be apparent for years because psychological damage suffered in childhood can sometimes only manifest itself in later life.

Dr Bijlani said: 'Episodes in childhood are often repressed, children often fear reporting abuse, and only later in life do these issues surface in the form of depression, stress and anxiety and other serious psychological conditions.

'This relatively new phenomenon of sexting – where explicit texts and pictures are sent between smartphone devices – seems to have become endemic, and we are not sure of the long-term consequences.

page 1 of 3

Worksheet 2.24
Young People & Pornography

Activity 2.8

'However, coupled with online bullying, we can expect an increasing number of people suffering issues of trust, shame and self-loathing, sometimes manifesting itself in self-harming.'

The psychiatrist, who is based at the Priory Hospital at Roehampton, south-west London, said she feared growing numbers of teenagers and adults will experience depression, anxiety, low self-esteem and other mental problems associated with their 'body image'.

Dr Bijlani said sexting can have 'nightmare consequences', and called for online bullying to be taken more seriously.

She said: 'The long-term effects of bullying can be prolonged and pervasive.

'Children are vulnerable to online sexual extortion.

'Much more focus needs to be given to how best educate young people about the risks of sending compromising images, and communicating with unknown others online, and how to cope with bullying via devices at school.'

The Priory Group disclosed that it had seen a sharp rise in the number pf under-18s treated for serious depression, anxiety and stress.

In 2010 it dealt with just 178 clients aged 12 to 17 for such issues, but last year the figure was 262, an increase of nearly 50 per cent, compared with a 25 per cent rise among adults over the same period.

A spokesman for the group said the figure could be the 'tip of the iceberg' because many young people may never have been diagnosed.

page 2 of 3

Worksheet 2.24
Young People & Pornography

Activity 2.8

A report by online safety group the Internet Watch Foundation and Microsoft, the technology giant, which worked together on the research, said they identified nearly 4,000 images and videos in a snapshot covering three months last autumn.

Of those, 667 (17.5 per cent) featured children who were 15 years old or younger and of those 286 were thought to be under 10.

Bob Lotter, the creator of online safety tool My Mobile Watchdog, said his company was dealing with growing numbers of 'sextortion' cases, in which children are lured into sharing naked photographs.

The children are told if they do not co-operate their sexual images will be distributed to friends and to their parents – luring the frightened youngsters to produce highly sexual photographs and videos.

Worksheet 2.25
Sexting Facts

Activity 2.8

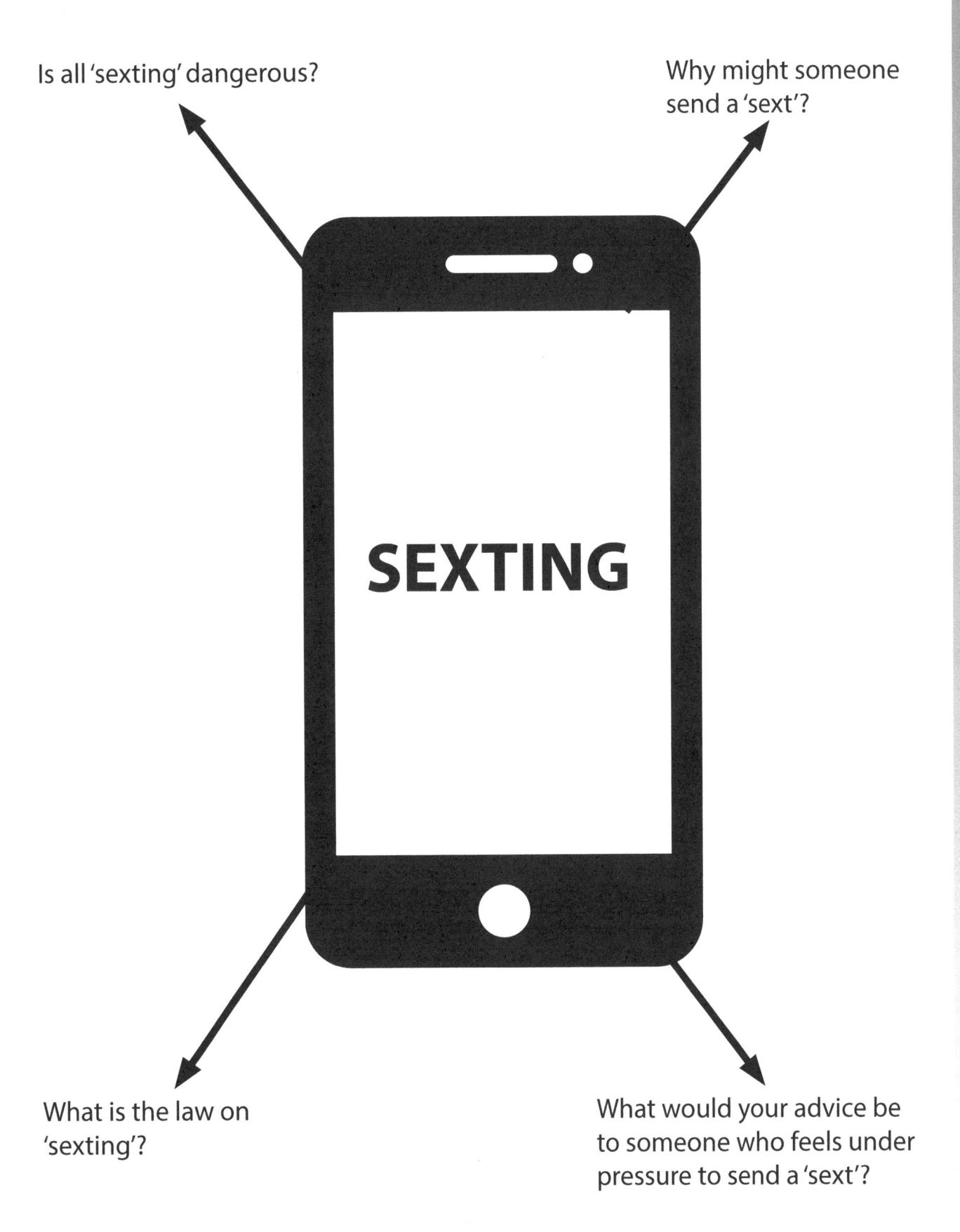

Is all 'sexting' dangerous?

Why might someone send a 'sext'?

SEXTING

What is the law on 'sexting'?

What would your advice be to someone who feels under pressure to send a 'sext'?

Activity 2.9
The Media & Other Influences 2

Aims

* For the students to feel safe & confident to participate in the session
* To be able to describe what a 'catfish' is
* To begin to explore how other people might feel if they are misled/lied to online
* To understand what personal information is safe to disclose online

Group Rules   2 mins

Materials: Worksheet 1.1 'Visual Timetable' (p. 27); Group Rules Chart created in Activity 1.1.

Using Worksheet 1.1 and the Group Rules Chart, remind the group of the structure of each session and of the rules that were agreed in Activity 1.1.

Talk Time   5 mins

Materials: Post-it notes.

Ask the students: 'What websites do you visit online?'

Students have the opportunity to discuss their answers, write them on post-its, or to reflect on their responses without sharing with the group.

Ice-Breaker   5 mins

Materials: flip chart & paper, flip-chart pen (or a whiteboard & dry-wipe pen).

The session consolidates the work completed over the past 2 sessions, with a focus on staying safe online and remaining in control of our personal information.

The session begins by presenting the idea of an online 'catfish'. What does it mean if you say someone is a 'catfish'?

As a group, discuss what the students understand by the term 'catfish'. It might be helpful to note responses on flip chart paper/a white board.

Core Activity 1: Who are You Talking To?   10 mins

Materials: safe access to the internet, computer with audio.

Having discussed the term 'catfish', the group are then invited to watch a clip from the reality TV series 'The Circle'. The aim of the show was to be the most popular contestant. However, the group never met face-to-face, so all their communication was done via a social media platform.

Watch the video clip of 'Kate' (aka Alex) on a virtual date with Mitchell (the link to the video appears in the *Daily Mail* article).

> https://www.dailymail.co.uk/femail/article-6183911/C4-reality-Circle-divides-viewers-contestants-compete-social-media-likes.html

After watching the video, the group are asked to discuss:

- Who does Mitchell think he's talking to?
- Who does Kate/Alex think she/he is talking to?
- How does Mitchell feel?
- How might Mitchel feel when he realises Kate isn't Kate?
- Why might someone pretend to be someone else?
- How might you know if someone is pretending?
- How can you protect yourself from a catfish?

Core Activity 2: Safe Profiles   20 mins

Materials: Worksheet 2.26 'Profile Page' (p. 169) (one each); colouring pencils/pens

In this activity, the students must consider what information is appropriate to display online. They should be encouraged to think back to previous sessions (including Activities 6 (Sexual Behaviours) and 7 (Online Behaviours) when considering what might be necessary and appropriate in order to keep themselves safe.

The students are each given the blank profile on Worksheet 2.26, which they can then fill in as they wish.

Areas which may be important to discuss include:

- Photos: what type of photograph would be appropriate? What type of photograph would be inappropriate? Who can see this photograph? What information can be gathered from the photograph? (For instance, if the young person is in a school uniform, does that provides additional information about their location?)

This page may be photocopied for instructional use only. The ASD Girls' Wellbeing Toolkit © Tina Rae & Amy Such 2019

* Personal info: consider how much detail to provide with regard to name, age, date of birth, address and school.
* Friends: who do they wish to be 'friends' with online? What does that friendship look like/actually mean? Is there a certain number of friends you need to have? Why?
* Status updates: what additional information does that provide? (For instance: 'big party at my house' could mean losing control of the guest list, 'going away with the family for a week' could say 'my house is empty'.)

Reflections & Feedback   5 mins

Materials: Facilitator Guide 1 'Reflections & Feedback' (p. 262).

Ask the students to focus on the questions on the facilitator guide.

Target-Setting   5 mins

Materials: Worksheet 1.4 'My Targets' (p. 30) (one each); pens.

Use Worksheet 1.4 to support each student in setting their weekly targets. They can do this in pairs and support each other to identify what they would like to work on during the coming week. Allow a little time for reflection on the achievement (or otherwise) of the previous week's targets.

Compliments to Close   5 mins

Materials: Each individual's 'Golden Scroll' & a gold permanent marker each; Facilitator's Guide 2 'The Golden Scroll' (p. 263).

The guide will support you in directing the group as they add positive comments to their Golden Scrolls.

Relaxation   10 mins

Materials: Facilitator Guide 3 'Guided Relaxation' (p. 264).

Use the script on the facilitator guide to support the students in deep relaxation.

Worksheet 2.26
Profile Page

Activity 2.9

ONLINE NAME

FRIENDS

( ) NUMBER

WHAT OTHER PEOPLE HAVE WRITTEN TO ME …

☺ ( ) 💬 ( ) 🚫 ( )

☺ ( ) 💬 ( ) 🚫 ( )

TODAY I AM FEELING ◯ BECAUSE …

INFORMATION
AGE:
LOCATION

Worksheet 2.26

This page may be photocopied for instructional use only. *The ASD Girls' Wellbeing Toolkit* © Tina Rae & Amy Such 2019

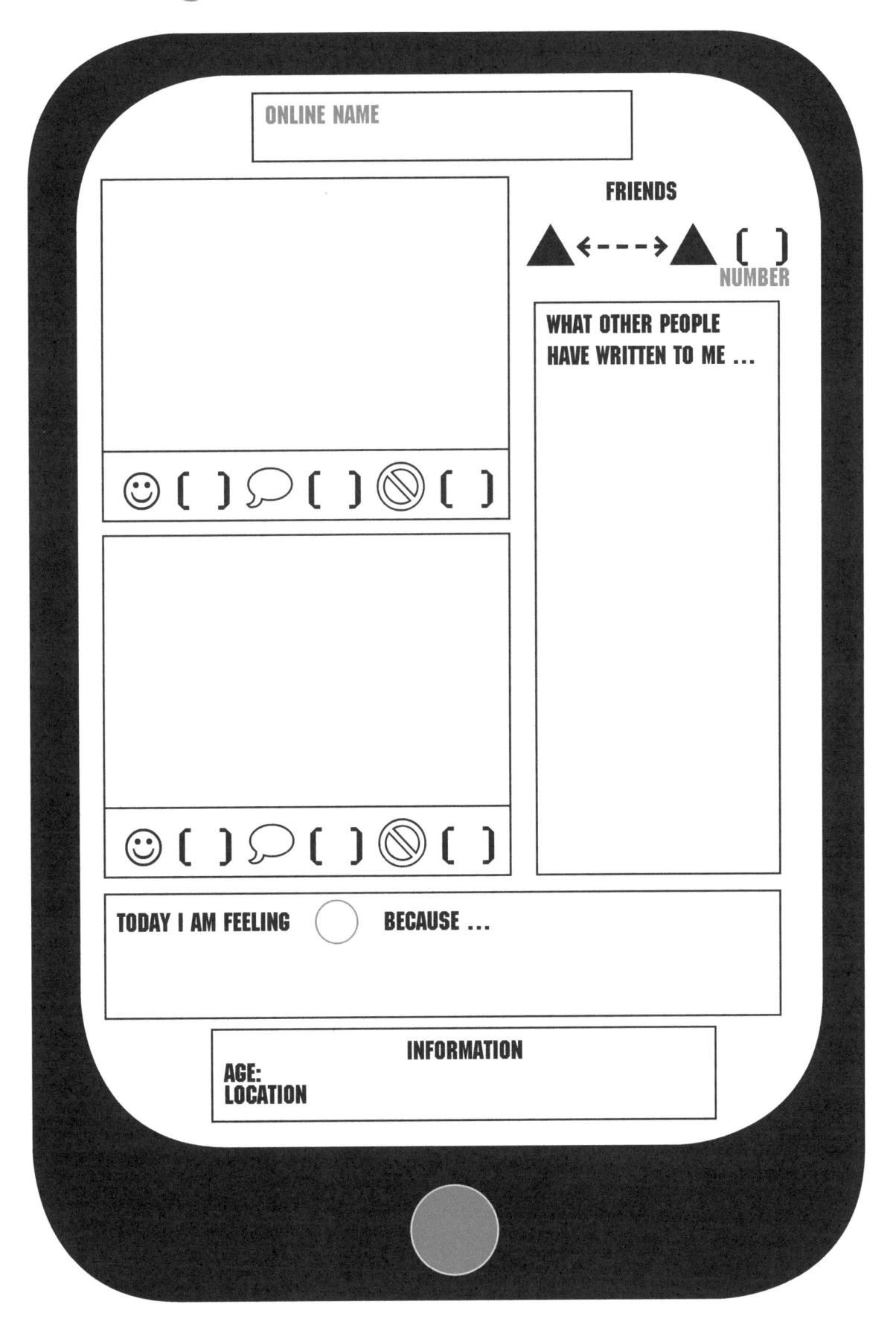

Activity 2.10
Risk-Taking

Aims

- For the students to feel safe & confident to participate in the session
- To be able to define 'peer pressure'
- To be able to identify situations where the students might experience increased peer pressure
- To formulate responses to experiencing peer pressure
- To begin to develop the skills needed to analyse and assess risk

Group Rules — 2 mins

Materials: Worksheet 1.1 'Visual Timetable' (p. 27); Group Rules Chart created in Activity 1.1.

Using Worksheet 1.1 and the Group Rules Chart, remind the group of the structure of each session and of the rules that were agreed in Activity 1.1. Ask if anyone would like to add a rule, or have a rule explained again.

Talk Time — 5 mins

Materials: Post-it notes.

Ask the students: 'Why might a friend tell you to do something you don't want to do?'

Students have the opportunity to discuss their answers, write them on post-its or to reflect on their responses without sharing with the group.

Ice-Breaker — 5 mins

Materials: Whiteboard and markers or flip chart & paper and flip-chart pen.

According to the Cambridge Dictionary, peer pressure is: 'The strong influence of a group, especially of children, on members of that group to behave as everyone else does.'

Ask the students if they agree with this definition. Ask them to reflect on a time when they have experienced peer pressure. On a whiteboard or flip chart, note does all the reasons that the girls can produce as to why is it difficult to say no to peer pressure.

Core Activity 1: Saying 'No' — 10 mins

Materials: Worksheet 2.27 'No, Because …' (p. 173) (one per pair); pens, flip chart & paper, flip-chart pen (or whiteboard & dry-wipe pen).

Previous activities in Part 2 have highlighted the significant pressures young people are subjected to by peers and adults. This activity supports the young people to develop their confidence in using scripts to negotiate some aspects of peer pressure.

It is important to stress that there is a context for supporting young people to develop scripts to resist pressure and there is no implication that young people have any responsibility for any abuse that they may have suffered.

As a whole group, ask the girls to share examples of when they think that young people face negative peer pressure. Examples may include to smoke, drink alcohol, use drugs, miss school, shoplift or treat others badly (bullying). Write the suggestions up on a flip chart/whiteboard and once the group have come up with different suggestions, allocate one to each pair.

Each pair needs to come up with arguments against the pressure, using sentences that start with, 'No, because …' Each pair should come up with as many different responses as possible on Worksheet 2.27.

Share these responses with the whole group.

Core Activity 2: Risk — 20 mins

Materials: Worksheets 2.28 'High Risk' (p. 174) & 2.29 'No Risk' (p. 175); Worksheet 2.30 'Risky Scenarios' (p. 176) (cut up into the individual scenarios).

This activity presents a variety of scenarios to the students and explores how they perceive and react to risk in different situations. The aim is to develop the young people's idea of risk, especially the risks posed by those they know and those who are strangers. The group are supported in understanding the factors that increase and reduce risk.

The whole room will be used as a 'risk scale'. Pick one side of the room and put up the sign on Worksheet 2.28 ('High Risk'); put the sign on Worksheet 2.29 ('No Risk') on the other side of the room. If it is not possible to use a whole room, scale the activity down by using either end of a desk.

Each young person takes a card from Worksheet 2.30 and places it somewhere on the scale, depending on how much risk they think is involved. You can model this first and think aloud as you describe how you are coming to a decision about the level of risk.

Once all scenarios have been placed on the scale, collect them back in and start to combine two or three scenarios, asking the group whether the combination increases or decreases the risk. Present a variety of combinations and explore the impact of this. For example, does combining 'drinking alcohol' with 'going to a house you haven't visited before' increase the risk or decrease the risk?

Finally, focus on ways to minimise risk. Split the group into pairs and ask each pair to imagine a scenario and come up with examples of how they would minimise the risk for that particular scenario.

Reflections & Feedback   5 mins

Materials: Facilitator Guide 1 'Reflections & Feedback' (p. 262).

Ask the students to focus on the questions on the facilitator guide.

Target-Setting   5 mins

Materials: Worksheet 1.4 'My Targets' (p. 30) (one each); pens.

Use Worksheet 1.4 to support each student in setting their weekly targets. They can do this in pairs and support each other to identify what they would like to work on during the coming week. Allow a little time for reflection on the achievement (or otherwise) of the previous week's targets.

Compliments to Close   5 mins

Materials: Each individual's 'Golden Scroll' & a gold permanent marker each; Facilitator's Guide 2 'The Golden Scroll' (p. 263).

The guide will support you in directing the group as they add positive comments to their Golden Scrolls.

Relaxation   10 mins

Materials: Facilitator Guide 3 'Guided Relaxation' (p. 264).

Use the script on the facilitator guide to support the students in deep relaxation.

Worksheet 2.27

No, Because …

Activity 2.10

No, because…

Worksheet 2.28
High Risk

Activity 2.10

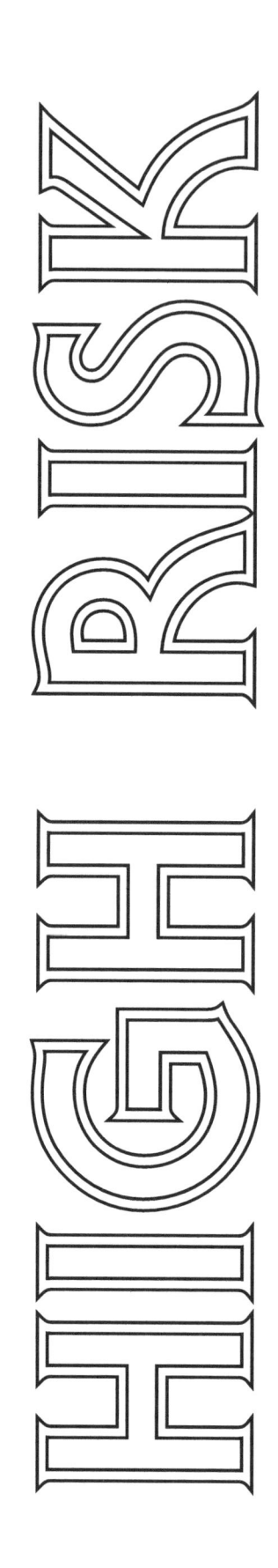

HIGH RISK

Worksheet 2.29
No Risk

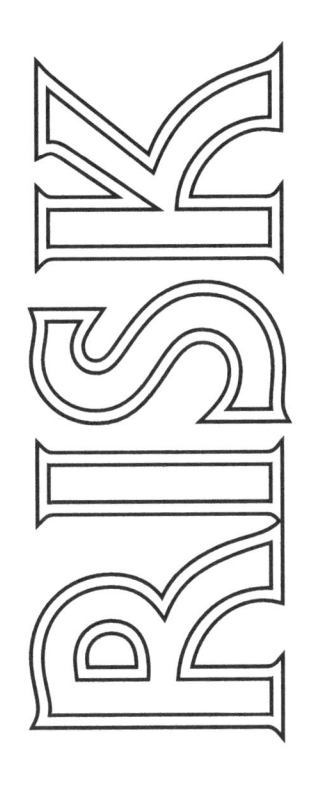

Activity 2.10

NO RISK

Worksheet 2.30
Risky Scenarios

Activity 2.10

Getting a late night bus/taxi with a friend	Getting a late night bus/taxi alone
Meeting up with your friends in your local town centre	Meeting up with someone you have met online
Going to a house you haven't been to before alone	Going to a house you haven't been to before with people you know
Kissing your boyfriend/girlfriend	Kissing someone you don't know
Chatting online to friends	Chatting online to people you haven't met and don't know
Taking a drink given to you by a stranger	Going to your friend's house for a party
Drinking alcohol	Taking drugs
Having unprotected sex with your boyfriend/girlfriend	Having unprotected sex with someone you don't know
Getting into the car of someone you don't know	Getting into the car of someone you have just met
Getting into your best friend's car	Giving your mobile number to a stranger
Accepting gifts from someone you have just met	Giving your mobile number to someone in your class
Posting your mobile number on your social network accounts (so that is can be viewed)	

Part 3
My Toolbox for Wellbeing & Future Health

1. Effective Thinking 1
   Positive Mental Attitude (PMA)
   Thoughts, Feelings, Behaviours

2. Effective Thinking 2
   NAT-Bashing
   Socratic Questioning

3. Relaxation & Mindfulness 1
   Explaining Mindfulness
   Mindful Mouthful

4. Relaxation & Mindfulness 2
   Relaxation Techniques
   My Mindful Timetable

5. Being Solution-Focused
   Problem-Free Talk
   Forgiveness

6. Future Hopes, Dreams & Realities 1
   Many Selves
   My Life Map

7. Future Hopes, Dreams & Realities 2
   A Preferred Future
   Looking Forward

8. Evaluation
   Situations Circles
   Trust Map

9. My Targets 1
   The Stages of Change
   Relapse Planning

10. My Targets 2
    Target-Setting
    My Positive Future

Activity 3.1
Effective Thinking 1

Aims

- For the students to feel safe & confident to participate in the session
- To introduce the concept of a Positive Mental Attitude (PMA)
- To be able to identify the cyclical relationship between thoughts, feelings and behaviours
- To begin to consider ways to break a cycle maintaining a negative internal dialogue

Group Rules — 2 mins

Materials: Worksheet 1.1 'Visual Timetable' (p. 27); Group Rules Chart created in Activity 1.1.

Using Worksheet 1.1 and the Group Rules Chart, remind the group of the structure of each session and of the rules that were agreed in Activity 1.1.

Talk Time — 5 mins

Materials: Post-it notes.

Ask the students: 'When do you think happy thoughts?'

Students have the opportunity to discuss their answers, write them on post-its, or to reflect on their responses without sharing with the group.

Ice-Breaker — 5 mins

Materials: Safe access for everyone to the internet, computer with audio, scrap paper, pens.

This activity is about developing and trying out a Positive Mental Attitude (PMA). This can be both uncomfortable and threatening, so ensure that it is introduced gently and with the understanding that we can try on these 'positive glasses' even if we are not feeling positive all the time, or much of the time.

Explain what a PMA is and have a look at a clip of somebody with a positive attitude. Whilst watching, try to notice the things they say that suggest they have a PMA and ask the students to note down any phrases that they hear that they think are particularly positive. You might choose one of the following to suit your group and the time available:

Serena Williams talking about coming back from being behind in tennis:

   https://www.youtube.com/watch?v=ZP8yNJefop4

Malala Yousafzai talking about fighting for education for girls:

   https://www.youtube.com/watch?v=A6Pz9V6LzcU

At the end of the clip, share some of the PMA messages that you heard with the group.

Core Activity 1: Positive Mental Attitude (PMA)   10 mins

Materials: Worksheet 3.1 'PMA Scenarios' (p. 181) (1 per pair/three). Optional: pens.

The group should now work in pairs/threes to talk over Worksheet 3.1. They do not need to fill in the sheet – discussion alone is fine. However, if they wish to fill in the sheet, this should also be encouraged.

After 8 minutes, pause the activity and give the students 1 minute to reflect individually on whether they feel they ever have a PMA and whether it is possible for all of us to have a PMA (maybe Serena and Malala are special or different to us?).

Core Activity 2: Thoughts, Feelings & Behaviours   15 mins

Materials: Worksheets 3.2 'The Link' (p. 182) & 3.3 'Negative Internal Monologue' (p. 183) (one each).

You can initially discuss with the group how our feelings, thoughts and behaviours are all linked. Using a visual diagram is always helpful. Introduce the group to the thoughts, feelings and behaviour diagram on Worksheet 3.2. Emphasise that this is a cycle and that each element impacts the others, maintaining the cycle.

The group can also be given Worksheet 3.3 to reinforce how these key aspects are linked and to generate discussion as to what this 'negative internal monologue' means for us as individuals. They can think about how easy it is to get stuck in such a cycle of negative thinking and how one negative thought can so easily lead to another.

Move the discussion on by requesting that each student provides an example of a negative thought that they have previously had and how this made them feel and how it affected their behaviours.

It is important to emphasise that it is human nature to have such thoughts. The problems really arise when our thinking is not entirely realistic and these thoughts make us feel bad and low, and subsequently stop us from living a fulfilled life and getting on with everyday tasks.

They may wish to focus on identifying how they might get out of such a cycle. What would they need to do in terms of changing their thinking and behaviour patterns? Who might help them in this process?

Reflections & Feedback — 5 mins

Materials: Facilitator Guide 1 'Reflections & Feedback' (p. 262).

Ask the students to focus on the questions on the facilitator guide.

Target-Setting — 5 mins

Materials: Worksheet 1.4 'My Targets' (p. 30) (one each); pens.

Use Worksheet 1.4 to support each student in setting their weekly targets. They can do this in pairs and support each other to identify what they would like to work on during the coming week. Allow a little time for reflection on the achievement (or otherwise) of the previous week's targets.

Compliments to Close — 5 mins

Materials: Each individual's 'Golden Scroll' & a gold permanent marker each; Facilitator's Guide 2 'The Golden Scroll' (p. 263).

The guide will support you in directing the group as they add positive comments to their Golden Scrolls.

Relaxation — 10 mins

Materials: Facilitator Guide 3 'Guided Relaxation' (p. 264).

Use the script on the facilitator guide to support the students in deep relaxation.

Worksheet 3.1
PMA Scenarios

Activity 3.1

Scenario	What might you think, do and feel if you take a positive mental attitude?	What might you think, do and feel if you have a negative mental attitude?
You get lost in a town you don't know	Think: Feel: Do:	Think: Feel: Do:
You find some money	Think: Feel: Do:	Think: Feel: Do:
Someone steals your phone	Think: Feel: Do:	Think: Feel: Do:
You get a really good mark in an exam	Think: Feel: Do:	Think: Feel: Do:

This page may be photocopied for instructional use only. *The ASD Girls' Wellbeing Toolkit* © Tina Rae & Amy Such 2019

Worksheet 3.2
The Link

Activity 3.1

- Thoughts create feelings
- Feelings create behaviours
- Behaviours reinforce thoughts

Worksheet 3.3
Negative Internal Monologue

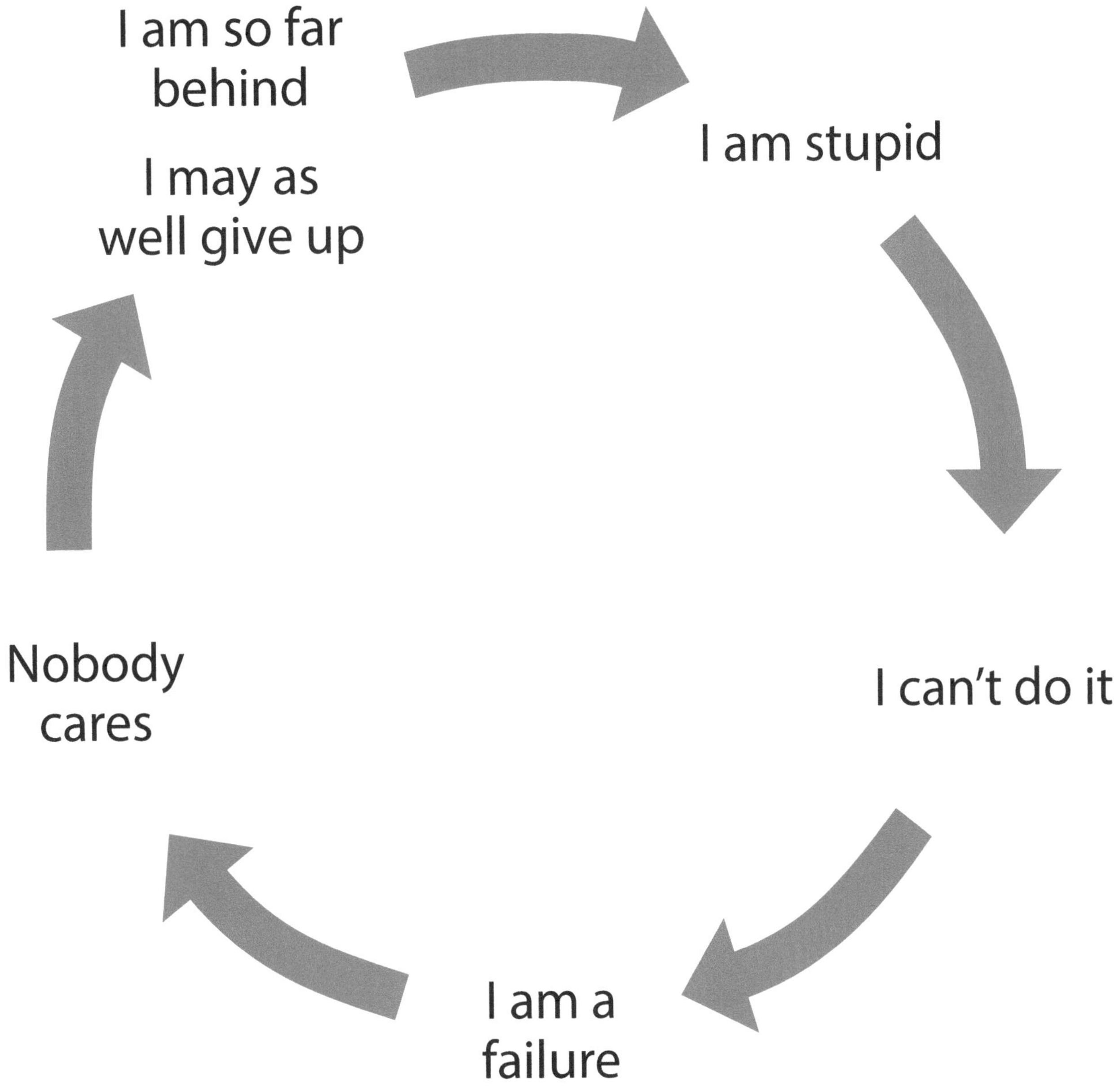

Activity 3.1

- I am so far behind
- I may as well give up
- Nobody cares
- I am a failure
- I can't do it
- I am stupid

Activity 3.2
Effective Thinking 2

Aims

* For the students to feel safe & confident to participate in the session
* To create an opportunity to general some positive thoughts
* To explore Negative Automatic Thoughts (NATs) and how they might impact on behaviour
* To begin to challenge NATs through techniques such as Socratic questioning

Group Rules — 2 mins

Materials: Worksheet 1.1 'Visual Timetable' (p. 27); Group Rules Chart created in Activity 1.1.

Using Worksheet 1.1 and the Group Rules Chart, remind the group of the structure of each session and of the rules that were agreed in Activity 1.1.

Talk Time — 5 mins

Materials: Post-it notes.

Ask the students to list some positive things that they have noticed today.

Students have the opportunity to discuss their answers, write them on post-its, or to reflect on their responses without sharing with the group.

Ice-Breaker — 5 mins

Materials: Worksheet 3.4 'What If …?' (p. 188) (one each); pens.

What if every time we worried about something happening, we also thought about the positive things that might happen?

Try to come up with 3 positive 'what if' examples for every 1 negative!

Core Activity 1: NAT-Bashing

Materials: Worksheet 3.5 'NAT-Bashing' (p. 189) (one each); pens.

This activity supports the students in challenging Negative Automatic Thoughts (NATs).

Explain that providing evidence against negative thoughts is believed to be a very powerful step towards accepting that they might not be true. Keeping a physical record can help the students to think things through, rather than just accepting the automatic thought. In turn this may lead them to thinking alternative thoughts that will help them to feel better and influence their actions in a positive way. It is a proven strategy to help them cope with difficult situations.

Ask the group for their own examples and take it in turns to present if they feel able to do so.

> Attention: This activity has to be handled carefully, so begin by providing an example of your own NAT, which could be quite light-hearted, for example: 'I am rubbish at speaking in front of other people.'

The idea is to encourage the group to see that not only is it normal to have negative thoughts, but it is also possible for us all to challenge them in order to come up with a more realistic thinking pattern that has less of a negative impact upon our overall behaviours and feelings.

Finally, give each person a copy of Worksheet 3.5, which provides a blank sheet for them to record and challenge NATs, as well as a completed example of the same sheet.

Core Activity 2: Socratic Questioning   15 mins

Materials: Worksheet 3.6 'Socratic Questioning' (p.191) (one each); pens.

Reflection is central to this activity and the task is underpinned by the **Socratic questioning** approach used in Cognitive Behavioural Therapy. This provides a framework for students to identify their thoughts and test them, as well as to look more deeply into assumptions that may be influencing them. This forms part of the process of **cognitive restructuring** – the process of noticing irrational or unhelpful thoughts and challenging them.

Examples of irrational or unhelpful thoughts experienced by young people who have been victims of bullying or exploitation might include black and white thinking, overgeneralisation, and emotional reasoning.

> Attention: It is vital that facilitators are mindful that some of the unhelpful thoughts the group hold may well be centred around shame and blaming themselves: it will be important that these thoughts are carefully and sensitively explored.

The first stage of this activity is to revisit the idea that what we think impacts how we feel and what we do. It may be useful to refer back to Worksheet 3.3, 'Negative Internal Monologue', as a visual prompt. Since we know that our thoughts impact us in this way, it is important for us to recognise our thoughts and realise that we can challenge them and change our thinking. Our thoughts can help us and our thoughts can harm us: during this activity we have an unusual chance to stop and observe our busy thoughts.

Ask everyone to pick one thought that they think is unhelpful. You might suggest that each person identifies their own unhelpful thought, however, if less time is available, or there quite a few students, you might ask the group to select a common unhelpful thought (e.g., 'I'm going to fail my exams', or 'no-one in my class likes me'). In this case, you might offer everyone their own copy of Worksheet 6.3 to complete away from the group, mentioning that you will be available later to discuss their thoughts individually, if they wish.

The chosen thought is written in the top box on the worksheet. Students should then be given a few minutes to read the questions that follow and select those they personally consider helpful in altering thought processes. The purpose is not to respond to every single question with brief answers. Instead, **the aim is to use between 3 and 5 questions** to gently gather in-depth answers. It is therefore important to allow time for the answers. The group may wish to record their responses on the worksheet.

Reflections & Feedback   5 mins

Materials: Facilitator Guide 1 'Reflections & Feedback' (p. 262).

Ask the students to focus on the questions on the facilitator guide.

Target-Setting   5 mins

Materials: Worksheet 1.4 'My Targets' (p. 30) (one each); pens.

Use Worksheet 1.4 to support each student in setting their weekly targets. They can do this in pairs and support each other to identify what they would like to work on during the coming week. Allow a little time for reflection on the achievement (or otherwise) of the previous week's targets.

Compliments to Close — 5 mins

Materials: Each individual's 'Golden Scroll' & a gold permanent marker each; Facilitator's Guide 2 'The Golden Scroll' (p. 263).

The guide will support you in directing the group as they add positive comments to their Golden Scrolls.

Relaxation — 10 mins

Materials: Facilitator Guide 3 'Guided Relaxation' (p. 264).

Use the script on the facilitator guide to support the students in deep relaxation.

Worksheet 3.4
What If …?

Activity 3.2

Negative What If …?	**Positive** What If …?
1	1
	2
	3

How does the **negative** 'what if …' make you feel?
_____

How does the **positive** 'what if …' make you feel?
_____

Which 'what ifs …' are more likely?
_____

Time to STOP! Ask yourself … am I catastrophising?

188   This page may be photocopied for instructional use only. *The ASD Girls' Wellbeing Toolkit* © Tina Rae & Amy Such 2019

Worksheet 3.5
NAT-Bashing

Activity 3.2

Thought	Support	Challenge	Others	Revised Thought
What is the thought? How much do you believe it?	Evidence for this thought	Evidence against this thought	What would my best friend say to me? What would I say to my friend? What would my mum/dad/carer say?	What do you think now?

page 1 of 2

Worksheet 3.5
NAT-Bashing

Activity 3.2

An example of how you can challenge those Negative Automatic Thoughts (NATs).

Thought	Support	Challenge	Others	Revised Thought
What is the thought? How much do you believe it?	Evidence for this thought	Evidence against this thought	What would my best friend say to me? What would I say to my friend? What would my mum/dad/carer say?	What do you think now?
I am going to fail my GCSEs. I believe it 95%.	I have not been concentrating in some of my lessons this year. I am behind on my coursework. I get anxious whenever anyone mentions the exams.	I normally do okay in tests and am predicted good grades. My teacher has said that we will have time off to revise and do our coursework. I have a revision timetable. We have Mocks to help with anxiety around exams.	They would say that I have always done well in exams and why would this be any different? I would tell them not to worry and that they have worked hard. Mum would say that I have plenty of time to revise and manage my anxiety before the exams.	I think that I am likely to do okay in my GCSEs. I believe this 70%.

Page 2 of 2

Worksheet 3.6
Socratic Questioning

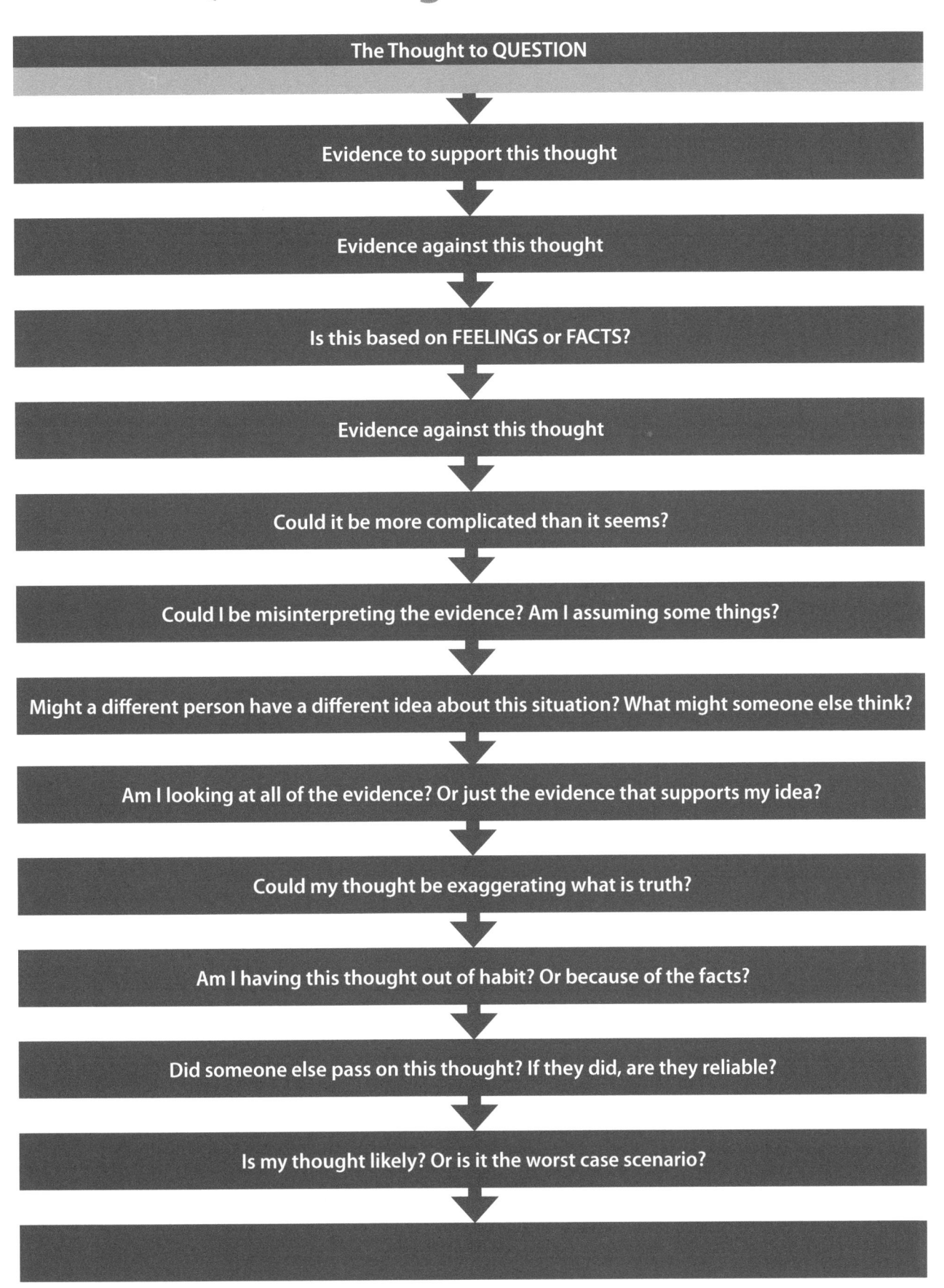

Activity 3.2

The Thought to QUESTION

⬇

Evidence to support this thought

⬇

Evidence against this thought

⬇

Is this based on FEELINGS or FACTS?

⬇

Evidence against this thought

⬇

Could it be more complicated than it seems?

⬇

Could I be misinterpreting the evidence? Am I assuming some things?

⬇

Might a different person have a different idea about this situation? What might someone else think?

⬇

Am I looking at all of the evidence? Or just the evidence that supports my idea?

⬇

Could my thought be exaggerating what is truth?

⬇

Am I having this thought out of habit? Or because of the facts?

⬇

Did someone else pass on this thought? If they did, are they reliable?

⬇

Is my thought likely? Or is it the worst case scenario?

⬇

This page may be photocopied for instructional use only. *The ASD Girls' Wellbeing Toolkit* © Tina Rae & Amy Such 2019

Activity 3.3
Relaxation & Mindfulness 1

Aims

* For the students to feel safe & confident to participate in the session
* To be able to describe what is meant by Mindfulness
* To be able to identify the benefits of incorporating a Mindfulness practice into our day-to-day lives
* To begin to practise simple Mindfulness techniques

Group Rules   2 mins

Materials: Worksheet 1.1 'Visual Timetable' (p. 27); Group Rules Chart created in Activity 1.1.

Using Worksheet 1.1 and the Group Rules Chart, remind the group of the structure of each session and of the rules that were agreed in Activity 1.1.

Talk Time   5 mins

Materials: Post-it notes.

Ask the students: 'What do you like to do to relax?'

Students have the opportunity to discuss their answers, write them on post-its, or to reflect on their responses without sharing with the group.

Ice-Breaker   5 mins

Start with a simple mindfulness activity, focusing on the breath. Focusing on breath is a good way to stay in the moment and introduce ourselves to the idea of: **paying attention, on purpose, non- judgementally.** Tell the group that it is not easy to train ourselves to do this, so we will do it step by step and will be kind to ourselves as we grow our skills. All we can do is our best.

> Before you start, ensure that everyone is comfortable, calm and knows what to expect. If they do not wish to take part at any point, that is fine.

Now read this script to the group:

- Sit still and relax
- Close your eyes
- Begin to focus on your breathing
- Direct your attention to the sensation of each breath in and out. In and out. In and out …
- Become aware of the feeling of air as it enters and then leaves your mouth or nostrils
- Thoughts will enter into your mind. Become aware of them, note them without judgement and let them pass. Imagine pinning your passing thoughts to a drifting cloud or a leaf that floats down the river
- Focus your attention on your breath. In and out, in and out …

Take some feedback and discuss how people found the exercise. What was most useful? Most difficult? What might be the point of doing something like this?

Core Activity 1: Explaining Mindfulness   15 mins

Materials: Worksheet 3.7 'Mindfulness' (p. 196) (one each); computer with audio and safe internet access, mobile phone with 'Headspace' app (if desired).

Using Worksheet 3.7, explain to the group that Mindfulness is considered to be 'paying attention, here and now, with kindness and curiosity'. It is about being 'in the moment' and focusing on the body, rather than being caught up in the world around us.

Mindfulness skills to develop:

- Attention: awareness of emotions, thoughts and feelings; greater concentration
- Balance: time for you, time for family and friends, time for school and studying
- Compassion: self-acceptance and forgiveness

Ask the students to think back to previous activities. Are any of these skills in keeping with the work they have been completing during The ASD Girls' Wellbeing Toolkit sessions?

To further explain Mindfulness, the students should then watch the following video:

> https://www.bing.com/videos/search?q=mindfulness+explanation+for+children+video&&view=detail&mid=0B8F9BD4664C377542820B8F9BD4664C37754282&&FORM=VRDGAR

Discuss how the students might be able to incorporate some Mindfulness practice into their day. They need to consider the importance of taking a few minutes every day to sit quietly and breathe, being sure to pay attention to their breath. Mindfulness needs to be planned into your life – it won't just happen! One way of doing this is to get a Mindfulness app for your phone. Techniques such a visualisation or keeping a gratitude diary can also help.

Present the students with another opportunity to engage in Mindfulness. This can either be done through downloading the 'Headspace' app and listening to Basics Session 1 (5 mins), or through the following website:

> https://www.youtube.com/watch?v=R9w7SjHaZmE

Core Activity 2: Mindful Mouthful   15 mins

Materials: Selection of tasty food items (e.g., cherry tomatoes, chocolate raisins, grapes, pieces of chocolate, Maltesers)

Before starting, prepare the group as you did with the ice-breaker: sit comfortably, relax, be aware of what is about to happen.

Now invite the students to each select an item of food and read through the script below. This activity draws awareness to our sense of taste and smell. When we eat, we often do so without really focusing on the taste, smell or texture of the food. Today we will eat mindfully.

> Bring your attention to the piece of food you have selected to eat. Look very closely at it, as if this were the first time you have seen it. Begin to notice how it feels in your hand … PAUSE … the texture of it in contact with your fingers. Look carefully, what do you notice about the colours?

> Notice and recognise any thoughts that you may be having about this food. Be aware of any feelings you may be having as you look at the food.

> Now, in your own time, begin to move the food up to your nose. Smell it. PAUSE. What do you notice? Once you have smelt it, take it to your mouth. PAUSE. As you are moving it towards to your mouth, be aware of your arm and hand moving … PAUSE.

> If your mind wanders … gently and non-judgementally bring it back.

> Slowly put the food into your mouth. Notice the taste, the texture and the sensation. Attend to these sensations … really notice the qualities of the food as you hold it in your mouth. PAUSE.

> Bring your attention to the sensations as you hold it in your mouth. PAUSE.

When you feel ready to swallow, notice the feeling and experience it with awareness. Once you have eaten the food, take your attention to the sensations and tastes left in your mouth.

Finally, direct the students' attention to any reactions and thoughts they had during their experience. Did the food taste the same, better or worse than usual? Did it feel the same eating in that way? What did they like? What did they not like?

Reflections & Feedback   5 mins

Materials: Facilitator Guide 1 'Reflections & Feedback' (p. 262).

Ask the students to focus on the questions on the facilitator guide.

Target-Setting   5 mins

Materials: Worksheet 1.4 'My Targets' (p. 30) (one each); pens.

Use Worksheet 1.4 to support each student in setting their weekly targets. They can do this in pairs and support each other to identify what they would like to work on during the coming week. Allow a little time for reflection on the achievement (or otherwise) of the previous week's targets.

Compliments to Close   5 mins

Materials: Each individual's 'Golden Scroll' & a gold permanent marker each; Facilitator's Guide 2 'The Golden Scroll' (p. 263).

The guide will support you in directing the group as they add positive comments to their Golden Scrolls.

Relaxation   10 mins

Materials: Facilitator Guide 3 'Guided Relaxation' (p. 264).

Use the script on the facilitator guide to support the students in deep relaxation.

Worksheet 3.7
Mindfulness

Activity 3.3

> **Mindfulness is:**
>
> *'Paying attention, here and now, with kindness and curiosity'*
>
> *(Association for Mindfulness in Education)*

Activity 3.4
Relaxation & Mindfulness 2

Aims

- For the students to feel safe & confident to participate in the session
- To be introduced to a range of relaxation techniques that are based upon the principles of Mindfulness
- To continue to practice Mindfulness techniques
- To begin to incorporate Mindfulness into their everyday routines

Group Rules   2 mins

Materials: Worksheet 1.1 'Visual Timetable' (p. 27); Group Rules Chart created in Activity 1.1.

Using Worksheet 1.1 and the Group Rules Chart, remind the group of the structure of each session and of the rules that were agreed in Activity 1.1.

Talk Time   5 mins

Materials: Post-it notes.

Ask the students: 'When might be a good time to practice Mindfulness?'

Students have the opportunity to discuss their answers, write them on post-its, or to reflect on their responses without sharing with the group

Ice-Breaker   5 mins

Materials: Worksheets 3.8 'Beach' (p. 203), 3.9 'Meadow' (p. 204) & 3.10 'Park' (p. 205).

Ask the group to think about some of their favourite places. When we spend time thinking about a place that is special to us, then we start to have feelings linked to this place. The human brain can create emotional responses based on our thoughts/memories/ideas. This relaxation technique is going to use our imagination to help us to feel calm.

This page may be photocopied for instructional use only. *The ASD Girls' Wellbeing Toolkit* © Tina Rae & Amy Such 2019

In a calm and quiet space, invite the young people to choose to reflect on a favourite, calming place. It is usually easier to do this activity with a place the young person knows, as it is easier for them to remember the place in detail. It does not need to be somewhere exotic: it could be playing with a pet, going for a walk in a local park, sitting in a garden, sitting on a beach, somewhere they went on a school trip, relaxing in their bedroom. However, if they appear to find this very difficult then you may wish to provide them with the options available on Worksheets 3.8, 3.9, or 3.10. Encourage them to make this image as precise and real as possible in their imagination.

Once they have imagined their place, invite them to go through each sense, one by one, and imagine their experience in the relaxing place.

To support them, you should encourage them to close their eyes. If there is space, they may wish to sit or lie on the floor. Go through each sense, providing the following prompts:

- **Sight** What can you see? Is it bright? Dark? What colours are around you? Is there lots of movement, or is it very still? Who else is about?
- **Sound** What can you hear? What is making that noise? People, animals, the wind, the sea? How loud is the noise? Is it near? Far?
- **Touch** What can you feel? What is beneath you? Is it soft? Hard? Smooth? Are you cold? Hot? Is there a breeze?
- **Taste** What can you taste? Is it sweet? Warm? Refreshing? Soothing?
- **Smell** What can you smell? What is around you that is providing a scent? Can you smell the fresh air? Can you smell the perfume of flowers? Can you smell the salt from the sea? Are there animal smells around?

At the end of the activity, pause briefly before bringing the students back into the room by asking them to begin to tune into the noises they can hear around them. Then ask them to begin to wiggle their fingers and toes before blinking their eyes open.

Core Activity 1: Relaxation Techniques   20 mins

Materials: Water, straws, glasses (one each); paper towel for everyone, to wipe any spillage.

This activity is an opportunity to introduce some basic ideas about how we react to acute stress: the 'fight-or-flight' response. Once this is explored, then relaxation techniques can be understood much more effectively in the light of our subconscious reaction to stress.

Explain 'fight-or-flight': When a person is confronted with something stressful or anxiety-provoking, the body undergoes several changes and enters a special state called the 'fight-or-flight' response. The body prepares to either fight or flee the perceived danger.

During the fight-or-flight response, it is common to experience a 'blank' mind, increased heart rate, sweating, tense muscles, and more. Unfortunately, while we can understand why the body behaves like this, these responses can be unhelpful.

Using a variety of skills, you can end the fight-or-flight response before the symptoms become too extreme. All skills improve with use, so we are now going to explore a few options that you might like to consider trying out after this session.

Now ensure a quiet, calm, reflective atmosphere and lead the group through the following relaxation techniques:

Relaxation Technique 1: Deep Breathing

When we are feeling relaxed, our normal way to behave is to take long, deep breaths. However, during the fight-or-flight response, breathing becomes rapid and shallow. Deep breathing reverses that, and sends messages to the brain to begin calming the body. Practice will make your body respond more efficiently to deep breathing in the future.

Now follow the script:

> Breathe in slowly through your nose, counting to 5 in your head. Each inward breath lasts at least 5 seconds. Pay attention to the feeling of the air filling your lungs.
>
> Hold your breath for 5 seconds (again, keep count). You do no't want to feel uncomfortable, but it should last quite a bit longer than an ordinary breath.
>
> Breathe out very slowly through your mouth for 5 seconds (count!).

Relaxation Technique 2: Deep Breathing

Now provide each student with a straw and a glass half filled with water. Ask everyone to hold the straw in their mouth and repeat the script in Technique 1. They should continue to breathe in through their nose, however, when they breathe out, they should breathe out through their mouth, creating bubbles in the water. Prompt the students to look at the bubbles and make sure they are all the same size. This means they are breathing smoothly and calmly.

They may wish to repeat this exercise.

Relaxation Technique 3: Simple Body Scan

Explain that during the fight-or-flight response our muscles become tense. This can lead to a feeling of tension and discomfort, or even back and neck pain. This is a simple version of the Body Scan used in Mindfulness practice, which teaches us to become more aware of the tension we are experiencing, so we can better identify and address stress and anxiety.

Ensure the atmosphere is calm and quiet, and then ask group members to sit or lie down somewhere comfortable. The idea is to deliberately tense each muscle, and then to release the tension. Follow the script:

> Tense the muscles in your toes by curling them into your foot. Notice how it feels when your foot is tense. Hold the tension for 5 seconds.
>
> Release the tension from your toes. Let your toes completely relax. Notice how your toes feel differently after you release the tension.
>
> Tense all of the muscles in your legs. Hold it for 5 seconds. Notice the feeling of tension in your leg. How does it feel?
>
> Release the tension from your legs. Take a moment to think about how the feeling of relaxation differs from the tension.
>
> Now tense the muscles in your bottom. Hold … How does it feel?
>
> And release.
>
> Move onto your torso, your lower stomach and back. Hold for 5 seconds.
>
> Release. How did that feel?
>
> Now tense your arms. Hold … release. Clench your fists. Squeeze.
>
> And release. Notice any feelings in your arms and hands.
>
> Move on to your neck. Tense your neck and your shoulders. Feel how your body changes. Hold … release.
>
> Finally, tense your face: your eyes, your nose, your mouth. Scrunch up your face. Hold … and relax.
>
> Take a minute to notice how your body is feeling.

Core Activity 2: Mindful Timetable 10 mins

Materials: Worksheet 3.11 'Mindful Timetable' (p. 206) (one each); pens.

Brainstorm ways you can get mindfulness into your life. Be realistic, but also encourage students to be creative.

For example:

- mindful breakfast once a week
- setting an alarm for 10 minutes earlier than usual and lying quietly, attending to the sounds around you
- being mindful of the feel of the toothbrush as you brush your teeth
- sitting in the car for 5 minutes at the end of the car journey home to take some deep breaths

Ask the students to have a go at planning some Mindfulness activities into their coming week, using Worksheet 3.11. Remind them to be realistic: the harder your plans are, the less likely you are to carry them out!

There is space on the worksheet for them to make notes about their chosen activities. These might relate to the activity itself, but they might also be about how easy/difficult it was to complete, or the practicality of their chosen times/locations, for example: 'house not calm enough before school to practise Mindfulness'.

Reflections & Feedback 5 mins

Materials: Facilitator Guide 1 'Reflections & Feedback' (p. 262).

Ask the students to focus on the questions on the facilitator guide.

Target-Setting 5 mins

Materials: Worksheet 1.4 'My Targets' (p. 30) (one each); pens.

Use Worksheet 1.4 to support each student in setting their weekly targets. They can do this in pairs and support each other to identify what they would like to work on during the coming week. Allow a little time for reflection on the achievement (or otherwise) of the previous week's targets.

Compliments to Close 5 mins

Materials: Each individual's 'Golden Scroll' & a gold permanent marker each; Facilitator's Guide 2 'The Golden Scroll' (p. 263).

The guide will support you in directing the group as they add positive comments to their Golden Scrolls.

Relaxation 10 mins

Materials: Facilitator Guide 3 'Guided Relaxation' (p. 264).

Use the script on the facilitator guide to support the students in deep relaxation.

Worksheet 3.8
Beach

Activity 3.4

Worksheet 3.9
Meadow

Activity 3.4

Worksheet 3.10
Park

Activity 3.4

Worksheet 3.11
Mindful Timetable

Activity 3.4

My Mindfulness Timetable

Activity	When? Where?	Thoughts/Feelings	Notes

Activity 3.5
Being Solution-Focused

Aims

* For the students to feel safe & confident to participate in the session
* To be introduced to a range of techniques used within solution-focused practices
* For the students to begin to think about ways of implementing solution-focused approaches within everyday life
* To continue to practise Mindfulness techniques

Group Rules   2 mins

Materials: Worksheet 1.1 'Visual Timetable' (p. 27); Group Rules Chart created in Activity 1.1.

Using Worksheet 1.1 and the Group Rules Chart, remind the group of the structure of each session and of the rules that were agreed in Activity 1.1.

Talk Time   5 mins

Materials: Post-it notes.

Ask the students: 'What are you good at?'

Students have the opportunity to discuss their answers, write them on post-its, or to reflect on their responses without sharing with the group.

Ice-Breaker   5 mins

Materials: small pieces of paper (at least one per person), large jar.

This is an opportunity for reflection and acceptance. Start by asking everyone to write down one thing they are grateful for on a slip of paper and to put it in a big jar (the 'gratitude jar'). Explain that these will be read out later in the session.

You may wish to keep filling this jar over the final few sessions, or you may want to suggest that each student creates their own 'gratitude jar' to keep at home. The students may wish to include their whole family in adding to the jar. Alternatively, students may like to keep a gratitude diary, in which they note down a couple of things each day that they are grateful for. Some people will prefer to spend a couple of minutes of quiet time each day reflecting on this alone.

Ask the students to reflect on how they feel after identifying something they are grateful for.

Core Activity 1: Problem-Free Talk   20 mins

Materials: Worksheets 3.12 'Case Study: Lisa' (p. 211) (one per pair) & 3.13 'Solution-Focused Cards' (p. 212) (printed and cut into separate cards, one set per pair); A4 paper & pens.

This activity is about trying out some techniques from solution-focused thinking (see Berg & de Shazer, 1993). Solution-focused thinking involves looking forwards and working on strengths: 'Looking **for** solutions rather than looking **at** problems' (Ajmal & Rees, 2004).

There are many ideas and techniques in this field that help us to see and explore things from a future-oriented and positive perspective. This is not to say that there are not problems in the world or our lives, or that we should avoid talking about them. It is just an opportunity to try out a different and potentially empowering way of seeing things.

The students will consider Lisa's story on Worksheet 3.12 in conjunction with the Solution-Focused Cards. The cards represent different solution-focused thinking techniques that the pairs could use to help support Lisa, if she were their friend.

1. Ask the students to form up into pairs, choosing partners that they are comfortable talking to, especially about sensitive subjects. Each pair has a set of Solution-Focused Cards.

2. Ask the pairs to imagine that they are Lisa's best friends. They should choose three solution-focused thinking techniques on the cards that might help them to brainstorm ideas to support Lisa.

3. Ensure there is time for feedback, debrief and information-sharing at the end of the activity.

4. Suggest that the group may even wish to go on to make a short video clip, presenting their solutions to Lisa.

Core Activity 2: Forgiveness   10 mins

Materials: Worksheets 3.14 'A Walk in the Woods' (p. 215) & 3.15 'Autumn Wood' (p. 217).

This is an opportunity for reflection and acceptance.

1. Ask the group to reflect back on the ice-breaker and the things that they are grateful for. Open the jar and read out each statement that the girls have submitted (without asking them to identify which is theirs). Once read, fold back up and return to the jar.

2. Next, ask the students to think about a time when they have forgiven someone. Ask everyone to reflect on the fact that we feel better when we forgive others, although this is hard.

3. Next ask everyone to take a comfortable place on the floor and begin to read them the visualisation on Worksheet 3.14.

    Following the visualisation, discuss:

    * Why might we want to think about gratitude and forgiveness today?
    * What do you think these have to do with Mindfulness and being solution-focused?

4. Try to draw out the idea that we often do not attend to how we feel and what we think, and that Mindfulness gives us a chance to do this. You may also like to highlight that showing gratitude can help us identify the resources we have that will help us move towards our preferred future.

Reflections & Feedback   5 mins

Materials: Facilitator Guide 1 'Reflections & Feedback' (p. 262).

Ask the students to focus on the questions on the facilitator guide.

Target-Setting   5 mins

Materials: Worksheet 1.4 'My Targets' (p. 30) (one each); pens.

Use Worksheet 1.4 to support each student in setting their weekly targets. They can do this in pairs and support each other to identify what they would like to work on during the coming week. Allow a little time for reflection on the achievement (or otherwise) of the previous week's targets.

Compliments to Close 5 mins

Materials: Each individual's 'Golden Scroll' & a gold permanent marker each; Facilitator's Guide 2 'The Golden Scroll' (p. 263).

The guide will support you in directing the group as they add positive comments to their Golden Scrolls.

Relaxation 10 mins

Materials: Facilitator Guide 3 'Guided Relaxation' (p. 264).

Use the script on the facilitator guide to support the students in deep relaxation.

Worksheet 3.12
Case Study: Lisa

Activity 3.5

Lisa's Story

I am 17 years old now and I have a job in the gym as a personal trainer. I have some friends. I was in foster care most of my life. I have been on my own most of my life. My mum left and my dad left and I was on my own. I ended up in foster care with a strange person. She took a dislike to me. So I went out all the time, walking the streets. Always out on the streets. I had to be out of the house and I came in late and I didn't talk to anyone. I sometimes went to school.

I ended up getting picked up by some men. They built the trust first. I was on the streets and they stopped and got me a taxi home. They gave me fags. They looked after me for ages. I thought this is the first time someone is looking after me. They took me off the streets. It was the first time I felt accepted. The first time I felt wanted. The first time I felt safe.

I had some friends in school but I stopped seeing them.

Then, when I was 15, I was raped. I didn't understand what happened. I didn't tell anyone. Then one day I spoke to a sexual health worker and said what happened and what was happening. She said it back to me and I heard it differently. She said this isn't right.

I spoke up and told the police, but I was ignored. I was told that this thing that happened to me was a horrific thing, but then nothing happened. So I went back to my sexual health worker and she helped me.

Worksheet 3.13
Solution-Focused Cards

Activity 3.5

Card Two: Resource activation

- You will need pen and paper.
- A resource is something that helps you, e.g., a person, a skill
- Person 1 asks Person 2 to think of something they have ever done that was successful – anything at all.
- Ask them to think about **what was it about them** that meant they could do this thing.
- Write down exactly what they say. Read it back.
- Keep asking them: Anything else? Anything else?
- Keep writing until you have a list of your partner's resources.

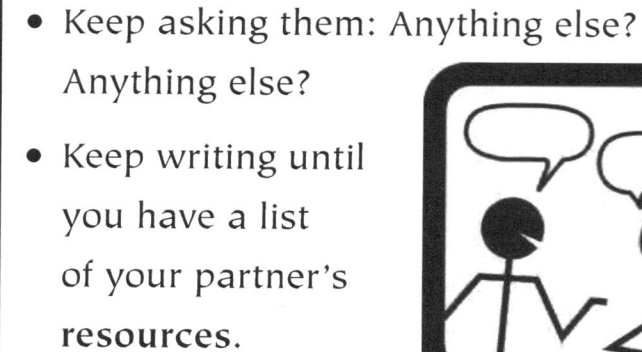

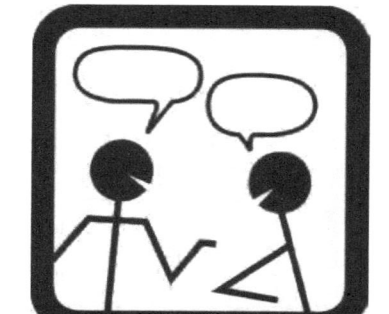

Card One: Problem-free talk

- Time 2 minutes of talk
- In that time, talk must **not** be about problems, but it can be about anything else you like.
- **TIPS FOR TOPICS:** weather, food, transport, weekend plans, clothes, the news, music, TV, animals …

Worksheet 3.13
Solution-Focused Cards

Activity 3.5

Card Three: How would you like things to be?

Talk or write about how you would like things to be – your preferred future.

Some things to think about:

- What would you be doing?
- Where?
- With whom?
- What would you be thinking?
- What would you be feeling?

Card Four: How could we get there?

- Think of a goal, even if it is a small one.
- Write it down, or say it out loud.
- Talk to your partner about how you could get there.
- What does it make sense to work on now? Try and come up with at least one thing.

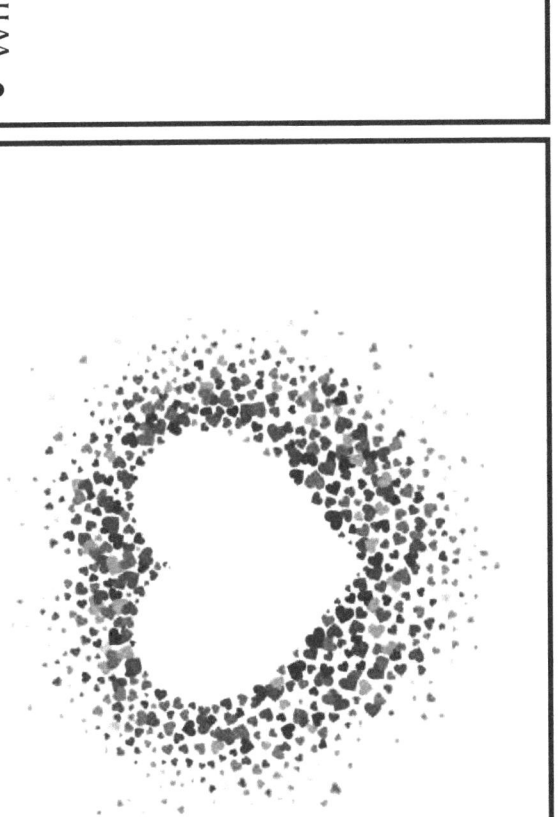

Worksheet 3.13
Solution-Focused Cards

Activity 3.5

Card Five: Identifying strengths

Start a countdown timer for 2 minutes

Take it in turns to write down or say as many of your strengths in that time, without thinking about it too much.

Card Six: Visualising

Think about your preferred future in a year's time. What will you be doing, thinking and feeling?

Find a relaxing place to close your eyes (if you are happy to) and really visualise this future – What would that look like?

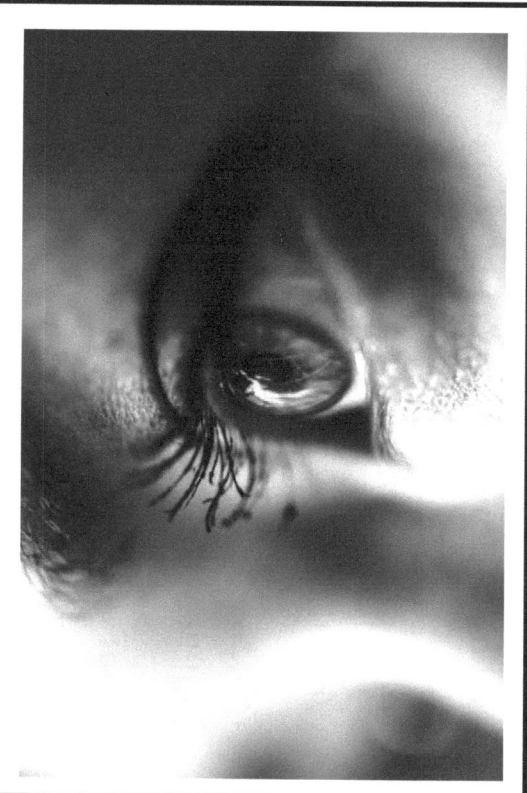

Worksheet 3.14
Walk in the Woods

Activity 3.5

A Walk in the Woods

Before you begin your walk, stretch your body as much as you can …

Lift your arms up and out to the side. Bend over to the left … and now, the right. Push your arms back to arch your back and now pull them in front of you, rounding your back. Now release your arms, relax and, if you feel comfortable to do so, shut your eyes.

Take a nice, deep breath in. Feel the air rushing into your body. You might notice your chest going out or your diaphragm moving up in your tummy. Hold. And breathe out. Slow, steady. Let's do that again. Deep breath in … 2 … 3 … 4 … and out. 2… 3… 4…

Now I want you to try and move your attention away from this room and we are going to enter our imagination.

We are now in the woods. It is a warm autumn day and you can see the sun glistening through the trees … orange, golden, brown, red.

As you took towards the shards of light coming into the wood, you can see particles of dust spinning and twirling as they float ahead of you. You breathe in … and out.

You take a step forward and the dried leaves that cover the woodland floor crunch under your feet. Crunch, crunch, crunch, crunch. In the trees, you can hear the rustling of twigs. What can you see? A squirrel? A bird? Take a good look around you.

page 1 of 2

Worksheet 3.14
Walk in the Woods

Activity 3.5

Breathe. In … out …

And you carry on walking, gliding, along the path. You feel light and effortless. Your tension drifts away as you float past the bluebells and foxgloves that line the path. What can you smell? Sweet perfume from the flowers. Sap from the trees.

And you breathe. Slowly. In and out. In and out.

You reach an old oak tree. The trunk is heavy, solid, stable. You reach out to touch the bark. How does it feel on your fingers? Cold? Rough? Bumpy? Fragile? Breathe.

As you walk away from the tree, you look up. Notice how big the canopy of leaves is above you. How comforting, protective. You feel safe. Feel the warmth from the sun as it peeks in between that canopy. Safe, secure.

In. 2 … 3 … 4 … Out. 2 … 3 … 4 …

[Pause]

We are now going to leave the wood. Imagine the sunlight, the leaf canopy, the thick tree trunk. It is beginning to fade. The colours, the smells, the sounds.

And, instead, have a listen to what you can hear around you right now. What can you smell? Taste? Slowly wiggle your fingers and toes and, when you're ready, you can blink your eyes open.

Worksheet 3.15
Autumn Wood

Activity 3.5

Activity 3.6
Future Hopes, Dreams & Realities 1

Aims

- For the students to feel safe & confident to participate in the session
- To begin to think about the different ways people present themselves and how this impacts on others
- To begin to consider past events and future dreams
- To explore how the past can influence how we feel about the future

Group Rules   2 mins

Materials: Worksheet 1.1 'Visual Timetable' (p. 27); Group Rules Chart created in Activity 1.1.

Using Worksheet 1.1 and the Group Rules Chart, remind the group of the structure of each session and of the rules that were agreed in Activity 1.1.

Talk Time   5 mins

Materials: Post-it notes.

Ask the students: 'Why might people behave differently around different people?'

Students have the opportunity to discuss their answers, write them on post-its, or to reflect on their responses without sharing with the group.

Ice-Breaker   5 mins

Materials: Worksheet 3.16 'Hand Template' (p. 222) (one each); paper, coloured pens, coloured pencils.

This activity is split into two parts: this first part considers the past and the follow-up (Activity 3.7, 'Ice-Breaker) imagines the future. This is a safe, dedicated time for the group to look creatively at their pasts and futures.

Ask the students to draw their own left hand, which represents the past, on the left side of a blank sheet of A4 paper, folded in half (they may find drawing around each other's hands easier). Alternatively, they may choose to use the template on Worksheet 3.16.

> Attention: As facilitator, it is important to be aware that there may be concerns that arise from past issues: consider carefully if this is an appropriate activity for your group.

Encourage the group to fill their left hand outline with drawings that represent their past. They do not need to draw each thing; they can include writing or even a colour or pattern that represents something. Ask them to consider the elements in the past that have shaped them:

- key moments
- key people
- important events
- important feelings
- key places
- special pets

Core Activity 1: Many Selves 15 mins

Materials: Worksheets 3.17 'Many Selves' (p. 223) & 3.18 'Self-Awareness Profile' (p. 224) (one each).

This activity aims to encourage the group to identify who and what they are and who and what they would like to be. Start by discussing the concept that we have 'many selves', using the information on Worksheet 3.17, and ensure that the group understands the distinctions between these 'selves'.

Real Self
This is how we see ourselves now! This is about our behaviour, thoughts and feelings as they are in this moment. This self is how we see ourselves now in our social and learning contexts.

Ideal Self
This is who, and what, we would like to be. This would be the best version of ourselves!

Fantasy Self
This is how we would like to be if reality did not figure or matter and we were not constrained by it – imagine winning the lottery, for example, so that money was not an object.

Open Self

This is the self that other people out there notice. For example, what would your friends say about you and how you behave, think and feel?

Hidden Self

This is the self that only you know about. For example, you may be a great dancer, but perhaps you are too shy to dance in front of others. As a result, others do not know that you dance well.

Present Self

This is you now and how you perceive your strengths and skills. For example, you may say that you are a good listener, or a hard worker, or generous.

Self in progress

This is the self as it is currently developing – like a work in progress. You might identify something that you would like to be good at, but find quite hard at the moment. For example, you may wish to feel more confident at speaking out in class, or when meeting new people, or when performing in a show.

Ask the group to really stop, think and reflect on each of these. Then ask them to use Worksheet 18.3 to compile their own self-awareness profile, noting down words or phrases that they feel relate to each of their own selves.

As they complete the activity, ask the group: do you see yourself as others see you? How accurate is your self-awareness and thinking?

Core Activity 2: Life Map   15 mins

Materials: Worksheet 3.19 'My Life Map' (p. 225) (one each); large sheets of paper, coloured pens.

This activity is designed to help the students further reflect on where they have been and where they would like to be going.

Give everyone a copy of Worksheet 3.19 and encourage them to produce their own life maps to reflect their personal experiences.

The group may need some support to identify key events within their lives, or to evaluate the shape of the road they will then draw, for example: 'When I moved to secondary school, I found it really hard, so the road went down quickly and steeply'; or 'When we bought our new puppy I was happy and the road went up a little bit.'

Reflections & Feedback   5 mins

Materials: Facilitator Guide 1 'Reflections & Feedback' (p. 262).

Ask the students to focus on the questions on the facilitator guide.

Target-Setting   5 mins

Materials: Worksheet 1.4 'My Targets' (p. 30) (one each); pens.

Use Worksheet 1.4 to support each student in setting their weekly targets. They can do this in pairs and support each other to identify what they would like to work on during the coming week. Allow a little time for reflection on the achievement (or otherwise) of the previous week's targets.

Compliments to Close   5 mins

Materials: Each individual's 'Golden Scroll' & a gold permanent marker each; Facilitator's Guide 2 'The Golden Scroll' (p. 263).

The guide will support you in directing the group as they add positive comments to their Golden Scrolls.

Relaxation   10 mins

Materials: Facilitator Guide 3 'Guided Relaxation' (p. 264).

Use the script on the facilitator guide to support the students in deep relaxation.

Worksheet 3.16
Hand Template

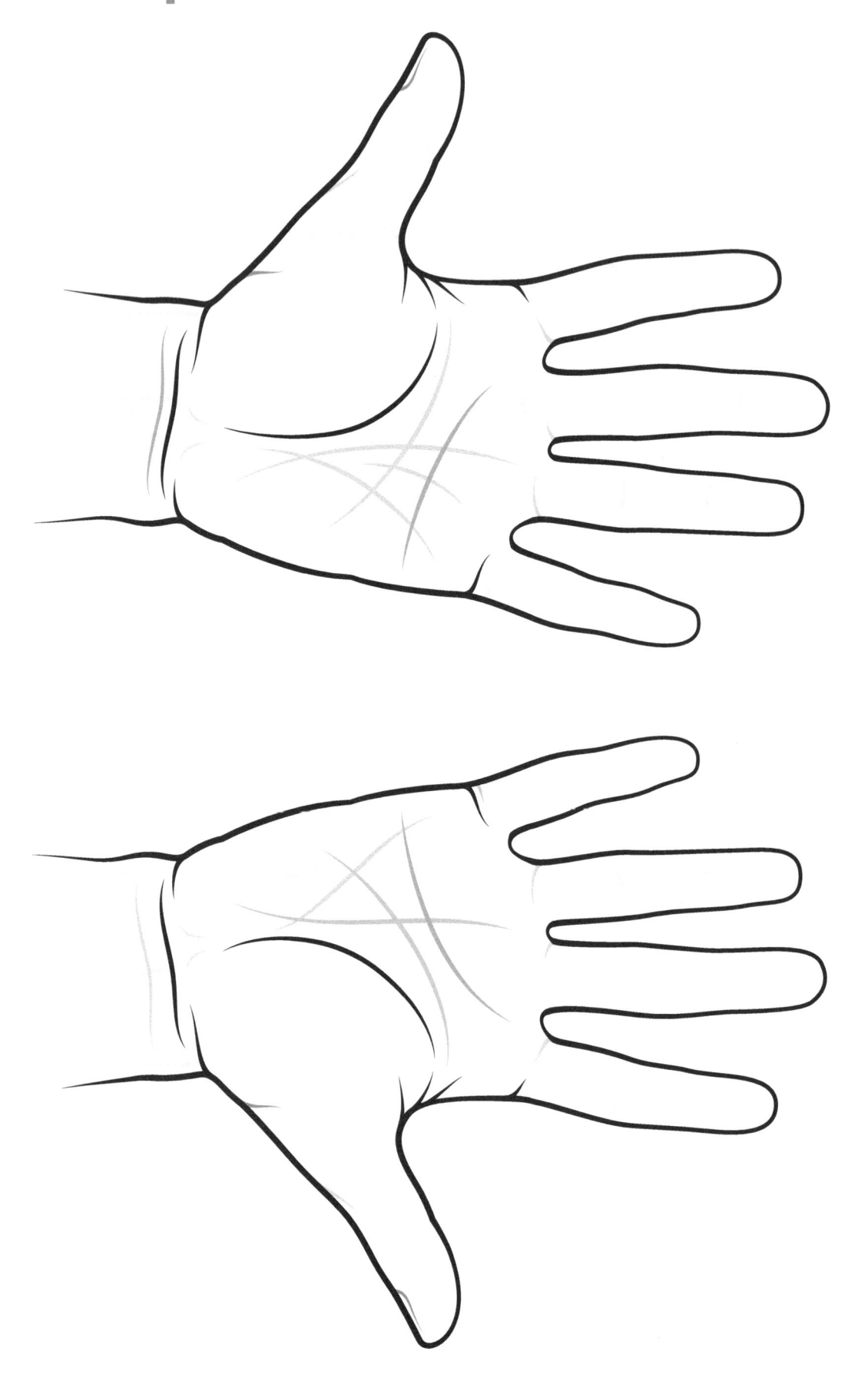

Activity 3.6

Worksheet 3.17
Many Selves

Activity 3.6

Many Selves

REAL SELF: this is us as we see ourselves now! This is about our behaviour, thoughts and feelings as they are in this moment. This self is how we see ourselves now in our social and learning contexts.

IDEAL SELF: this is who, and what, we would like to be. This would be the best version of ourselves!

FANTASY SELF: this is how we would like to be if reality didn't figure or matter and we were not constrained by it – imagine winning the lottery, for example, so that money was not an object.

OPEN SELF: this is the self that other people out there notice. For example, what would your friends say about you and how you behave, think and feel?

HIDDEN SELF: this is the self that only you know about. For example, perhaps you are a great dancer, but you are too shy to dance in front of others. As a result, no one knows how well you dance.

PRESENT SELF: this is you now and how you perceive your strengths and skills. For example, you may say that you are a good listener, or a hard worker, or generous.

SELF IN PROGRESS: this is the self as it is currently developing – like a work in progress. Perhaps you can identify something that you would like to be good at, but find quite hard at the moment? For example, you may wish to feel more confident at speaking out in class, or when meeting new people, or when performing in a show.

Worksheet 3.18

Self-Awareness Profile

Activity 3.6

Self-Awareness Profile

- Ideal self
- Real self
- Fantasy self
- Open self
- Present self
- Hidden self
- Self in progress

Worksheet 3.19
My Life Map

Activity 3.6

Memo

Memo

Success

03

01

02

Topic

Time

Total

Idea

Searching

MY MAP

Inner

Connection

Imagination

Connection

Break

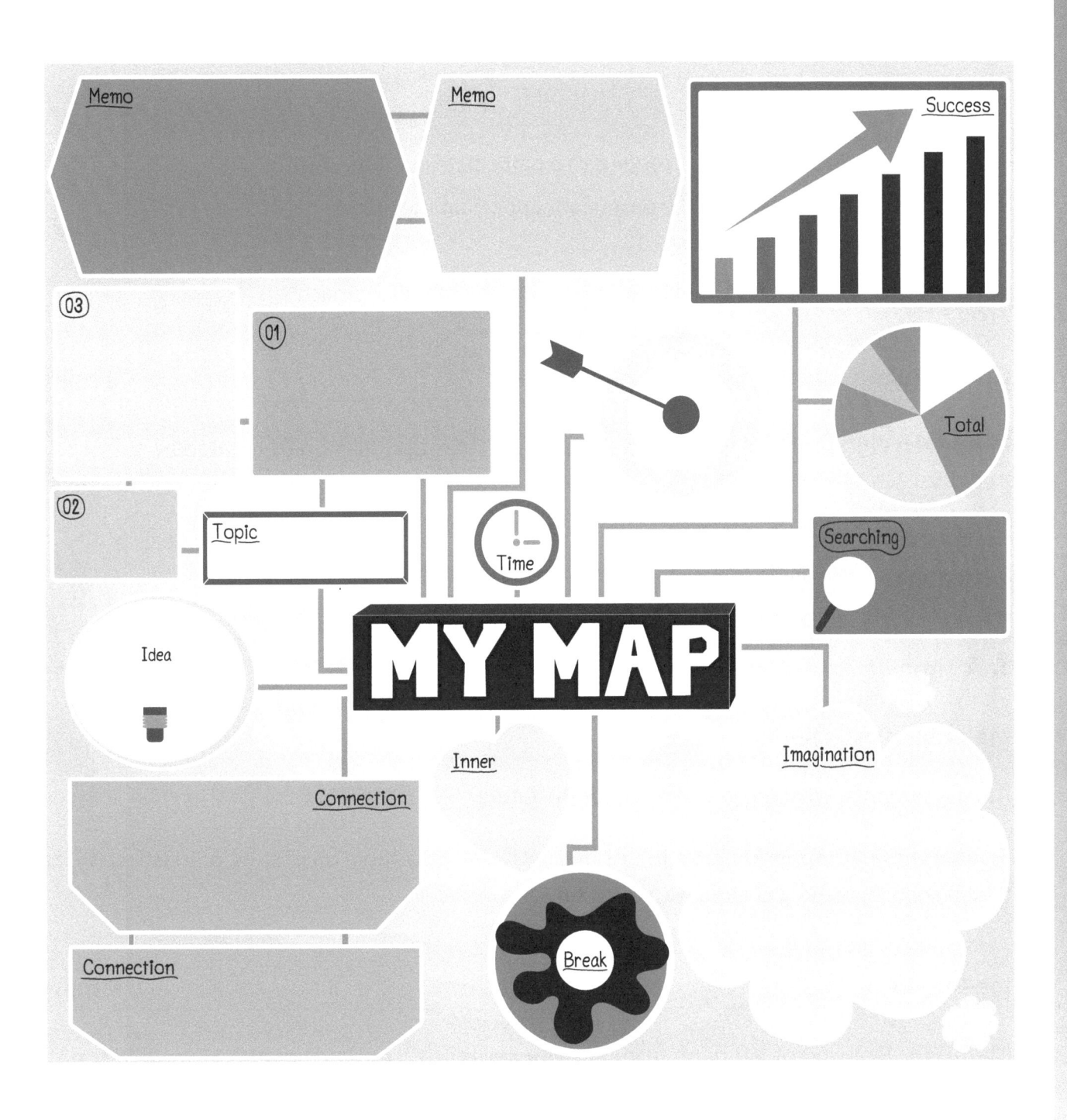

Worksheet 3.19

This page may be photocopied for instructional use only. *The ASD Girls' Wellbeing Toolkit* © Tina Rae & Amy Such 2019

225

Activity 3.7
Future Hopes, Dreams & Realities 2

Aims

* For the students to feel safe & confident to participate in the session
* To continue to explore how the past might impact on the future
* To consider future hopes and dreams
* To begin to plan for the future by using a strengths-based approach

Group Rules   2 mins

Materials: Worksheet 1.1 'Visual Timetable' (p. 27); Group Rules Chart created in Activity 1.1.

Using Worksheet 1.1 and the Group Rules Chart, remind the group of the structure of each session and of the rules that were agreed in Activity 1.1.

Talk Time   5 mins

Materials: Post-it notes.

Ask the students: 'What are your dreams for the future?'

Students have the opportunity to discuss their answers, write them on post-its, or to reflect on their responses without sharing with the group.

Ice-Breaker   5 mins

Materials: Drawing of left hand from Activity 3.6 (p. 218), or Worksheet 3.16 (p. 222) (one each); coloured pens, coloured pencils.

Provide the students with the drawings created in Activity 3.6 (or their copies of Worksheet 3.16).

Unfold the paper and ask the students to draw around their right hand on the other side of the paper (they may wish to draw around each other's' hands if this is easier).

The right hand represents the future and their hopes moving forward. As with the left hand, ask the students to fill their hand with drawings of the future. They do not need to draw each thing; they can include writing or even a colour or pattern that represents something. Ask the group to consider these elements:

- key moments
- key people
- important events
- important feelings
- key places
- special pets

They may then want to compare their two hands, past and future.

Core Activity 1: Preferred Future   20 mins

Materials: Worksheet 3.20 'Preferred Future' (p. 229) (one each); coloured pencils.

Identifying our preferred future is an important step in the process of behavioural change. For this activity, the group is asked to consider: What would you like to be like in the future?

To answer this question, suggest that they might set goals for different areas of their lives. Give each person a copy of Worksheet 20.3 and ask them to draw a quick sketch of themselves in each of the three mirrors, to represent themselves in 5 years', 10 years' and 20 years' time. If they would rather, they could write key words inside the mirrors, rather than making drawings of themselves.

Then ask them to consider, and record on the worksheet, their goals in the following areas:

- What kind of person would they like to be?
- What kind of friends and family would they like to have?
- What kind of school/job would they like to be in?
- What kind of place would they like to live in?
- What kind of hobbies would they like to have?

It will be important to emphasise the choices they have and the potential benefits they can gain from the choices they make. It is never too late to make good choices, and this process starts by identifying one area to improve and setting an appropriate goal with regard to that.

It may be difficult for some of the group to identify future plans, so it can be helpful in these circumstances to consider the opposite of the task. What kind of future do you *not* want? This may prompt them to consider what they *do* want.

Core Activity 2: Looking Forward   10 mins

Materials: Worksheet 3.21 'Looking Forward' (p. 232) (one each, plus spares).

The aim of this activity is to provide a positive and strengths-based structure to allow the young people to look ahead and identify their hopes for themselves and their relationships with others. This is about imagining an ideal future and then exploring it in depth.

This is a personal activity and the young people will not be asked to share their worksheets. The group may be offered additional copies of the worksheet if they want to develop their ideas independently, or discuss these further with either you or another trusted adult.

Reflections & Feedback   5 mins

Materials: Facilitator Guide 1 'Reflections & Feedback' (p. 262).

Ask the students to focus on the questions on the facilitator guide.

Target-Setting   5 mins

Materials: Worksheet 1.4 'My Targets' (p. 30) (one each); pens.

Use Worksheet 1.4 to support each student in setting their weekly targets. They can do this in pairs and support each other to identify what they would like to work on during the coming week. Allow a little time for reflection on the achievement (or otherwise) of the previous week's targets.

Compliments to Close   5 mins

Materials: Each individual's 'Golden Scroll' & a gold permanent marker each; Facilitator's Guide 2 'The Golden Scroll' (p. 263).

The guide will support you in directing the group as they add positive comments to their Golden Scrolls.

Relaxation   10 mins

Materials: Facilitator Guide 3 'Guided Relaxation' (p. 264).

Use the script on the facilitator guide to support the students in deep relaxation.

Worksheet 3.20
Preferred Future

Activity 3.7

5 YEARS' TIME...

Personal Goal: _____

_____

Friends and Family Goal: _____

_____

School/Work Goal: _____

_____

Home Goal: _____

_____

Hobbies Goals: _____

_____

page 1 of 3

Worksheet 3.20
Preferred Future

Activity 3.7

10 YEARS' TIME...

Personal Goal: _____

_____

Friends and Family Goal: _____

_____

School/Work Goal: _____

_____

Home Goal: _____

_____

Hobbies Goals: _____

_____

page 2 of 3

Worksheet 3.20
Preferred Future

Activity 3.7

20 YEARS' TIME...

Personal Goal: _____

_____

Friends and Family Goal: _____

_____

School/Work Goal: _____

_____

Home Goal: _____

_____

Hobbies Goals: _____

_____

Worksheet 3.21
Looking Forward

Activity 3.7

Choose a timeframe to think about for this activity. It could be to your next birthday or one year from now.

Timeframe:

What would you like to achieve during this timeframe?

What are you looking forward to during this timeframe? Try to give at least 4 examples.

Worksheet 3.21
Looking Forward

Activity 3.7

What relationships would you like to strengthen during this timeframe? What would these stronger relationships look like?

What could you do to help/support others during this timeframe?

In your ideal future, how will your life be different at the end of this timeframe? Give specific details.

page 2 of 2

Activity 3.8
Evaluation

Aims

* For the students to feel safe & confident to participate in the session
* For the students to feel connected and be able to identify the strengths within their group
* To evaluate situations in which it might be appropriate to request additional support
* To begin to consider who the students might be able to turn to for support in the future

Group Rules   2 mins

Materials: Worksheet 1.1 'Visual Timetable' (p. 27); Group Rules Chart created in Activity 1.1.

Using Worksheet 1.1 and the Group Rules Chart, remind the group of the structure of each session and of the rules that were agreed in Activity 1.1.

Talk Time   5 mins

Materials: Post-it notes.

Ask the students: 'Who can you go to for support?'

Students have the opportunity to discuss their answers, write them on post-its, or to reflect on their responses without sharing with the group.

Ice-Breaker   5 mins

Materials: Worksheet 3.22 'Bricks' (p. 238) (2 copies each, cut into individual bricks); bricks (or brick alternative), stickers, coloured pens, stapler, large sheet of paper/wallpaper, photographs of group members.

The group will cooperate to build a 'positive wall', brick by brick. Ideally this forms a 2D or 3D display, with each brink representing a positive thing about an individual or the group as a whole.

Provide the students with a pile of bricks or brick alternatives: 3D 'bricks' made from old boxes, or the 2D bricks on Worksheet 3.22. Ask the students to label the bricks, using photographs or the decorated names of individuals within the group to illustrate, then writing the strengths of that individual next to their name or photograph, for example: friendly, resilient, discrete. Some bricks may be used to describe the strengths of the group as a whole.

Once everyone has completed at least 2 bricks, you should have enough to begin to build your wall. You might want to build a physical 3D wall, or perhaps staple the 2D wall to a large sheet of paper or roll of wallpaper.

Core Activity 1: Situations Circles   15 mins

Materials: Worksheets 3.23 'Situations Circles' (p. 239) (cut up, one set per pair) & 3.24 'Decision Grid' (p. 240) (one per pair).

This activity focuses on asking for support or help and the role of others in helping us to be assertive. Remind the group that **assertiveness is about developing the skills to identify and communicate our feelings and needs**. Mention that sometimes we can do this on our own, and at others we need support – these are times when we are in danger and at risk. It is not always easy to recognise these situations.

Ask everyone to find a partner. Each pair has a copy of the Situations Circles on Worksheet 3.23 and must use the headings on the Decision Grid (Worksheet 3.24) to sort their Circles into the following categories:

- **NO:** I can deal with this on my own
- **YES:** I need to get some support from someone with this
- **MAYBE:** I might need to get some support from someone with this

Once all the situations have been sorted, open up some discussion by comparing the different decisions that have been made: there is no right or wrong answer for many of the situations. The key is to engage in open discussion and ensure that everyone is listened to and able to express their opinion.

Discuss one Situation Circle that has been placed in the 'Yes' pile and brainstorm **WHO** the person in the circle could go to, **HOW** they might do this and **WHAT** outcome they might be looking for.

> Attention: It is important not to ignore and dismiss any past negative experiences of help-seeking, and to clarify that this exercise is not about telling the girls that they should seek help from professionals.

Core Activity 2: Trust Map   15 mins

Materials: Worksheet 3.25 'Sources of Support' (p. 241) (one each); large piece of paper each, coloured pencils, pens, glue, magazines, one photograph of each group members, small post-it notes, rulers.

The group are asked to make their own personal Trust Map, which enables them to think about who they might turn to for support and how they might do this (Worksheet 3.25 offers some suggestions).

Make the map as follows:

1. Each person takes a large piece of paper and places an image to represent themselves in the centre of the page. They may do this in any way they wish: a stick person, a drawing, a photo, their name, a picture of something that they like.

2. On post-it notes, the students should write down, or draw, any person/agency/professional/group that has ever helped or supported them. Reflection time will be needed for this, as well as discussion of what is meant by 'help' and 'support'. Broad definitions of these concepts should be used, so as to generate as many names as possible.

3. Next they position the post-it notes on their sheets – the nearer they place the post-it to the representation of themselves, the more important they feel this person or agency is.

4. Now each person uses single or double arrows to show 'reciprocity': those on the sheet who the student has helped or supported in return should have a double arrow to show this; those that have helped or supported them in any way, a single arrow. Again, encourage the students to think broadly about what it means to help someone, so that they may identify when they have been helpful in return.

Conclude by drawing on similar questions to those posed at the end of Core Activity 1. Ask the students to consider **HOW** they can ask for support, focusing on three post-its they have positioned closest to them on their Trust Map.

The students should then be given Worksheet 3.25 to take away with them.

Reflections & Feedback   5 mins

Materials: Facilitator Guide 1 'Reflections & Feedback' (p. 262).

Ask the students to focus on the questions on the facilitator guide.

Target-Setting   5 mins

Materials: Worksheet 1.4 'My Targets' (p. 30) (one each); pens.

Use Worksheet 1.4 to support each student in setting their weekly targets. They can do this in pairs and support each other to identify what they would like to work on during the coming week. Allow a little time for reflection on the achievement (or otherwise) of the previous week's targets.

Compliments to Close   5 mins

Materials: Each individual's 'Golden Scroll' & a gold permanent marker each; Facilitator's Guide 2 'The Golden Scroll' (p. 263).

The guide will support you in directing the group as they add positive comments to their Golden Scrolls.

Relaxation   10 mins

Materials: Facilitator Guide 3 'Guided Relaxation' (p. 264).

Use the script on the facilitator guide to support the students in deep relaxation.

Worksheet 3.22
Bricks

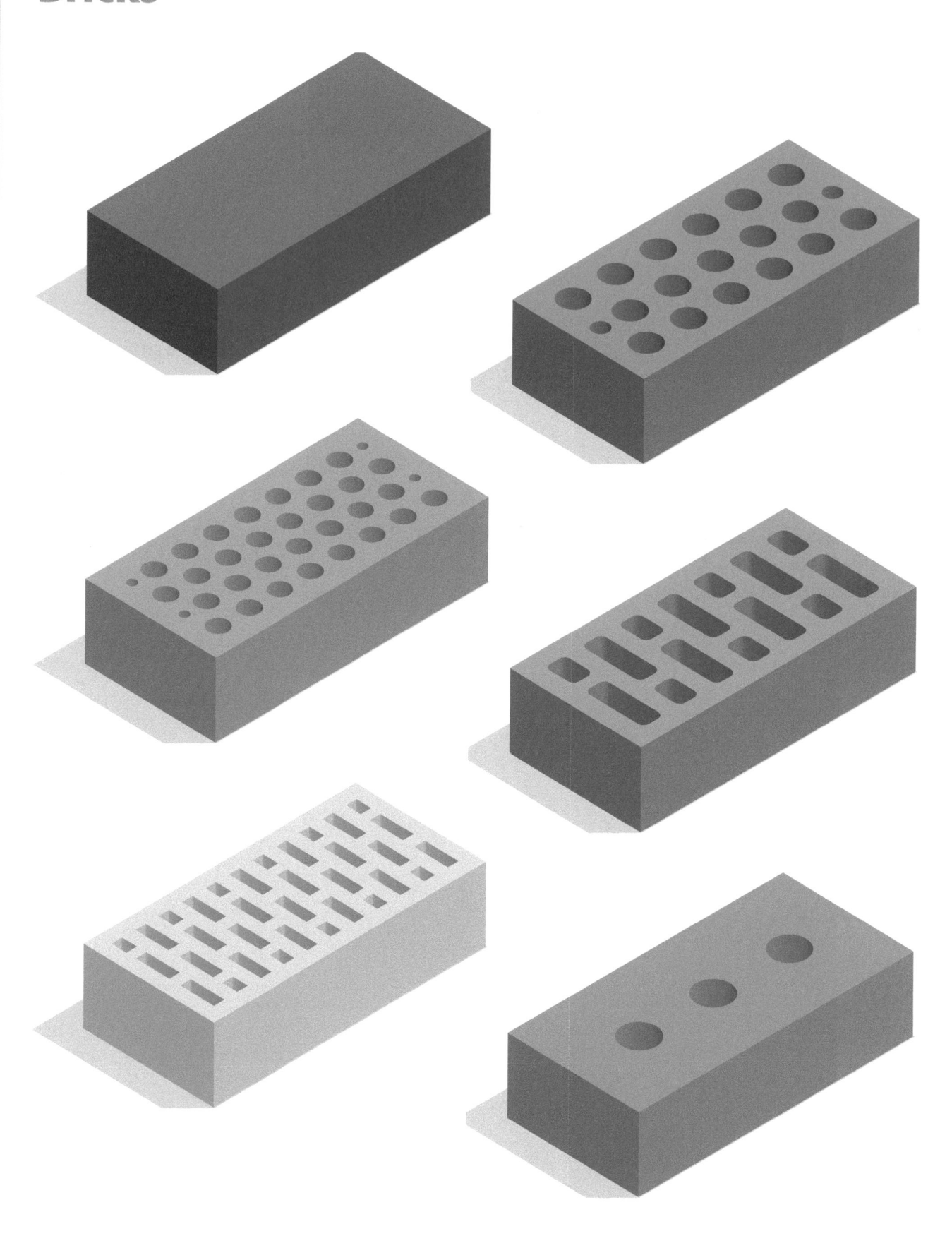

Activity 3.8

Worksheet 3.23
Situation Circles

Activity 3.8

- You think you are pregnant
- You are worried about your health
- You get into trouble at school
- Your friend is annoying you
- Your boyfriend is pressuring you to have sex with him
- You hear your dad on the phone say that you will be moving to live with your mum and her new boyfriend soon. No-one has said anything about this to you.

Worksheet 3.24
Decision Grid

Activity 3.24

NO	YES	MAYBE

Worksheet 3.25

Sources of Support

Activity 3.8

★ SOS ★

(Sources of Support)

People

▶▶ Parents _____

▶▶ Friends _____

▶▶ Head of Year _____

▶▶ SENCO _____

▶▶ Police _____

▶▶ Doctor _____

Websites

▶▶ National Autistic Society (NAS): www.autism.org.uk

▶▶ YoungMinds: www.youngminds.org.uk

Helplines

▶▶ Samaritans: phone 116 123; email jo@samaritans.org

▶▶ Childline: phone 0800 1111

Books

▶▶ *M is for Autism*, by the students of Limpsfield Grange School & Vicky Martin

▶▶ *M in the Middle*, by the students of Limpsfield Grange School & Vicky Martin

▶▶ *The Independent Woman's Handbook for Super Safe Living on the Autistic Spectrum*, by Robyn Steward

Activity 3.9
My Targets

Aims

- For the students to feel safe & confident to participate in the session
- To discuss the role of 'hope' within our lives
- To begin to move towards a positive future by establishing the need for targets
- To consider alternative support strategies for when we are unable to meet our targets

Group Rules — 2 mins

Materials: Worksheet 1.1 'Visual Timetable' (p. 27); Group Rules Chart created in Activity 1.1.

Using Worksheet 1.1 and the Group Rules Chart, remind the group of the structure of each session and of the rules that were agreed in Activity 1.1.

Talk Time — 5 mins

Materials: Post-it notes.

Ask the students: 'Why do people set themselves targets?'

Students have the opportunity to discuss their answers, write them on post-its, or to reflect on their responses without sharing with the group.

Ice-Breaker — 5 mins

Materials: Large pieces of paper (one each, or per pair), coloured pens, whiteboard or flip chart & paper, appropriate marker pens.

This warm-up activity aims to encourage the students to identify the notion and importance of hope. Having hope for the future is all about being optimistic, thinking about what we want to achieve, and being a 'doer', so that we can make things happen.

Ask the students to create a Mind Map, containing everything that comes to mind when they think of the word 'hope'. They can work alone, in pairs, or as a whole group.

You may wish to contribute to the discussion with the following thoughts:

* Hope is active; you have to do something about it/with it.
* Hope involves setting yourself a very clear goal.
* It's important to know what success means to you in order to have hope.
* Hope involves willpower, energy and persistence and doing something every day to achieve your goals; a little can achieve a lot.
* Hope means using your brains to plan how to make your goal happen (lots of things fail because they never start).
* Hope helps you to understand that there will be challenges along the way, but that these challenges are there to be overcome.
* Hope allows you to set yourself a deadline that is not too easy to achieve.
* Hope means every day imagining your goal as though you have already achieved it.

It may be useful to prompt the group to think further about hope by asking them to identify examples of people they know in the news, the media, history, or stories who have been really hopeful about the future and have consequently made things happen and achieved their goals.

Conducting this kind of inspirational discussion is very important. It is one of those 'happy habits' that we probably should engage in regularly in order to maintain motivation and further build our resilience. Thinking about and recognising our achievements can frequently give us hope for the future.

Core Activity 1: Stages of Change   15 mins

Materials: Worksheet 3.26 'Stages of Change' (p. 246) (one each); pens.

This activity encourages the group to focus on and gain a further understanding of the process of change and its potential benefits.

To begin, everyone should be supported in 1) identifying one aspect of their behaviour they wish to change and 2) asking themselves how ready, or otherwise, they are for making that change. It is also vital to emphasise that relapse is a normal and natural part of the whole cycle of change. Reassure the group that relapsing does not equate to failure – it simply means that you begin the process/cycle again.

Worksheet 3.26 describes some possible stages in the process of change that might be involved when an individual is deciding that they want to get along with teaching staff and have better results in school. It provides examples of what that person might say to themselves at each stage in the process.

1. **Pre-thinking:** the statement might be, 'I don't care if teachers don't like me. I'm really not bothered at all.'

2. **Thinking:** the statement might be, 'I realise that sometimes the lessons go better when I don't try to get on the teacher's nerves.'

3. **Deciding:** the statement might be, 'I'm going to try and get on better in more of my lessons so that people feel better about me in general.'

4. **Doing:** the statement might be, 'I'm working harder now and paying more attention in most of my lessons.

5. **Maintaining:** the statement might be, 'I haven't had a detention or a fixed-term exclusion for over six weeks now.'

6. **Relapsing:** the statement might be, 'I told Mr Francis where to go when he told me I wasn't trying hard enough in my maths project.'

Encourage the group to formulate their own examples of what they might say to themselves at each stage in the process of changing the aspect of their behaviour they have chosen to focus on. Using their own experience, they can record their statements/thoughts in the empty boxes on Worksheet 3.26.

Core Activity 2: Relapse Planning   15 mins

Materials: Worksheet 3.27 'Relapse Plan' (p. 247) (one each); pens.

When we relapse and revert back to old behaviour after trying hard to change it, we can feel angry or sad and experience some difficult emotions and questions:

- Why did I let myself down?
- Why did this go wrong?
- Why couldn't I be successful?

We can have a tendency to blame ourselves or others for this and to get caught up in a negative cycle of thinking and behaviour, falling into the self-fulfilling prophecy trap.

Encourage the group to work through the Relapse Plan on Worksheet 3.27, in order to plan in advance for what they might do if they relapse during the process of changing the behaviour they have chosen to focus on during this activity.

Reflections & Feedback 5 mins

Materials: Facilitator Guide 1 'Reflections & Feedback' (p. 262).

Ask the students to focus on the questions on the facilitator guide.

Target-Setting 5 mins

Materials: Worksheet 1.4 'My Targets' (p. 30) (one each); pens.

Use Worksheet 1.4 to support each student in setting their weekly targets. They can do this in pairs and support each other to identify what they would like to work on during the coming week. Allow a little time for reflection on the achievement (or otherwise) of the previous week's targets.

Compliments to Close 5 mins

Materials: Each individual's 'Golden Scroll' & a gold permanent marker each; Facilitator's Guide 2 'The Golden Scroll' (p. 263).

The guide will support you in directing the group as they add positive comments to their Golden Scrolls.

Relaxation 10 mins

Materials: Facilitator Guide 3 'Guided Relaxation' (p. 264).

Use the script on the facilitator guide to support the students in deep relaxation.

Worksheet 3.26
Stages of Change

Activity 3.9

Sample behaviour I'd like to change: 'I'd like to get along with my teachers better and work harder in school'.

Pre-thinking: I don't care if teachers don't like me, I'm really not bothered at all

Thinking: I realise that sometimes the lessons go better when I don't try to get on the teacher's nerves

Deciding: I'm going to try and get on better in more of my lessons so that people feel better about me in general

Doing: I'm working harder now and paying more attention in most of my lessons

Maintaining: I haven't had a detention or a fixed term exclusion for over six weeks now

Relapsing: I told Mr Francis where to go when he told me I wasn't trying hard enough in my maths project

Worksheet 3.27
Relapse Plan

Activity 3.9

Coping with Relapse & Making the Plan

When we relapse and revert back to old behaviour after trying hard to change it, we can feel angry or sad and experience some difficult emotions and questions. *Why did I let myself down? Why did this go wrong? Why couldn't I be successful?* We can have a tendency to blame ourselves or others for this and to get caught up in a negative cycle of thinking and behaviour, falling into the self-fulfilling prophecy trap.

What we SHOULD do is make a plan for when we relapse! Work through the stepped approach as follows:

* **Identify the change that you would like to make now:**

  _____

  _____

* **If you relapse, identify the following:**

  1. Who will help me to talk it through and give me the best support, advice and encouragement? My residential worker? A friend? A member of my family?

     _____

  2. What 3 practical steps will I take to try again? What should I think about? What can I plan to do?

     a _____

     b _____

     c _____

page 1 of 2

Worksheet 3.27

Relapse Plan

Activity 3.9

3 Identify how these steps are better or more appropriate than the ones I took last time:

   a _____

   b _____

   c _____

4 I will take my three steps in this order:

   a _____

   b _____

   c _____

5 What self-talk or script can I develop to feel positive again about trying once more?

   _____
   _____
   _____

6 My 'top talk' script will be as follows:

   _____
   _____
   _____
   _____
   _____

Activity 3.10
My Targets 2

Aims

- For the students to feel safe & confident to participate in the session
- For the students to increase their understanding of what a goal is and why we set them
- To identify individual goals and targets for the future
- To reflect on the personal learning journey each student has undertaken and to leave the group with a positive outlook on the future

Group Rules — 2 mins

Materials: Worksheet 1.1 'Visual Timetable' (p. 27); Group Rules Chart created in Activity 1.1.

Using Worksheet 1.1 and the Group Rules Chart, remind the group of the structure of each session and of the rules that were agreed in Activity 1.1.

Talk Time — 5 mins

Materials: Post-it notes.

Ask the students: 'What will you remember from coming to this group?'

Students have the opportunity to discuss their answers, write them on post-its, or to reflect on their responses without sharing with the group.

Ice-Breaker — 5 mins

Materials: Worksheet 3.28 'Famous Goals' (p. 253) (one each). You will need to source photos of these or other famous people and copy them onto the worksheet.

Ask everyone to look at the photos of the four celebrities on Worksheet 3.28 (Lionel Messi, Jacqueline Wilson, Gemma Collins and Justin Bieber).

As a group, discuss what targets these celebrities might have set themselves over the past 5 to 10 years. Consider things such as:

- Why did they set themselves these targets?
- Who else might have a similar target?
- Do any of the targets overlap with the other celebrities/students in the group?

Core Activity 1: Target-Setting 10 mins

Materials: Worksheets 3.29 'SMART Targets' (p. 254) & 3.30 'Target-Setting' (p. 255) (one each).

In some approaches to behavioural change young people are encouraged to identify personal goals, but this is not always done in a SMART (**S**pecific, **M**easurable, **A**chievable, **R**ealistic, **T**imely) manner, and the goals are very rarely separated out into long-term and short-term aims. It is also quite unusual to clearly specify the action steps needed to reach the goals.

This activity aims to ensure that the students work through the target-setting process in a systematic way, stating the problem and then identifying short-term goals and action steps that will bring them nearer their long-term goals.

Give everyone a copy of Worksheets 3.29 and 3.30. Tell them to consider the criteria of a SMART target listed on Worksheet 3.29, and explain to them that overall goals or ambitions can be achieved, step-by-step, if we set ourselves short-term SMART targets.

Tell the group that Worksheet 3.30 offers them a framework for setting their goals.

1. Reflect on a behaviour you want to change, or are already working on, and then identify a problem area or area of concern that will need to be overcome.

2. State the problem: what is it that you want to do differently? Clarify this. Present the problem in the form of a 'how to' statement.

3. Long-term goal: what would be different in your life if you changed your behaviour and how will you know that things are better for you and others around you?

4. Short-term/SMART goal: this goal must be achievable within 30 days. What would be different over the next few days and weeks if you make this change? What will you be doing or saying differently as a result of the change? What is the greatest barrier to change?

5. Action steps: write down a list of action steps that will be achieved in order to meet the short-term goal.

6   Finally set a date when you will review this with someone who is important to you and has your best interests at heart. (You may need to support the students in identifying this person. It might be that you volunteer to be that person for them).

Core Activity 2: My Positive Future   20 mins

Materials: Worksheets 3.31 'Front Cover' (p. 256), 3.32 'Things I Want in My Future' (p. 257), 3.33 'Sentence Stems' (p. 259) & 3.34 'My Top Three' (p. 260) (one each of all); glue, scissors, coloured pencils, hole punch and treasury tags (or stapler), sheets of A4 (per person).

During the activity the group are asked to identify things they want, need and hope for and to make a booklet that describes the future they wish to make reality. The activity should provide long-term support for the students and draws the ASD Girl's Toolkit sessions to a hopeful conclusion.

Before starting to make up the booklet, allow 5 to 10 minutes for people to discuss 'My Positive Future' with a partner.

Make up the booklet as follows:

1   Illustrate the front cover of your booklet, 'My Positive Future', using Worksheet 3.31.

2   Sort the images on Worksheet 3.32 into 'things I want' and 'things I don't want'. Stick these into your booklet under the two headings.

3   Complete Worksheet 3.33 and add it to your booklet.

4   Use Worksheet 3.34 to write about or illustrate the three key things you hope for in the future, for example: to work as a personal trainer, to feel safe, to get a pet, to feel better, to improve my maths, to have a relationship, to live in the country, to travel to new places, and so on.

Once complete, attach the individual pages together to create a booklet for each student. They can then share booklets as they wish. They may like to take them away to show their class teacher, family or friends. They may like to keep building up their booklets over time with any information or ideas linked to their positive future.

Reflections & Feedback   5 mins

Materials: Facilitator Guide 1 'Reflections & Feedback' (p. 262).

Ask the students to focus on the questions on the facilitator guide.

Target-Setting 5 mins

Materials: Worksheet 1.4 'My Targets' (p. 30) (one each); pens.

Use Worksheet 1.4 to support each student in setting their weekly targets. They can do this in pairs and support each other to identify what they would like to work on during the coming week. Allow a little time for reflection on the achievement (or otherwise) of the previous week's targets.

Compliments to Close 5 mins

Materials: Each individual's 'Golden Scroll' & a gold permanent marker each; Facilitator's Guide 2 'The Golden Scroll' (p. 263).

The guide will support you in directing the group as they add positive comments to their Golden Scrolls.

Relaxation 10 mins

Materials: Facilitator Guide 3 'Guided Relaxation' (p. 264).

Use the script on the facilitator guide to support the students in deep relaxation.

Worksheet 3.28

Activity 3.10

Famous Goals

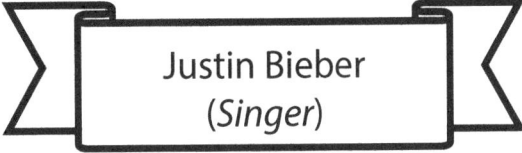

Lionel Messi
(*Footballer*)

Jacqueline Wilson
(*Author*)

Gemma Collins
(*TV Personality*)

Justin Bieber
(*Singer*)

Worksheet 3.29
SMART Targets

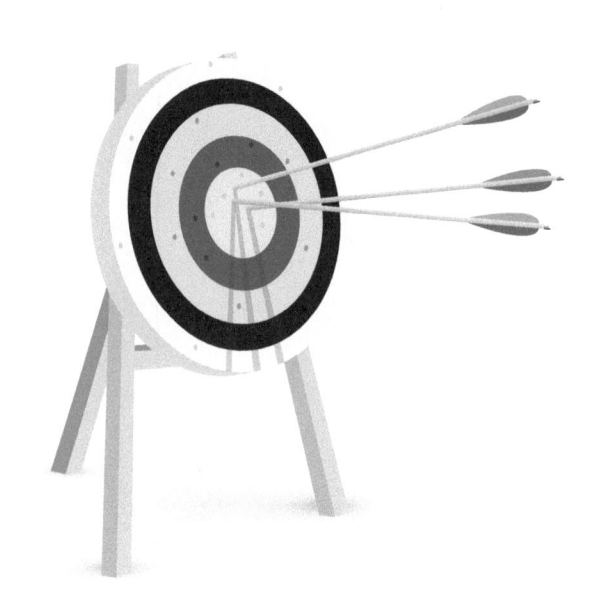

Specific

Measurable

Achievable

Realistic

Timely

Worksheet 3.30
Target-Setting

Activity 3.29

Target Setting

1. What behaviour do you want to change/are you already working on?

   _____

   _____

2. What is the problem? How do you want to do things differently?

   How to _____

   _____

3. My long-term goal is:

   _____

4. My short-term goal is (make sure it's SMART!):

   _____

   _____

5. Action Steps:

   a _____

   b _____

   c _____

6. Review date: _____ Reviewer: _____

P This page may be photocopied for instructional use only. *The ASD Girls' Wellbeing Toolkit* © Tina Rae & Amy Such 2019

Worksheet 3.31

Front Cover

Activity 3.10

My Positive Future

My Name _____

Worksheet 3.32

Activity 3.10

Things I Want in My Future

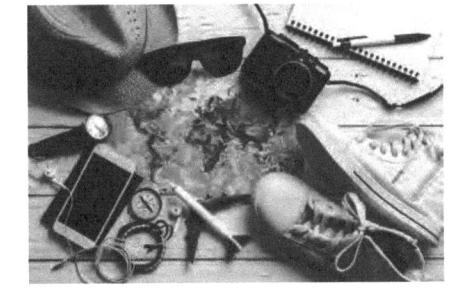

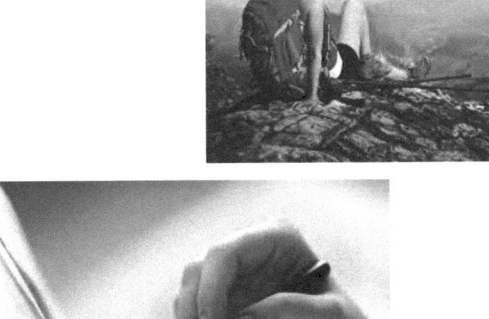

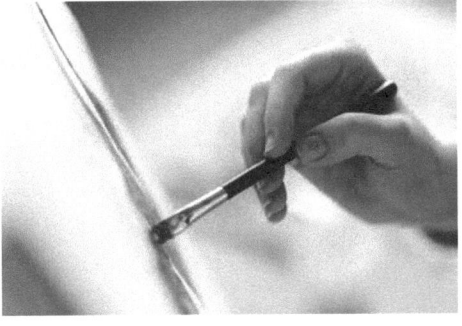

?

page 1 of 2

This page may be photocopied for instructional use only. *The ASD Girls' Wellbeing Toolkit* © Tina Rae & Amy Such 2019

Worksheet 3.32

Things I Want in My Future

Activity 3.10

Things I want ...

- -

Things I don't want ...

page 2 of 2

Worksheet 3.33
Sentence Stems

Activity 3.10

Sentence Stems

I can _____

_____

I will _____

_____

I want to _____

_____

I am excited about _____

_____

I am looking forward to _____

_____

I am interested in _____

_____

I have _____

_____

I am good at _____

_____

Worksheet 3.34
My Top Three

Activity 3.10

My Top Three

1

2

3

Resources

Facilitator Guides

Templates & Information Sheets

Useful Agencies, Websites & Support Systems

References & Bibliography

Facilitator's Guide 1
Reflections & Feedback

All activities

Use this checklist to prompt reflection at the end of each session:

- What have we learnt in this session?

- Have we increased our knowledge?

- Have we gained any further useful strategies or techniques?

- Did everyone feel supported and comfortable?

- What was the most useful?

- What was the least useful?

- How would you change or adapt this session to make it more engaging and useful for other students in the future?

Facilitator's Guide 2
The Golden Scroll

> All activities

In Activity 1.1 each member of the group has the opportunity to create their own 'Golden Scroll', which they may use to record their positive attributes and achievements throughout the series of sessions.

Group members may receive spontaneous compliments from you or other members of the group during the course of an activity. Reinforce these positives by encouraging students to identify one thing that each member of the group has done well during the session – and then make sure it is recorded on that person's 'Golden Scroll'.

You might choose to have all the group members sit in a circle and focus on each member of the group in turn. Everyone should choose an attribute or specific skill that they feel the person 'in the spotlight' has demonstrated during that session.

It will be important to ensure that each student is given a compliment. If necessary, highlight the following behaviours or responses as worthy of positive comment:

- Listening well and attentively
- Taking turns, or waiting for a turn
- Showing empathy or concern for others
- Being thoughtful
- Supporting someone who found responding or contributing difficult
- Working hard in activities during the session
- Building on others' ideas and not putting anyone down
- Overcoming any initial embarrassment or fear and trying to contribute
- Being honest and reflective about themselves
- Making a contribution
- Having a go and being positive in the session

The scrolls are added to each week and awarded to the students at the end of the programme.

Facilitator's Guide 3
Guided Relaxation

All activities

Guide students through this relaxation technique at the end of each session.

1. Sit in a chair with both feet planted firmly on the ground and legs uncrossed. Put your hands in your lap and close your eyes if you feel comfortable to do so.

2. Clench your fists – hold them, feel the tension, then let your fingers loose and relax. Feel yourself relax all over. Then repeat.

3. Bend your arms up from the elbow and tense up your biceps. Feel the tension, then stretch your arms out and let them relax. Repeat. Really feel the tension and the relaxation in your muscles.

4. Straighten up your arms so that you feel the tension in the upper parts – within the muscles on the backs of your arms. Then let your arms hang loose and feel the tension disappear. Repeat.

5. Close your eyes extremely tightly. Feel the tension in your eyelids and around your eye sockets. Then relax your eyes, still keeping them closed, and enjoy the sensation. Repeat.

6. Frown and pull the muscles in your forehead together. Then relax and feel your forehead becoming smooth and relaxed. Repeat.

7. Close your lips together tightly. Then relax and focus on the difference between the relaxed position and the tensed position. Feel yourself relax all over your face, in your mouth and in your throat. Repeat.

8. Lift your head up and let it drop back as far as you can (without any straining). Feel the tension in your neck. Move your head from left to right and right to left, feeling the tension moving into each side of your neck. Next lift your head forwards and press your chin downwards against your chest. Then return your head to an upright position and relax. Repeat.

9. Lift your shoulders up and hold in the tension – then drop and relax. Feel this relaxation spreading to your back and all the parts of your face and neck. Repeat.

Facilitator's Guide 3
Guided Relaxation

All activities

10. Concentrate on relaxing your whole body and breathe slowly in and out. Each time you exhale, imagine all the tension leaving your body. Next breathe in – inhale deeply and hold your breath. Then breathe out, feeling your chest relax. Breathe in deeply through your nose, counting slowly to five. Then exhale slowly, letting your breath free to the count of five. Repeat.

11. Next, tighten up your stomach muscles. Hold your stomach in as tightly as you can and then let the muscles relax. Concentrate on the two different sensations of tension and relaxation.

12. Next push your stomach out and hold in this position – then relax the muscles again. Repeat.

13. Tighten up your thighs and buttocks – and then release and relax. Press down on your heels and then relax. Repeat.

14. Press your feet into the floor and feel your calf-muscles tensing. Release and relax. Repeat.

15. Bend up your ankles towards your body and hold them tightly. Then release and feel them relax. Repeat.

16. Curl up your toes as tightly as you can. Hold them tightly. Relax and release them. Repeat.

17. Finally, let yourself relax all over – from your toes, through your feet, ankles, calves, shins, knees, thighs, hips, stomach and lower back. Feel the tension escape. Relax your upper back, chest, shoulder, arms and fingers. Feel your neck, jaws and facial muscles relax. Breathe in deeply and then slowly let your breath out. Count slowly from 1 to 10 and then open your eyes. You are now truly relaxed.

Letter Template 1
Letter to Parents & Carers

Dear parents/carers

There is an increasing amount of research that suggests that young people today may experience a range of issues from low self-esteem and anxiety to other behavioural difficulties. This is particularly the case for girls and young women with ASD. The wellbeing of our students is a priority for our school and therefore during this year we will be delivering a 30-session programme called 'The ASD Girls' Wellbeing Toolkit', which will specifically focus upon and support this group of girls.

The programme aims to target girls exhibiting difficulties and those who appear to be somewhat vulnerable in terms of their levels of confidence and self-esteem, in order to prevent escalation of any problems and to provide them with a range of skills and strategies that will help and support them throughout their lives. Enclosed is an information sheet that provides more information about the programme.

We hope you appreciate the importance of this programme for the personal, social and emotional development of your child and will support them as they work through the sessions.

Thank you

If you have any concerns about this programme or require any further information, please contact:

_____

Letter Template 2

Letter to Parents & Carers with Consent Form

The ASD Girls' Wellbeing Toolkit

Dear parents/carers

_____ school is offering your child the opportunity to take part in a ____ week 'Wellbeing Toolkit' Group starting on _____.

The group will be run by _____ with a member of school staff. It will take place on _____ at _____.

The programme aims to help children and young people learn a range of techniques and ideas to support their wellbeing in school and out of school.

Enclosed is an information sheet that will provide more information about the group. Please fill in and return the slip on the next page to _____ if you would like your child to take part, and please do get in touch if you would like more information.

Yours sincerely,

_____

Letter Template 2

Letter to Parents & Carers with Consent Form

Consent and Permissions

I agree to let my child participate in the sessions.

I understand that I can withdraw my child from the sessions at any time and do not have to state a reason.

Signed _____ (parent/carer)

Print name _____

Date _____

> If you have any concerns or queries about this programme, or require any further information please contact:

School information
_____

Information Sheet 1

The ASD Girls' Wellbeing Toolkit: Information for Students

Dear Student,

During this academic year we will complete a 30-session programme for girls called 'The Girls' Wellbeing Tool Kit'. We hope this leaflet answers some of the questions you may have about these sessions. Please talk to your form tutor or head of year if you would like any further information.

What is The ASD Girls' Wellbeing Toolkit?
The Girls' Wellbeing Toolkit is a 30-session programme that will help you to make positive changes in your life. Each session will teach you some new skills that will help your own personal development and give you the chance to practise these skills in a safe environment. These skills will be useful to you throughout your whole lives and at school.

What will I gain by taking part in these sessions?
The programme will help you identify behaviours you might wish to change, and you will have the opportunity to think about your wellbeing and how you can improve this – decreasing anxiety levels and increasing your confidence at school and in social settings. You will also learn about techniques and strategies from a range of therapeutic approaches to help you achieve success and reach your goals.

What will be expected of me?
You will be encouraged to listen and respond in group discussions. You will also be asked to try out strategies in each session, but you will not have to share confidential information with the rest of your group unless you want to. You will be expected to be respectful to others in your group and support each other in developing your skills and knowledge.

Information Sheet 2

The ASD Girls' Wellbeing Toolkit: Information for Parents & Carers

Promoting the mental, physical & emotional health of girls with ASD

This comprehensive 30-session programme is designed to support the development of good mental health and overall wellbeing in girls and young women with ASD. It is designed to specifically support them in managing both the internal and external pressures and stressors they may experience on a daily basis as they progress through adolescence.

We now know that if autism in girls remains undiagnosed, they are at high risk of developing mental health difficulties, such as anxiety, depression, self-harm and eating disorders. This also impacts upon their ability to engage in the learning process and, in turn, achieve their full potential. Navigating the complexities of modern media platforms is stressful for all children and young people, but there are also significant concerns for the young women on the ASD continuum who do not necessarily have the skill-set to analyse and accurately interpret the content and behaviour of other users that will enable them to manage this without experiencing high levels of stress and anxiety. These difficulties include anxiety disorders, social phobias, self-harm and eating disorders. Of most concern to many professionals has been the prevalence of self-harm behaviours within this group.

We have therefore decided to deliver a programme to specifically address these concerns and provide these young women with opportunities to develop the skills that they need within the context of a nurturing group. The programme will be ASD-friendly, with predictable session formats, ASD-friendly teaching and learning strategies, as well as opportunities for addressing individual needs and concerns.

The activities aim to:

* promote personal and social skills development
* develop pupils' self-esteem and self-awareness
* empower young people to explore the many aspects of sexuality and healthy personal relationships

- encourage pupils to accept personal responsibility for keeping the mind and body safe and healthy
- help pupils to evaluate and access confidently a range of local and national sources of information, support and advice
- address contemporary issues that are relevant to young people

Each session ensures that the following elements are considered:

- Reinforcement: copious opportunities for over-learning key skills and concepts
- Clarity: language that is very clear and explicit at all times
- Concrete examples: in each session, so as to facilitate comprehension
- Role-play: practising key social skills and problem-solving challenges met in the real world of relationships with both genders
- Structure & routine: each session structured in the same way so as to reduce anxiety. Structure emphasised at the beginning of each session and any changes discussed and prepared for
- Reading others' intentions: using role-plays in order to try to develop skills in reading behaviours
- 'I do not have to copy that': used as a mantra throughout the sessions to reinforce the importance of taking control and not being manipulated by images in the media or others' behaviours and choices
- Self-awareness: 'If I do not feel comfortable, what should I do?' Real-life examples of other girls' experiences of being used or exploited, due to not 'reading it right'. Participants supported in the development of problem-solving skills by using structured frameworks

The 30 sessions are structured as follows:

- Welcome
- Group Rules
- Talk Time
- Ice-Breaker
- 2 Core Activities
- Reflections & Feedback
- Target-Setting
- Compliments to Close
- Relaxation

Contents of the programme (which can be delivered over a whole year or used flexibly as needed) are as follows:

Part 1 (first term) – Me & My Mental Health

1. About Me
   Group Rules
   Layers of Myself

2. Physical & Mental Health
   Mental & Physical Fitness Ideas
   Key Energisers & Motivators

3. My Self-Concept
   Building Confidence
   Learning from Failure

4. Resilience
   Control Spectrum
   Noticing Beliefs

5. Self-Esteem
   My Self-Esteem
   A Good Friend

6. Managing Stress & Anxiety 1
   What is Stress?
   Stress-Busting

7. Managing Stress & Anxiety 2
   Stress versus Anxiety
   Understand Panic

8. Managing Stress & Anxiety 3
   The Worry Tree 1
   The Worry Tree 2

9. Self-Harm 1
   Amie's Story
   Keeping Safe

10. Self-Harm 2
    Letter from Sally
    My Safety Plan

Part 2 (second term) – Relationships & Communication Skills

1. Non-Verbal Communication
   Non-Verbal Communication
   Photo Stories

2. Verbal Communication
   What is Assertiveness?
   My Scripts

3. Relationships 1
   Speak & Guess Cards
   Other People

4. Relationships 2
   Beliefs about Relationships
   Good Partners versus Toxic Partners

5. Relationships 3
   Challenging Controlling Behaviour
   The Effects of Kindness

6. Sexual Behaviours
   Exploitation
   Sources of Support

7. Online Behaviours
   Online Grooming
   Online Grooming Case Study

8. Media & Other Influences 1
   Online Images
   Sexting

9 Media & Other Influences 2
Who Are You Talking To?
Safe Profiles

10 Risk-Taking
Saying 'No'
Risk

Part 3 (third term) – My Toolbox for Wellbeing & Future Health

1 Effective Thinking 1
Positive Mental Attitude (PMA)
Thoughts, Feelings, Behaviours

2 Effective Thinking 2
NAT-Bashing
Socratic Questioning

3 Relaxation & Mindfulness 1
Explaining Mindfulness
Mindful Mouthful

4 Relaxation & Mindfulness 2
Relaxation Techniques
My Mindful Timetable

5 Being Solution-Focused
Problem-Free Talk
Forgiveness

6 Future Hopes, Dreams & Realities 1
Many Selves
My Life Map

7 Future Hopes, Dreams & Realities 2
Preferred Future
Looking Forward

8 Evaluation
Situations Circles
Trust Map

9 My Targets 1
The Stages of Change
Relapse Planning

10 My Targets 2
Target-Setting
My Positive Future

For further information on the programme please contact _____.

You will also have the opportunity to attend an introductory training session that describes the programme in more depth on _____. Please contact _____ to receive further information about the arrangements for this event.

Information Sheet 3
Creating an ASD-Friendly Classroom

Some tried and tested ideas to support the ASD child or young person in the classroom.

Create a familiar, predictable environment

Pupils are often ritualistic in their approaches to routines and can find disruptions extremely disturbing. The following elements may contribute:

Seating plan

Using photographs and/or name labels to reinforce where each child is required to sit can provide a sense of security and order for *all* children. The child will benefit from a preferential seating position towards the front of the class and, importantly, away from busy 'traffic routes' and from constant sources of sound, such as a noisy radiator, or humming fluorescent lighting. Select a place for the child alongside peers who provide appropriate models of behaviour. It may also be helpful to give the pupil their own personal space, for example, seating the child at the end of a table rather than between two children. It may be necessary to clearly mark the boundaries of the child's space with masking tape.

The child should also be provided with a workstation within the classroom that allows the pupil to work alone. Ideally, this will consist of two tables: one for individual teaching and the other table for independent work. The tables should be positioned against a plain wall, minimising how much a child can see the rest of the class. If possible, there should be screens around the workstation to reduce distraction. Surrounding wall space should be kept free of displays and equipment should be kept in storage boxes. On the table for independent work there should be two labelled containers. Work to be completed by the child should be placed in a container on the left and finished work in a container on the right.

Visual timetable

Provide a continuous opportunity for pupils to predict activities, rewards, breaks and daily and weekly events. This visual timetable may contain photos, drawings or words, depending on the ability of the child. The child needs to be talked through the timetable at regular intervals, either daily or half-daily.

Approaches to learning

Children find it easier to cope with activities that involve rote learning or applying rules, rather than activities that require spontaneity, independence or creativity. In literacy for example, the child may struggle with comprehension, inferencing and creative writing. Difficulties with 'central coherence' (i.e., an inability to see the bigger picture) can mean that children have difficulty understanding what the point of an activity is and they can therefore be poorly motivated.

- Encourage children to make connections for themselves. The child may learn best when materials are presented in a structured, sequential format, for example: lists, multiple choices, and so on. Instructions on materials should be clear and orderly and where possible illustrated by diagrams or pictures.
- Tasks must be meaningful for the child and have a reward that is tangible and motivating.
- Opportunities will need to be provided for newly taught skills to be practised in a range of situations.
- Expectation about quantity of work output needs to be explicit and detailed. The child should be shown examples of the end product and provided with an individual 'to do' list, which divides the task up into small, specific, sequential steps.
- The child may need to be taught specific strategies to support their learning, including the use of task-planning sheets, highlighting relevant information, making a list of what has to be done, and so on. Encourage the child to predict how to go about tasks. Initially an adult will need to teach these strategies and then gradually reduce support as the child becomes more independent.
- Where possible, teach areas of the curriculum through the child's 'special interests' and also use them as a source of reward and motivation, for example: 'If you complete this work by 10.30, then you can have 10 minutes to work on your project'.
- Do not attempt to stop harmless ritualistic behaviour, such as rocking or flapping. It may be the only way the individual has of calming down. Provide an appropriate time and place for this behaviour to take place.
- If appropriate, provide the child with opportunities to show knowledge and understanding of topics in ways that require little or no writing. Alternative ways of recording may include use of a computer, tape recorder or dictaphone.

Tailored communication

* Instructions should be short, simple and to the point, and delivered in small 'chunks' with time in between to allow the child space to process the information.
* Provide opportunities for the child to pre-learn subject-specific vocabulary.
* Instructions may also need to be repeated individually, emphasising what is to be done rather than what is not to be done.
* Let the child know in advance the question you want to ask them and tell them you will ask them the question after a certain amount of time.
* If the child appears confused, stressed or agitated, or does not do as asked, speak LESS rather than MORE, emphasise key words and repeat instructions rather than rephrasing them.
* Reinforce the verbal message with visual cues such as symbols or picture sequences and, if the child can read, write down key instructions.
* Sharing equipment is very difficult, so provide the child with the necessary labelled equipment and plan opportunities to teach the child how to share and take turns.

Friendships

The child will need to be given clear, explicit information about how to behave in particular social situations and why other people behave in the way they do. It is important not to assume that the child will read 'between the lines' and work out what is happening. The child may need to be taught about everyday social situations, such as: how to tell if someone is joking (as opposed to bullying); how another person might be feeling in specific situations; and how to tell if someone had done something 'on purpose' (rather than by accident). It may also be necessary to teach the child the particular behaviours to deal with routine situations, such as eating lunch in the canteen and how to behave in assembly. The pupil may need to be praised and rewarded for specific appropriate social behaviour that may be taken for granted in other children.

Managing behaviour

Pupils may have anxieties that are intense and may lead to challenging behaviour. Sensory difficulties can also be the trigger for difficult behaviour. As behaviour is always determined by what is going on in the environment, there is always a trigger for it. It is therefore essential to identify the trigger and any possible reinforcers by:

* Defining the behaviour
* Gathering information: when/where the behaviour occurs, what it looks like, the frequency of the behaviour

- Examine what happens before, during and after the behaviour
- Identify the cause of the behaviour
- Plan an intervention and monitor it. One strategy may be to enable the children to monitor their anxiety levels by using a 'feelings thermometer' in order to assess themselves where they are on the scale and if they need to take action to prevent the anxiety level rising further
- Allow the use of a special place to withdraw to when the child becomes anxious.

Information Sheet 4
Parents & Carers: Autism in Girls

What does autism in girls look like?

In simple terms – it looks different. Boys with ASD tend to be less social than their peers and display prominent and obvious areas of obsessive interests and compulsions. In contrast, girls with autism appear to be more able to follow or imitate social actions. In the early years they can mimic socially appropriate behaviour without understanding what they are doing, or why they are doing it. This can result in the masking of their difficulties and we feel that this is directly linked to the under-diagnosis of autism in girls.

Social interaction

Girls with autism are often aware of and feel the need to socially interact. They can join in play, but are often led by their peers. They may not initiate social contact, but will react to it, and can appear socially passive or socially odd. They feel that they would like to have friends, but do not understand how to make friends. This can cause much unhappiness and create feelings of isolation.

Social communication can be difficult, since ASD girls may not understand why we would want to communicate with other people.

Recognising facial expressions and what emotions they express can be challenging for girls with autism, making it hard for them to read a situation. This can mean that people's responses to them are surprising and bewildering. Appropriate social communication can be difficult, with the girls having little or no understanding about social hierarchies. This can result in them speaking to adults as though they were their friends, and not changing their language to suit the social situation they are in. This can cause problems at school and in wider society.

Imagination

Often girls on the spectrum have a good imagination and, compared to boys with autism, are relatively good at 'pretend play'. They can spend time indulging in elaborate fantasy worlds, which can be complex and full of detail, and can be sustained over long periods of time. Their fantasy world can dominate play; the girls might be able to talk about their world in depth, and often the line between fantasy and reality can become blurred.

Girls with autism often have special interests. When they are young, these interests can include age-appropriate topics, such as horses or animals, boy bands or certain books or films. This is, in itself, not unusual. It is the intensity of their interest and how long the special interest lasts that will be different.

As other girls move on to other areas of interest, girls with autism often do not. This causes gaps to appear between their social development and that of their peers, often resulting in them becoming increasingly socially isolated as areas of common ground disappear.

Sensory needs

Sensory needs can also add to an already complicated picture.

Autistic girls may be particularly sensitive to loud noises, bright lights or touch; may hate wearing tight clothing or particular fabrics; or, conversely, may love to be tucked into very tight clothes, or need to have their hair tied back in a tight ponytail.

Eating issues & self-harm

Eating can be a difficult area for parents to manage, with girls only prepared to try certain foods and textures. Not eating or controlling their food intake is another characteristic, and there is ongoing research into the prevalence of anorexia amongst women and girls with Asperger's.

There is also a direct link to self-harming behaviours, which some may resort to in order to manage their feelings of extreme anxiety or social isolation. It is important to further investigate both areas to empower yourself and ensure that you access the appropriate professional support if necessary.

Anxiety & meltdowns

A high level of anxiety is common among girls with autism, for whom the world can be a confusing and unpredictable place. To minimise this, they may need to exert a high level of control on their environment and the people in it. This can result in quite ritualised behaviour, inflexible routines and meltdowns when unplanned events occur.

Autistic girls are often 'people pleasers' and will spend all day at school trying very hard to conform. As a result home life often suffers, as they vent their frustration and anxiety for hours at the end of every school day when they are in a context in which they feel that they do not have to conform and hold in all the anxiety that they have been experiencing.

Helping your autistic daughter

* Clear routines and structure at home can be helpful. A timetable of what is happening, with pictures, can help to make a girl feel less anxious or nervous.

* Communication is essential and it is vital to make everything explicit. Explain why you are doing something, or why you talk to someone in a certain way.

* You can use egg timers or sand clocks to count down at the end of an activity, so that changing activity or focus does not come as a surprise.

* It is important to try to identify triggers for crisis points or meltdowns. You can create a calm box in your home, and if it looks as if anxiety or anger is building, use it to avoid meltdown moments. Fill it with items such as stress balls, toys that light up or reflect light, tactile toys – or any other object or tool that you know helps your child to calm down.

* Display clear visual rules in your home and refer to them. This will generally mirror the approach taken by your child's school.

* Talk about emotions as they happen and name/label them to help her understand how she feels physically and the label for the emotion she is experiencing.

* Explain, explain, check understanding and explain again. Reinforcement is key.

Keep optimistic, as we know that with appropriate support and intervention, girls with autism can become successful, self-aware, happy and independent young people.

Information Sheet 5
Tips for Teens Managing Stress & Anxiety

> **Stress** is a feeling of mental strain that can affect your wellbeing
>
> **A stressor** is anything that causes stress, for example, exams
>
> **Anxiety** is an unhelpful feeling of intense fear that affects your wellbeing
>
> **A phobia** is an intense fear of something that poses little or no actual danger
>
> **A panic attack** is a rush of intense anxiety with physical symptoms, for example, shortness of breath
>
> **Remember:** A bit of stress can help you do things (e.g., try something new), but too much can be bad for your wellbeing. You are the best person to notice what 'too much' is.

- Try to identify your stressors. Sometimes keeping a journal can help you do this.
- Try to identify what it feels like when you are stressed. Draw or write it down.
- Try to identify what calms you down and makes you feel good, and plan it in.
- Think about sharing this knowledge with friends, family, or teachers.
- Remember that lots of people feel stressed and anxious and that stress and anxiety can both be managed and treated. Don't suffer in silence; think about who you could talk to, or where you could go for help.
- Here are a few places that might be helpful to find out more:
    * https://www.apa.org/helpcenter/stress-teens.aspx
    * http://kidshealth.org/en/teens/stress.html

A few stress-busting ideas to consider

- Plan in some exercise
- Spend time with people who make you feel good
- Write or draw a journal
- Spend time with pets
- Get a Mindfulness app on your phone and build some meditation into your day

Information Sheet 5

- Join a yoga class
- Recognise the rituals and routines that make you feel good
- Keep a gratitude diary – write down one thing each day that you are grateful for, however small
- Do some small acts of kindness
- Watch 'Melvin and the Magical Mixed Media Machine' on YouTube
- Write a list of things you are good at
- Get a friend or family member to write a list of things you are good at
- Watch a film
- Listen to music
- Grow something
- Play
- Volunteer
- Write a letter

Information Sheet 6
Parents, Carers & Staff: Self-Harm

A common concern for parents, carers and staff is that talking about self-harm may make more students think about doing it. We have included this topic in *The ASD Girls' Wellbeing Toolkit* as we know that the evidence, in fact, suggests that the opposite is true, and this is clearly an area of concern for many of our young people. Talking to young people about self-harm is going to give them knowledge, confidence and an understanding of how to support themselves and others. The role of the facilitator in the sessions is to demystify a topic that can be very powerful and upsetting for young people. By talking about it and signposting support, young people can be empowered.

Key facts to hold in mind

- The prevalence statistics suggest that perhaps one in 12 young people self-harm. However, given that self-harm is very under-reported, the real figure is thought to be much higher. This conservative statistic suggests that in a class of 30 young people, at least two will have self-harmed at some point. *Therefore it is crucial to signpost young people towards appropriate within-school support (such as a school counsellor) at the start of the ASD Girls' programme.* It is vital to keep this in mind.

- If a young person discloses self-harm, the person they are most likely to tell is a peer – not a family member or teacher. Therefore, it is likely that other young people in the group will have experienced the stress, worry and upset of having been confided in by a friend about their self-harm. This is incredibly isolating for young people and one focus of the sessions will be to develop the confidence of young people to know how to support their friends and point them towards the right help.

- Self-harm among young people is the number one issue affecting their peer group that young people themselves are concerned about, in a list that includes gangs, bullying, drug use and binge drinking.

- Three in four young people don't know where to turn to talk about self-harm.

- Only one in 10 young people are comfortable seeking self-harm advice from teachers, parents or GPs, whereas over half would go online, despite only one in five thinking that is where they should be going.

Dispelling the myths

Self-harm is a topic surrounded by myths and misunderstandings, which make it even more difficult for young people to seek the help that they need. Challenging these myths and developing confidence for staff and young people is vitally important.

Self-harm is not usually a suicide attempt, or a cry for attention; instead, it is often a way for young people to release overwhelming emotions, a way of coping. So, whatever the causes, it should be taken seriously. We have addressed some of the myths surrounding self-harm in the table below:

Statement		What are the FACTS?
It's just a phase – they will grow out of it	Myth	Self-harm is not about being young or immature. When someone self-harms they are coping with more than they feel that they can manage.
		People of any age can self-harm as a way of trying to cope with emotional pain, trauma, stress, or other issues. Some people who have self-harmed as young people will turn to this coping mechanism again in adulthood when they experience stress or difficult life-events.
		People do not 'grow out' of self-harming behaviours. The way to make progress is through developing alternative coping mechanisms. To develop alternative coping mechanisms people need time and support.
		It is vital to understand self-harm as a coping mechanism. Some young people will self-harm infrequently and others do so regularly. Some people will self-harm consistently for a number of years, or when they experience particular difficulties or stresses in their life.
		Self-harm is not a phase, it is a coping mechanism. Therefore, in addressing self-harm, it is vital to address the underlying issues that are causing distress. If you tell someone who is self-harming to 'just stop it', this will not be helpful, but is likely to alienate them further. It will not work, because it does not help the person to address what is causing them to self-harm. It is also likely to make a young person feel guilty, ashamed and/or pressured.
		To make positive progress young people need support to develop alternative coping strategies.

Statement		What are the FACTS?
They are doing it to get attention	Myth	Seeing self-harm as 'attention seeking' is incredibly common. The opposite is true and it is important to start seeing self-harm as 'attention needing'. Self-harm is a very personal and private thing and considerable research has shown that people who self-harm will make lot of effort to hide it. The vast majority of self-harm is never reported. When self-harm does bring attention, that attention is usually negative attention. For some young people self-harm is to cope with a difficult situation – they will deal with it in private and cover it up. Self-harm is not a manipulative behaviour. Sometimes it is seen that way, because it is upsetting for those close to the young person who is self-harming. However, many young people are not aware of the impact that their self-harm is having on those around them. Sometimes young people do not know how to ask for the help that they need. So, instead, they might show a friend an injury they have caused themselves, or send them a photo. This can feel very overwhelming and young people need to know that it is okay to tell a trusted adult when this happens and that this is not a betrayal of their friend's trust. Others are very aware of this and find it even more isolating and upsetting to know that they are upsetting people who they care about. This results in feelings of guilt and shame and makes it even harder for young people to talk about what is happening for them. It is important to focus on the fact that seeking help usually will come after weeks, months or even years of hiding self-harm and feeling shame and guilt. When someone does disclose self-harm it requires real bravery. Self-harm can be usefully seen as a communication – a young person who is self-harming is expressing (to themselves): 'This is a bad situation; I am not in a good place and I am finding it hard to cope.'

Information Sheet 6

Statement		What are the FACTS?
Self-harm is only done by girls	Myth	It is not at all true that only girls or women self-harm. It is also not true that it is 'mostly' women who self-harm. A number of studies show that both men and women will self-harm. Self-harm is a behaviour people use to cope with emotional difficulties or stressful situations. Self-harm is not based on whether you are a man or woman.
If the injury is small, it is no problem	Myth	It can be easy to think that if the damage done to a person's body is bad, then this means someone is more seriously emotionally distressed. This is not true at all. The seriousness of the self-harm does not link to the level of distress. The physical side of self-harm does not necessarily reflect the emotional issues/stresses. Someone can feel extremely distressed and their self-harm can appear relatively minor. It is important to care for any wounds or other injuries. But the main focus needs to be on the factors that caused the young person to self-harm. If a young person is self-harming, this is never okay, even if they do not leave damage on their body. If someone is self-harming, it means that they are in distress and all people in distress need help and support.
Self-harm is a 'suicide attempt'	Myth	Self-harm is a coping behaviour to try to manage emotional distress – a way of coping, rather than a 'suicide attempt'. It is a way of staying alive and coping; it is, in fact, the opposite of a 'suicide attempt'. The reason behind why people self-harm is not to take their own life. The reasons are complex. ChildLine and other support lines for young people think that unaddressed emotions such as unhappiness, anger and frustration may often be reasons for self-harm. Stresses at home or feeling powerless are reasons why young people tell us that they self-harm. Think about occasions when you have felt distressed or that you have no control. You may have cried, or gone to someone for help – these are ways of coping with upsetting feelings and events. For some young people self-harm is their way of coping with these emotions.

Statement		What are the FACTS?
It is a 'fashion' or a 'trend'	Myth	This is an important misunderstanding/myth. Self-harm is not a lifestyle choice – it is a way of coping with emotional difficulties. Young people do not self-harm because of the music they listen to, the clothes they wear, or the friends that they hang out with. Self-harm is because someone is trying to cope with difficult and stressful issues. Self-harm is done by people of all ages, genders, backgrounds, races. Anyone can be affected by self-harm.
Self-harming means that you are mentally ill	Myth	Self-harm is a behaviour; a behaviour to cope with emotional distress or stress. Self-harm is not a diagnosis. Self-harm does not *necessarily* mean that you are mentally ill. You may be experiencing significant stress at a particular time and turn to self-harm as a way of coping with this. Every one of us has a state of 'mental health', just as we all have a state of 'physical health'. Our mental health is not fixed and we can all have times when we are feeling well and times when we are not, and we may need help. The charity, Mind, have found that in a single year one in four people will experience some form of mental health problem. So, anyone can be affected. Self-harm indicates that someone is experiencing mental or emotional distress, not *necessarily* that they are mentally ill.
The only form of self-harm is cutting	Myth	This statement is a myth. Self-harm includes a large number of behaviours that are used to attempt to cope with or relieve emotional distress. Cutting is one type of behaviour, but there are many, many others. However someone harms themselves, the focus needs to be on: * Tending to any wounds/injuries * Addressing the REASON for the self-harm, the thing that is causing the emotional distress.

Information Sheet 6

Once we understand self-harm as a coping behaviour, we can start thinking of other strategies to cope in order to prevent anyone reaching the stage where they feel that they need to self-harm to manage. This is why we have included such advice in the Toolkit sessions.

Ideas might include:

- Talking to friends
- Going for a run or a walk
- Spending time with family
- Having a bath
- Watching a movie
- Spending time with a pet, for example, taking the dog for a walk
- Playing a sport
- Eating chocolate

Useful Agencies, Online Support & Books

Agencies

Ambitious About Autism: www.ambitiousaboutautism.org.uk

Autscape (organises a three day conference, run by and for adults on the autism spectrum): http://www.autscape.org/

Mind UK (information on self-harm): https://www.mind.org.uk/information-support/types-of-mental-health-problems/self-harm/#.WTP1f2yrPRM

National Autistic Society (NAS): www.autism.org.uk. NAS has developed an extremely helpful module:

> https://www.autism.org.uk/professionals/training-consultancy/online/women-and-girls.aspx
> http://www.autism.org.uk/about/what-is/gender.aspx

Selfharm UK: https://www.selfharm.co.uk/

YoungMinds UK (information on self-harm): https://youngminds.org.uk/find-help/feelings-and-symptoms/self-harm/

Online support

Asperger & ASD (online forum): http://www.asd-forum.org.uk/

Asperclick (online forum): http://asperclick.com/forum/7-friendrelationship-advice/

Asperger United Magazine (NAS magazine)

Aspie Village (a friendly UK-based social group for adults with Asperger syndrome and similar conditions): https://aspievillage.uk/

Limpsfield Grange (NAS school in Wales): https://www.youtube.com/watch?t=18&v=oZhZ0k1lyF8;

Maja Toudal (ASD public speaker & consultant): http://www.majatoudal.com/

Purple Ella (ASD blog): https://www.purpleella.com/; https://www.youtube.com/channel/UCzske-KMAJYQn84rz6oD_yA

Robyn Steward (public speaker/author with ASD) speaking about friendships, relationships & the autism spectrum: http://www.ambitiousaboutautism.org.uk/understanding-autism/are-you-age-16-25-and-on-the-spectrum/myvoice/relationships

Talia Grant interviews:

> https://www.digitalspy.com/soaps/hollyoaks/a861222/hollyoaks-talia-grant-autism-loose-women/

> https://www.youtube.com/watch?v=A0Os79fTyls

The Curly Hair Project ('social enterprise aiming to help girls and women with Asperger's Syndrome and their neuro-typical loved ones', based in Richmond, UK): http://thegirlwiththecurlyhair.co.uk.

Wrong Planet (web community for those with ASD): http://wrongplanet.net/asperger-love-searching-for-romance-when-youre-not-wired-to-connect/

Books

Steward, R. (2014) *The Independent Woman's Handbook for Super Safe Living on the Autistic Spectrum*, Jessica Kingsley Publishers, London.

The students of Limpsfield Grange school and Vicky Martin (2015) *M is for Autism*, Jessica Kingsley Publishers, London.

The students of Limpsfield Grange school and Vicky Martin (2016) *M in the Middle: Secret Crushes, Mega-colossal Anxiety and the People's Republic of Autism*, Jessica Kingsley Publishers, London.

References & Bibliography

Ajmal Y. & Rees I. (Eds), 2004, *Solutions in schools* (2nd edn), BT Press, London.

American Psychological Association (APA), 2007, *Task Force on the Sexualization of Girls*, Report of the APA Task Force on the Sexualization of Girls. Retrieved from http://www.apa.org/pi/women/programs/girls/report-full.pdf

Berg, I. K., & de Shazer, S., 1993, 'Making numbers talk: Language in therapy', in S. Friedman (ed.), *The New Language of Change: Constructive collaboration in psychotherapy*, Guilford Press, New York.

Boorman S., 2009, *NHS Health and Wellbeing: Final report*, Leeds, NHS Health and Wellbeing Review. Available at: www.nhshealthand.org

Carpenter, B., Happe, F. & Egerton, J. (eds), 2019, *Girls and Autism Educational, Family and Personal perspectives*. London: Routledge

Chida Y. & Steptoe A., 2008, 'Positive Psychological Wellbeing and Mortality: A quantitative review of prospective observational studies, *Psychosomatic Medicine* 70, pp741–56. doi: 10.1097/PSY.0b013e31818105ba.

Coid J., Yang M., Roberts A., 2006, 'Violence and Psychiatric Morbidity in the National Household Population of Britain: Public health implications', *British Journal of Psychiatry* 189, pp12–19.

Crane L., Adams F., Harper G., Welch J. & Pellicano E., 2018, 'Something Needs to Change': Mental health experiences of young autistic adults in England, *Autism*, p.477-493

Cridland E.K., Jones S.C., Caputi P. & Magee C.A., 2014, 'Being a Girl in a Boy's World: Investigating the experiences of girls with autism spectrum disorders during adolescence', *Journal of Autism and Developmental Disorders* 44, pp1261–74.

Culpin I., Mars B., Pearson R.M., Golding J., Heron J., Bubak I., Carpenter P., Magnusson C., Gunnell D. & Rai D., 2018, 'Autistic Traits and Suicidal Thoughts, Plans, and Self-Harm in Late Adolescence: Population-based cohort study', *Journal of the American Academy of Child & Adolescent Psychiatry* 57:5, pp.313–20.

References & Bibliography

Deacon B. J. & Farrell N., 2013, 'Therapist Barriers in the Dissemination of Exposure Therapy', Storch E. & McKay D. (eds), *Treating Variants and Complications in Anxiety Disorders*, Springer Press, New York.

Department for Education, 2014, *Mental Health and Behaviour in Schools*, HMSO, London.

Dweck C., 2006, *Mindset: the New Psychology of Success*, Ballantine Books : New York.

Eaton J., 2017, *A Guide to Mental Health Issues in Girls and Young Women on the Autism Spectrum: Diagnosis, intervention and family support*, Jessica Kingsley Publishers, London.

Eder D., 1995, *School Talk: Gender and adolescent culture*, Rutgers University Press, New Brunswick, NJ.

Hedley D., Uljarević M., Wilmot M., Richdale A. & Dissanayake C., 2018, 'Understanding Depression and Thoughts of Self-Harm in Autism: A potential mechanism involving loneliness', *Research in Autism Spectrum Disorders* 46, pp1–7.

Kelly, G., 1955, The Psychology of Personal Constructs. Vol. I and II. London, Norton (Reprinted by Routledge 1990)

Kester K.R. & Lucyshyn J.M., 2018, 'Cognitive Behavior Therapy to Treat Anxiety among Children with Autism Spectrum Disorders: A systematic review', *Research in Autism Spectrum Disorders* 52, pp37–50.

Keyes C.L.M., 2005, 'Mental Illness and/or Mental Health? Investigating axioms of the complete state model of health', *Journal of Consulting and Clinical Psychology* 73, pp539–48.

Keyes C.L.M., Dhingra S.S. & Simoes E.J., 2010, 'Change in Level of Positive Mental Health as a Predictor of Future Risk of Mental Illness', *American Journal of Public Health* 100(12), pp2366-71.

Krassas N., Blauw Camp J.M. & Wesselink P., 2001, 'Boxing Helena and Cosseting Eunice: Sexual rhetoric in Cosmopolitan and Playboy magazines', *Sex Roles* 44, pp751–71.

Luxford S., Hadwin J.A. & Kovshoff H., 2017, 'Evaluating the Effectiveness of a School-Based Cognitive Behavioural Therapy Intervention for Anxiety in Adolescents Diagnosed with Autism Spectrum Disorder', *Journal of Autism and Developmental Disorders* 47(12), pp3896–908.

Lyubomirsky S., Schkade D. & Sheldon K., 2005, 'Pursuing Happiness: The architecture of sustainable change', *Review of General Psychology* 9(2), pp111–31.

MacConville R.M. & Rae T., 2012, *Building Happiness, Resilience and Motivation in Adolescents: A positive psychology curriculum for wellbeing*, Jessica Kingsley Publishers, London.

Martellozzo E., Monaghan A., Adler J.R., Davidson J., Leyva R. & Horvath M.A.H., 2016, *I Wasn't Sure it Was Normal to Watch It*, NSPCC, London.

McKinley N.M. & Hyde J.S., 1996, 'The Objectified Body Consciousness Scale', *Psychology of Women Quarterly* 20, pp181–215.

Mills P., Kessler R., Cooper J. & Sullivan S., 2007, 'Impact of a Health Promotion Program on Employee Health Risks and Work Productivity', *American Journal of Health Promotion* 22(1), pp45–53.

Moran, H. J., 2006, A very personal assessment: using personal construct psychology assessment technique (Drawing the Ideal Self) with young people with ASD to explore the child's view of the self. Good Autism Practice, 7(2), October 2006, pp. 78-86.

National Institute for Health & Care Excellence, 2009, *Social and Emotional Wellbeing in Secondary Education*, NICE, London.

NHS Foundation Trust for Central & North West London, 2014, *Brent Adolescent Team Self-Harm and Safety Plan*, CAMHS & Me, HMSO, London.

Nichter M., 2000, *Fat Talk: What girls and their parents say about dieting*, Harvard University Press, Cambridge, MA.

O'Donohue W., Gold S.R. & McKay J.S., 1997, 'Children as Sexual Objects: Historical and gender trends in magazines', *Sexual Abuse: Journal of Research and Treatment* 9, pp291–301.

Olfson M., Wall M., Wang S., Crystal S., Bridge J.A., Liu S.M. & Blanco C., 2018, 'Suicide after Deliberate Self-Harm in Adolescents and Young Adults', *Pediatrics*, p.e20173517.

Pressman S.D. & Cohen S., 2005, 'Does Positive Affect Influence Health?', *Psychological Bulletin* 131, pp925–71.

Rae T., 2001, *Strictly Stress Effective Stress Management*, Lucky Duck Publishing, Bristol.

Rae T., Bunn H. &. Walshe J., 2019, *The Essential Guide to Using Positive Psychology with Children and Young People*, Hinton House Publishers, Banbury.

Rae T. & Giles P., 2018, *The Essential Guide to Using Cognitive Behaviour Therapy (CBT) with Children and Young People*, Hinton House Publishers, Banbury.

Rae T., Thomas M. & Walshe J., 2018, *The Essential Guide to Using Solution Focused Brief Therapy (SFBT) with Children and Young People*, Hinton House Publishers, Banbury.

Rae T., Walshe J. & Wood J., 2017, *The Essential Guide to Using Mindfulness with Children & Young People,* Hinton House Publishers, Banbury.

Rae T. & Weymont D., 2006, *Supporting Young People Coping with Grief, Loss and Death*, Sage Publishers, London.

Sayal K., Hornsey H., Warren S., MacDiarmid F. & Taylor E., 2006, 'Identification of Children at Risk of Attention Deficit/Hyperactivity Disorder: A school-based intervention', *Social Psychiatry and Psychiatric Epidemiology 41,* pp806–13.

Seligman, M.E.P., 2011, Flourish: A Visionary New Understanding of Happiness and Wellbeing. Free Press, New York.

Simonoff E., Pickles A. & Charman T., 2008, 'Psychiatric Disorders in Children with Autism Spectrum Disorders: Prevalence, comorbidity, and associated factors in a population-derived sample', *Journal of the American Academy of Child and Adolescent Psychiatry* 47(8), pp921–9.

Visser K., Greaves-Lord K., Tick N.T., Verhulst F.C., Maras A. & van der Vegt E.J., 2017, 'An Exploration of the Judgement of Sexual Situations by Adolescents with Autism Spectrum Disorders versus Typically Developing Adolescents', *Research in Autism Spectrum Disorders* 36, pp35–43.

Weare K., 2000, 'Work with Young People is Leading the Way in the New Paradigm for Mental Health – Commentary', *International Journal of Health Promotion* 4(4), pp55–8.

Yaull-Smith D., 2007, 'Girls on the Spectrum', *Communication* Spring.